My THEATRE *of* MEMORY

A Life in Words

MIROLAND IMPRINT 39

Canada

ONTARIO ARTS COUNCIL
CONSEIL DES ARTS DE L'ONTARIO
an Ontario government agency
un organisme du gouvernement de l'Ontario

Canada Council   Conseil des arts
for the Arts   du Canada

Guernica Editions Inc. acknowledges the support of
the Canada Council for the Arts and the Ontario Arts Council.
The Ontario Arts Council is an agency of the Government of Ontario.
We acknowledge the financial support of the Government of Canada

Adriana A. Davies

My THEATRE
of MEMORY

A Life in Words

GUERNICA
EDITIONS

TORONTO · CHICAGO · BUFFALO · LANCASTER (U.K.)
2023

Guernica Founder: Antonio D'Alfonso

Connie McParland, Michael Mirolla, series editors
Michael Mirolla, editor
Cover and interior design: Rafael Chimicatti
Guernica Editions Inc.
287 Templemead Drive, Hamilton, ON L8W 2W4
2250 Military Road, Tonawanda, N.Y. 14150-6000 U.S.A.
www.guernicaeditions.com

Distributors:
Independent Publishers Group (IPG)
600 North Pulaski Road, Chicago IL 60624
University of Toronto Press Distribution (UTP)
5201 Dufferin Street, Toronto (ON), Canada M3H 5T8
Gazelle Book Services
White Cross Mills, High Town, Lancaster LA1 4XS U.K.

First edition.
Printed in Canada.

Legal Deposit—First Quarter
Library of Congress Catalog Card Number: 2022944734
Library and Archives Canada Cataloguing in Publication
Title: My theatre of memory : a life in words / Adriana A. Davies.
Names: Davies, Adriana A., 1943- author.
Identifiers: Canadiana (print) 20220412065 | Canadiana (ebook) 20220412170
ISBN 9781771837705 (softcover) | ISBN 9781771837712 (EPUB)
Subjects: LCSH: Davies, Adriana A., 1943- | LCSH: Historians—Canada—Biography.
LCSH: Museum curators—Canada—Biography.
LCGFT: Autobiographies.
Classification: LCC FC151.D38 A3 2023 | DDC 907.2/02—dc23

To my sons Alexander and William Davies,
my daughters-in-law Catherine and Sabrina,
and my grandsons Ciaran, Oliver, Dawson and Miles.

I also dedicate this to my extended family, friends, mentors
and anyone who has been part of this journey.

CONTENTS

CHAPTER 1

Remembering

A MEMOIR, OF COURSE, is about remembering. Why do people write memoirs? Is this act the result of a bloated sense of self-worth? Or can someone write about events in their lives and retain a sense of modesty? At the most basic level, I suppose it is a way of passing on information to those who care about us – family and friends being foremost. On the other hand, a larger audience may be sought through publication if elements in one's life might be deemed to be of interest to a larger public. This is particularly true if one's employment has involved work that is in the public interest, or in the public domain. That is why politicians, movie stars and others who live in the fish bowl of media interest write about their lives sometimes dishing "dirt" on other famous people.

I think that there are other reasons for writing memoirs. Various works, both philosophical and literary, have been written about memory, and the act of remembering. It would seem that the act of remembering is essential to the human condition. Our minds allow us to move back in time effortlessly, and reflection enables the inventorying of experiences, whether our own or those of others. The mind does not, of necessity, distinguish between personal experience, that of others, or characters we have read about in works of fact or fiction.

This happens whether we like it or not and is as normal as breathing and dreaming. In fact, dreaming is an aspect of remembering since, in dreams, we frequently relive past experiences that we have shut away from our conscious thoughts. Human beings quickly learn to forget what is painful and remember what is pleasant. Dreams bring those painful memories into our lives again, and who has not awoken crying? I certainly have.

In Marcel Proust's *À la recherche du temps perdu,* the act of drinking a *tisane* and biting into a *petit madeleine* unleashes a flood of memories. Sensory triggers result in the evocation of past times associated with those tastes and smells. For me, crushing the leaves of oregano or basil in my hands evokes memories of my mother preparing a meal, just as on entering a coffee shop the smell reminds me of my mother roasting coffee beans in the kitchen hearth in our little house in Calabria in southern Italy.

But personal memory can also be impinged upon by cultural memory and there are numerous books that have dealt with this. In her classic work published in the 1960s titled *The Art of Memory,* Frances A. Yates studied memory from ancient Greece to the Middle Ages, the Renaissance and beyond. She examined the works of thinkers and philosophers such as Giulio Camillo (ca. 1480-1544) and Giordano Bruno (1548-1600).

Camillo, in the early decades of the sixteenth century in a book titled *L'Idea del Teatro* (The Idea of the Theatre), envisioned a three-dimensional "theatre of memory" that allowed individuals to open cupboards and cases filled with writings and artifacts that would reveal the entire learning of mankind, and the universe. Of course, the theatre was impossible to build (although recently a web-based attempt has been made). The cabinets of curiosities of collectors, which in the nineteenth century became museums, are a tangible representation of the concept: all of the world's history and culture represented through collections of artifacts housed in a building that was the house of the muses.

Even as a child I reflected on things. I asked questions and read voraciously. My father Raffaele Albi was both a skilled master carpenter and a storyteller. He would take fairy tales and embroider on them, adding rude elements that would make us – my older sister Rosa and younger brother Giuseppe, and me – laugh.

I continued to read fairy tales until I was eighteen, and the princes and princesses, fairy godmothers, witches, haunted woods and magical creatures were a part of my world. I was always in a corner with a book in my hands, and family and friends joked about my head "exploding" because of everything that I was putting into it. My mother Estera got used to calling me repeatedly for meals or to do household tasks because, when I was reading, I was in a different world, and it was difficult to get me out of it.

I read every possible fairy tale collection including those of Charles Perrault, the Brothers Grimm and Andrew Lang, as well as literary fairy tales by Hans Christian Andersen, John Ruskin, Frances Browne and George MacDonald. I also had a huge collection of comics and my father either destroyed them or gave them away for some wrongdoing that I can no longer remember committing.

My father had succumbed to a door-to-door magazine salesman when I was ten or eleven and ended up with subscriptions to a movie magazine, an architectural magazine and also a building trade magazine. I read them all, as well as the one-volume encyclopedia that he also purchased. I thought of becoming an architect or a diplomat and, finally, a journalist. In the end, I studied English and French literature at university and became a lecturer in adult education specializing in English literature, as well as a researcher, writer, editor, museum curator, cultural executive director and historian.

While in my professional life I analyzed the great body of English (and some French) literature and also wrote and edited prose, I somehow knew that I was a poet at heart. For me poetry was a different language, a language of the heart. This was something I learned from my University professors Henry Kreisel and Eli Mandel. With Henry I studied twentieth century English poetry, and his classes were a delight as we mined verse for the different layers of meaning. In my graduate year, I studied Tennyson and Browning with Eli but was also introduced to contemporary Canadian poetry, his own and that of Earle Birney and Leonard Cohen.

I wrote my first poems when I was a sessional instructor in 1967-68 at the University of Western Ontario. I don't know whether they were any good because I didn't keep them. I wrote a very short poem for my first lover in London, England, shortly after. It was several lines long and I cut each line out and taped the pieces together so that I could roll it up into a tight roll. I inserted this into a snail shell and presented it to him as a token of my love. He was impressed but I think that my intensity (and my literary knowledge) frightened him, and he once described me as looking like an "avenging angel" as I waited for him to come home, knowing full well that he was seeing someone else!

I suppose that Sylvia Plath scared Ted Hughes in the same way though mine is a much sunnier temperament than hers. Her suicide was very much in the minds of anyone pursuing university studies in London in the late 1960s. I accompanied a fellow Canadian graduate student friend, Tony Saroop, to various poetry readings around London. We discovered sound poetry, concrete poetry and all sorts of other "happening" writing.

I lost Tony's friendship the night we went to hear poet Adrian Henri at a pub in Hampstead. I was very taken with his Scottish guitarist but it was Adrian who invited me, alone, to his Hampstead flat. I thought it was for a party but he had other ideas. We had a wonderful conversation and, after a couple of hours, he was seriously making moves on me and I felt that I needed to leave. I was prepared to walk out into Hampstead Village and try to find a taxi but, gentleman that he was, he called a taxi and I made it home to Willesden Green. Tony never forgave me since he was doing his PhD thesis on contemporary poets and I had somehow edged him out of the picture. Oh, to be young and romantic and in love with not only the idea of poetry but also poets.

I turned to poetry again when traveling between Edmonton and Red Deer in the mid-1980s. I was working as an instructional designer for the Local Government Studies Program at the University of Alberta, and had to go down to assist in the presentation of professional development workshops. I would take the Greyhound bus around 6 a.m. and, once we left the city lights behind, cocooned in darkness, I allowed my imagination free rein to roam back and forth through time. These few poems depicted the landscape juxtaposing its permanence with the transience of human life. I still have them somewhere, these first works in which I began to reflect on my life.

Like many writers, it took an emotional crisis to spur me to write. While others might seek help from professionals, I knew instinctively that Tennyson was right when he wrote "a use in measured language lies." But it was through prose that I began my interior journey. I started a journal on September 1, 1997, as the stresses in my marriage became visible, like fault lines in granite.

On the surface, they were about my English husband Hugh not being happy in Canada. But they grew to be larger than that – about who we had become within the marriage, and what other things we wanted to do, and be. We were both very successful in our lives but, somehow, this was not enough. In spring of 1998, unrhymed lyric poems became interspersed with the prose passages in the journal that I was keeping as I questioned, poured out my fears and doubts, and some joys too. The stuff of my life became my subject matter and while in life I could not impose order on the chaos of feelings, writing about it somehow allowed me to go on.

As I wrote, I developed a personal vocabulary drawing from my readings but also from my working life. I had always been fascinated by nature and remember happily watching documentaries on television with my father. At the University of Alberta, I had to take three science courses to complete my BA degree. I chose botany, statistics and genetics. Unlike the typical Arts student for whom science courses were a trial, something to get over, I really enjoyed them. I got the highest mark in introductory botany and was approached by the department chair, Dr. Brodie, to change my major. I said, "No," because at that point I was going to be a truth-seeking journalist and help to change the world. The love of English literature ultimately led me to forsake journalism and to pursue graduate studies.

The critical thinking, research and writing skills that I developed became the basis of all of my future jobs. As Senior Editor in charge of science and technology for Mel Hurtig's iconic *The Canadian Encyclopedia*, I created the framework for all of the articles dealing with Canada's flora and fauna, geology, physical geography, as well as the development of the various science and technology fields. The work involved appointing specialist advisors as well as the authors. This subject area also enriched my vocabulary and became a part of my personal theatre of memory.

Thus, when I began to write poems, in spring, 1998, I could not help but refer to favourite authors – not only in terms of their language and themes but also for their insights into the human condition. I remembered what nineteenth century poet Gerard Manley Hopkins described as the process of "selving." Hopkins was influenced by medieval philosopher Duns Scotus, who believed that human beings could understand the universe by examining the "thisness" of all objects on Earth. For Scotus, each thing in the Creation asserts itself and what it was made to be by the Creator. Hopkins applied this to animate and inanimate objects, and wrote in the poem "As Kingfishers Catch Fire, Dragonflies Draw Flame":

Each mortal thing does one thing and the same;
Deals out that being indoors each one dwells;
Selves – goes itself; *myself* it speaks and spells,
Crying What I do is me: for that I came.

As I began to re-examine my life to see what it was that I was
meant to be, I envisioned writing a collection of poems that I titled
"Selves." I performed these poems as I wrote them at a poetry series at
the Grounds for Coffee café in Edmonton's inner city, which eventually became the Raving Poets (a dynamic performance poetry experience in which the Raving Father's Band intuited the kind of musical
accompaniment that a reading required).

I was mapping my inner life and sharing it with others, who were
also doing the same thing. Though I was among the oldest poets at the
readings, my questioning was no different from that of the youngest.
I did what my older son Alex accused me of doing – "I spilled my
guts in poetry!" Neither he nor his brother William was comfortable
with this. Alex even said, "Mum, why don't you write nature poetry?"

I shared some of the poems with a psychologist friend, Richard
Lang, who did his PhD thesis on memory. He introduced me to the
concept of the "theatre of memory" and the works of Rollo May. After
our discussions, I came to see "theatre of memory" not only as it was
envisioned by Camillo but also as theatre – the drama of my life.
My memories were not just of situations and events involving strong
feelings; they were also small dramatic scenes, involving one or more
characters – myself at the centre of them. There were also soliloquies:
self, speaking to self. This inner dialogue, I suppose, has been a part of
my thinking process from my earliest days since I have always reasoned
through questioning.

As a person who has been torn between the poles of rationality
and feeling, or as Jane Austen would have it, sense and sensibility,
there is a desire in me to understand the unfolding of my life and
how I have ended up where I am. This memoir, in part, describes this
process mostly, for myself, but also for others who might be interested
in what it was like coming of age in the 1960s, and my evolution as
an independent and privileged woman.

The second poem that I wrote in my journal on March 15, 1998,
on a trip to Montreal, sets the tone for this exploration.

Changing Skins

I read somewhere that a snake must change its skin to grow, or die.
My skin has felt uncomfortably tight for some time.
I tried dieting, but it didn't work.
I then worked out for increased definition but that too didn't work.

So I went back to the writers of my youth—
Gerard Manley Hopkins, T. S. Eliot, Emily Dickinson, W. B. Yeats.
Began a quest for the historical Jesus,
And pursued old, and new, loves.

I am waiting now to wake up some morning with my old skin
                                        [next to me in bed,
I will rise up and face the day and, Jesus, that Old Enchanter,
Like Prospero, will quieten the tempest,
And bring me forth, reborn.

CHAPTER 2

Emigration

WHEN YOU ARE BORN in another country, leaving it becomes the line drawn in your personal chronology; there is the time before leaving, and the time after. It is a deeply personal thing that, as an adult, has led me to study and gain some expertise in immigration history. Why do people leave a place where they are at home and part of an extensive network of kinship, and where they are tied to the land both in its cultivation and also as the resting place of their family members who have gone into that "dark goodnight"?

My family's immigration history is typical of people who leave a place not because of the "horrors" of history (war, famine, discrimination, violence) but for economic improvement and adventure. For many southern Italians, beginning in the second half of the nineteenth century, leaving to improve their lot in life was an economic necessity. But even for those who had land and education, the allure of foreign countries beckoned, simply because they were new and they were there to be discovered.

My family represents three generations of immigration history both on the paternal and maternal side. My maternal great-grandfather – Francesco Potestio – went to Colorado, USA, in the 1880s where he likely worked as a labourer. His family joined him including my grandfather Vincenzo who was a small boy. At least some members of the family returned to their home town Grimaldi, including Vincenzo. Around 1905, he married Assunta Mauro and their first child, a son, was born in 1906 and subsequently died. My aunt Teresa was born in

1908; my mother Estera, in 1921; and my aunt Livia, in 1924. My grandfather returned to the US in 1913 with his friend Francesco Albo, my paternal grandfather. Members of his family also went to the US in the 1880s, and were among the founding families of Spokane, Washington. The family name was changed to Albi early in the 20th century either by an immigration official or a family member entering the US. That begins my paternal family's story. I've learned from my father that his father, the youngest of seven sons, was supposed to stay in Grimaldi to look after his mother Rosa. But he couldn't stay in Italy while his older siblings were in the US making money and adventuring. He was prepared to risk family censure and decided to go, arriving at Ellis Island in 1913 and making his way to Spokane. According to family history, he was shunned by his brothers and ended up in Revelstoke, BC working on the railways.

When I was growing up, on trips to visit family in Vancouver, I know that Dad stopped in Revelstoke to try to find his father's grave but had no success. I was told that he had died as a young man as a result of pneumonia or other chest infection. In my heart, I believe it was heartbreak and loneliness that killed him though I have no evidence for this. He left a widow, Alessandra, in Grimaldi, with one son, my uncle Giuseppe, and another born after he left, my father.

In 2015 while working on an exhibit on the bootlegger Emilio Picariello for the Fernie Museum, I visited the Revelstoke Museum and the director kindly did a search in their digital newspaper archive and found an obituary in the *Mail Herald* dated February 12, 1916 with the following information:

Son of Joseph Albi and Rose Veltrie

The death occurred on Tuesday at the Queen Victoria hospital of Frank Albi. The late Mr. Albi who was 29 years of age was born in Italy and came to Revelstoke about a year ago. Besides a wife in Italy he leaves a brother John B. Albi, railroad contractor, of Spokane, who arrived in Revelstoke to take charge of the remains. The funeral, which was under the direction of Howson and Company took place from St. Francis church at 2 o'clock yesterday afternoon, Rev. J.C. McKenzie officiating.

I was able to obtain a death notice and discovered that his middle initial was "M." While seeing to his burial, his brother John did not purchase a gravestone so I could only find the location of the grave by looking at the list of burials and their locations provided by the City of Revelstoke.

Subsequently, I've done online searches on John Albi and discovered that he was an extremely successful railway contactor. He completed a number of contracts in the interior of BC for the building of the Grand Trunk Pacific Railway from 1906 to 1914; it followed the northern route through Jasper and the Yellowhead Pass suggested by Sir Sanford Fleming. Over 6,000 men were working on the line in 1912, hired by a range of contractors. In the same year, John purchased a large, two-storey house in Spokane with a turret and stone cladding on the exterior walls. He and wife Mary lived there until 1929. The home is on the list of historic homes, befitting a man of substance. The fact that he did not purchase a gravestone for his brother suggests that he lacked the milk of human kindness, though the Spokane families sent some money to Frank's widow, Alessandra, in Grimaldi to help her raise her two sons.

On my return to Edmonton, I visited my mother in her long-term-care facility and shared the story of finding the site of her father-in-law's burial. She was happy about this and enjoyed looking at the photos that I took of the graves around it, most with the names of Italians. I felt a kind of closure in finding information about a long-dead ancestor; however, I was no closer to understanding his story. His was a tragic end to an immigration journey that started with hope. I imagine that my grandfather wanted to make a fortune like his brothers had to improve the lot of his young family. He was no different from the hordes of young men who left Italy at the end of the nineteenth, and early part of the twentieth centuries, to make their fortunes in North America.

Immigration resulted in the fragmentation of family life but it was a risk many men were willing to take. If they could make money, then, they could return to the home town and, if they didn't have ancestral lands, perhaps buy their own plot and build a house. The immigrants in the earliest eras of immigration did not imagine that they would want to settle in the New World and were described as "sojourners," or itinerant labourers.

My maternal grandfather, Nonno Vincenzo, was a true sojourner: he traveled back and forth between Ontario where he worked on the railways, and Grimaldi. He never had his wife and daughters join him though he gave Uncle Paul, his oldest daughter Teresa's husband, the money to go to the US. The last time he returned to Grimaldi, he stayed from 1939 to 1949. (My mother told me that he could not return because of the war.) In 1949, he made his final trip to Canada, dying there alone on August 17, 1950. Because of his stay in Italy, my sister Rosa and I as well as our brother Giuseppe got to know him. Not everyone was lucky like this.

I was a wartime baby, born September 17, 1943, as the Canadians and other Allies moved up the boot of Italy. My mother has told me of rushing out to the countryside, heavily pregnant, as the planes dropped bombs. The effects of the war could be seen, even by a child, in my hometown. There were still bombed-out houses that had not been rebuilt and were barricaded with wooden shutters and fence posts. Stone walls of public buildings had remnants of posters with Mussolini's name on them. Of course, I was not aware of the war when I noticed these things at the time but could sense a vague uneasiness when I overheard the talk of the old people.

When I reflect back on my childhood in Grimaldi, a series of snapshots come into my mind – all associated with special places and strong feelings. The small town meanders down the hillside ending in a natural stone piazza – *L'Aria di l'Impelichiato*. At that time, white oxen still ground down the grain by turning heavy millstones. The natural stone terrace had been worn down by this activity carried on for centuries. My paternal home was just up the hill from *L'Aria* and, in the early years of their marriage, my parents lived there. The stone houses are all linked together and march up the hill, the narrow streets paved with cobblestones. Behind some houses there are walled gardens at the time filled with grapevines, fruit trees, vegetables and flowers. The real countryside stretched up and down hills and in small valleys around the town. The arable land was planted with crops and fruit trees. I discovered the countryside on visits to ancestral land holdings with my grandmothers, Nonna Alessandra and Nonna Assunta. The town itself I explored with my sister and friends.

I remember the day that my brother Giuseppe was born. I was three years old and was staying at Nonna Assunta's place. This house was on the East side of the town and close to another flat area, which was the scene of a Saturday market. It was close to the river and was located next to the flour mill with its pond and mill race. It is morning and my grandmother is trying to untangle my sausage curls, which my mother painstakingly brushed and curled around her fingers every morning. I've seen them in photographs taken before Papa went off to Canada when I was six years old. One of the curls on top of my head has a big floppy bow made from a ribbon. Nonna is in a hurry because Giuseppe had been born and we were going to see him. I don't remember my sister Rosa being there. I looked up to her and likely was even jealous of her because she could do so many more things than I could. Like every young girl of her age and generation, she was learning to embroider and knit clothes for her dolls. But I also remember that she didn't finish things very often so that I got to carry on from where she left off.

On Saturday mornings, animals would be taken to the market to be sold as well as a range of other merchandise. When I was five or six, I found clay in the slope next to the house we were renting and shaped it into market animals and also little people. I also loved painting outlines of houses, like doll houses open in the front. The houses were multi-storey like the ones I saw around me. I painted in tiny furniture. Another favourite subject was chickens, roosters and chicks. I suppose this is not unusual since many families also had chicken coops in their back gardens, or in the farms surrounding the town.

What to say about this period in my life, which was distinct not only because it was so long ago but also because it was in a different country from the one in which I've lived for most of my life? The remembered country is lush and green and fruitful; in comparison to my adopted country, its scale is small and offers a contrast to Canada, which is large and cold.

The scenes that make up my memories are real but they've been shaped by all of the readings that I've done since. My childhood has taken on the character of fairy tales like the ones that Papa read me. I remember one, in particular, about a child who is working for an ogre and who is helped by magic hands – *manine di fate* (fairy hands). I related to the heroes and heroines in fairy tales, feeling that I was somehow set apart, special, waiting for my adventures to begin.

I believed in magic as, I suspect did many of the old people in the town. As a tiny girl I knew that you had to beware of *il malocchio* (the evil eye) and guard against it by wearing a small gold or coral horn attached to a bracelet or necklace. You could also make a horn by curling your second and third fingers into your hand with the first and fifth fingers straight out, but you did this secretly, hiding your hand behind your back or below your clothing so no-one could see that you were doing it.

Most of the old women were dressed in black and there seemed to be more of them than old men. I remember Nonna Alessandra taking me to visit an old woman in a convent which, I suppose, acted as a seniors' residence as well. She insisted on kissing me and I knew that I could not turn away and wipe my face because it was rude. I suspect that I somehow sensed that she was close to death and death was something to be feared.

Whenever the church bells tolled outside of Mass times, every-one knew that someone had died. In such a close community, you could not avoid death. I remember that a neighbour's baby died and Rosa and I went to view him. He was dressed in his embroidered white Baptismal robe and looked like a wax doll. Down the road, a young girl of thirteen or fourteen died. The causes of death were shrouded in mystery and, therefore, it appeared to me as a young child that death could come to claim any of us.

Black crows cawing were a bad omen and there was always the need to guard against not just the evil eye but also "*l'affascino*," which as I understood was that someone could envy your beauty, good health, good fortune, and that you would lose them. To counteract this, there were certain "holy women" who could say special prayers to reverse this "minor curse." Everyone knew about this but you didn't talk about it. You also did not flaunt your looks or wealth to avoid becoming a target, thus promoting a kind of natural modesty. The other thing that it instilled in me was the belief that good things and happiness could not last; that they needed to be paid for, frequently, in pain and grief.

Most of the town's men had immigrated to Canada since the US was accepting fewer immigrants from Italy. It seemed that everyone had a family member in Canada and many were waiting to be sponsored. There were some women whose husbands formed other attachments in Canada and who waited, without hope, for the papers to come. The elders talked about this in hushed voices, as they did about unplanned pregnancies and shotgun weddings. As a child, I felt that all of the elders had a secret knowledge that they did not share with children.

Health was a huge issue, particularly if you were intending to emigrate. When the papers came from a family member, or a labour agent, a trip had to be made to Rome for a full physical examination and only those who passed it could leave.

My father was sponsored by Ottavio Iachetta, a labour agent from Winnipeg, and ended up working on a dairy farm after his arrival in 1949. As a skilled master carpenter, who was also a talented amateur musician (mandolin and clarinet), as well as a hunter, farm work was not to his liking. As soon as possible, he went to Edmonton to work for Italian-owned New West Construction.

We lived without Papa for two years. We moved into a small house near Nonna Assunta's place, which my mother rented. My mother was 28 and had three small children to look after. I know that at times she was very sad and had difficulty disciplining us. That is not because we were difficult and willful but simply because, as a gentle soul, she needed the support of my father. She had married in 1937 at the age of sixteen and had my sister in 1940 (she had a miscarriage, the previous year); I followed in 1943, and my brother in 1946.

Every one of our illnesses was a trial for her. When my sister Rosa contracted rheumatic fever, my mother became terrified of us all becoming ill or dying. Thankfully, my sister got better. I remember that we had to take various tonics to strengthen our systems. The one that I particularly liked was an egg yolk beaten with sugar and topped up with Marsala wine or caffè latte. Caffè latte was our morning break- fast drink in which we dunked *fresine* – fennel-seed buns baked, halved and then baked again to preserve them. My mother would roast her own coffee beans in our cooking hearth and I loved that smell.

There were so many good, and some bad, things to smell. The bad things were the chamber pots and outside lavatories. Inside plumb- ing did not come to my hometown until the 1960s, long after we had left for Canada. There were wonderful things to smell – flowers and shrubs as well as food. In town, almost every house had flowerpots on balconies or hanging from window boxes. Geraniums and roses were popular flowers but housewives also grew pots of basil, which was used to flavour tomato sauce as well as other dishes. In the gardens there were other herbs – rosemary, oregano, tarragon – as well as flowering shrubs and trees. Arbours were formed by grapevines that provided shelter from the heat. It was that heat in summer that released all of those natural scents, both good and bad, and made the air shimmer.

In the afternoon when we were forced to nap, you could hear the crickets and cicadas. My sister and I would lie in bed in our white cotton slips with the sweat trickling down our faces, unable to sleep.

The countryside was literally around us, embracing the town. With either of my grandmothers, we would go and visit family land holdings around the town. Nonna Assunta's farm was just across the river from the town. In the woods surrounding it, tiny violets blanketed the grass. There was a small house that was used for storage and it was surrounded by fruit trees (apple, pear, peach, figs, apricot and cherry) and rows of grapevines. She also grew tomatoes and salad makings as well as wheat. At seeding and harvest, she would hire labourers to help and she would prepare wonderful food for them.

She also kept hogs and had them butchered and prepared the various parts to produce prosciuttos, sausages, salamis, blood puddings as well as lard. In my last two years in Italy, I was allowed to stay home to see these preparations though this did not involve the actual killing of the hogs.

Everything was done in a traditional way intended to preserve things for the winter. The dead hogs, after the hair had been removed, hung from large hooks in the ceiling and were bled before they were butchered. My grandmother allowed Rosa and me to help stir the blood pudding, which was sweet rather than savoury (like a thick chocolate sauce). The fat was rendered and the bits of meat left in the bottom of the pan were delicious. We dipped crusty, home-made bread into the drippings as I am sure children have in farming communities around the world.

I remember walks in the woods where we had chestnut and almond trees. Nonna Alessandra would take us walking out beyond the small shrine to the Virgin Mary on a hillside outside town. We had to cross a small hanging bridge over a narrow ravine and I was convinced that an ogre lived down there. We would end up in a flat area criss-crossed by streams spreading out from a series of waterfalls. The sound of falling water was so loud that you had to shout to be heard. This would change when indoor plumbing was installed in the houses in nearby villages, and the water table was lowered to a dangerous degree by over-consumption and drought.

Some summers, Nonna Assunta would take Rosa and me to stay on a small neighbouring farm. We had daily hikes in the woods and she would pick mushrooms, some so large that they resembled cow patties. She would cook them fresh, frying them with olive oil, garlic and oregano, and we would eat them with crusty home-made bread. I remember also going out with childhood friends and taunting water-snakes that had fallen into stone irrigation tanks on my grandmother's farm. The boys would lift them with long poles and they would slither off. We knew to beware of snakes because there were poisonous ones about.

My childhood was one of freedom – freedom to discover and explore – within the security of an extended family, and a close-knit community. Everyone knew everyone else and I was Mastro (master based on his trade as a carpenter) Raffaele's daughter. By the age of five, my days were given structure by going to kindergarten, initially with the nuns in a local convent. I still remember the cool terrazzo floors made up of small black and white squares. The nuns would show us the embroidered cloths that they were making for their chapel as well as other places of worship. On special occasions when Nonno Vincenzo came to collect me, I would wait anxiously for him on the balcony and I would see him making his way through the town to the convent.

I was also extremely close to my father perhaps because, when Rosa was born in 1940, Papa was serving in the military and based in Ethiopia. His contracting malaria turned out to be a blessing because he was sent back to Italy to a desk job. This also spared him being taken a prisoner-of-war; this happened to my uncle Giuseppe, who was sent to England and spent his time at Kew Gardens. Mother said that Papa was able to spend more time with me and therefore we bonded. I remember even as a child of three being allowed to go to his workshop, though my mother had dressed me in a pretty dress and had shaped my hair into perfect curls. Papa's workshop was full of wood and half-finished pieces of furniture he was making for clients. I quickly learned the names of tools and would get them for Papa when he called for them, like a doctor calling for a scalpel. Sometimes I got too close as he was planing a piece of wood or lifting a wooden plank, and would get a bruise on my head. I don't remember ever crying because I knew it was a privilege to be in Papa's workshop. Sometimes, he would also take Rosa and me to gather honeycomb from the hives that he kept.

I loved learning and, particularly, drawing. I started school at age six in a small concrete building next to the river. There was one teacher – an old man – who taught multiple grades. His teaching methods would not pass muster today. If you were bad, however, he chose to define it, you would be sent to the corner and had to wear a dunce's cap or, if you were particularly bad, you had to kneel on corn kernels. I remember wanting to please him very much and, I think that he, and my father, stimulated my love of learning. At a very early age, my father introduced me to *Gulliver's Travels*. The idea of very large and tiny people intrigued me and, I too, wanted to go adventuring.

Within two years of his leaving, in 1949, my father was able to sponsor us. The adventure began with a trip to Rome. We were accompanied by a male cousin who went to help my mother. I remember the train journeys and the physical examination in Rome. My mother wore a wonderful perfume and talcum powder that smelled of violets and this, somehow, seemed to keep at bay the motion sickness that I suffered from, particularly in cars that at the time smelled heavily of gasoline.

When we returned to Grimaldi to pack, I gave away all my dolls and other toys, because I was convinced that everything was going to be better in Canada. While it was a joy for us, it was much harder for my mother, who had to choose very carefully among her possessions as to what to take to Canada. She had a wonderful trousseau of woven sheets, pillow cases and towels, all of which she had embroidered and personalized with her initials. Into the one trunk went Papa's mandolin and clarinet. Everything else she gave away to friends. We traveled to Naples, where we embarked as did many other families. However, the majority of travelers were men going to make their fortune in Canada.

We left Naples at the beginning of August 1951 and the weather stayed fine as we crossed the Mediterranean and the excitement was palpable, even to young children, as we neared the Straits of Gibraltar. The women cried at leaving the land of their birth and not knowing whether they would ever return to see their mothers and others left behind. Once beyond the Straits, the weather changed in the North Atlantic and it became stormy. Mother, suffering from seasickness, stayed in the cabin with my brother who was likely to run amuck and fall overboard – at least that is what she feared.

My sister and I were free to roam the decks in a ship that for a few days seemed to be absent of adults other than the crew. Rosa, who was older than me, really sensed what she was giving up and missed her friends. She spent a lot of time crying and complaining, which added to the pressure on Mother. As the middle child, I was somehow more placid and accepting and less demanding of her attention. Meal times were enjoyed by all. The food was plentiful, and, because, we ate little, we were popular with the men at our table, who would finish whatever we could not eat.

I remember being called on deck to see whales and other marine life. Finally, after 10 days, we arrived in Halifax at Pier 21. There was a lot of anxiety among the women because they knew that their luggage was going to be searched and that things could be confiscated. One woman, in particular, was distraught because she had packed her belongings in straw and this meant that everything was confiscated. I didn't realize at the time that agricultural items were prohibited to prevent transmission of insect pests. It just seemed that, in this country we had come to, there were many regulations that made life difficult for immigrants.

We boarded the train to Montreal where we stayed with some family friends for a couple of days. My father, thoughtfully, arranged this to ease our journey. We then took the train heading West, and the journey appeared interminable. Trees and giant rocks went on forever. In the middle of the night (likely the second night of our journey), our train stopped in Winnipeg (perhaps it was for a change of crew) and then we continued. Sadly for my mother, my smallpox vaccination began to itch and swell so that she now had to comfort three crying children. I am certain that the trip for her held many horrors and stretched her patience to the limit.

Eventually, we arrived in Edmonton and were greeted by my father, who was now a stranger to us. The first thing I noticed was that the end of his first finger on his right hand was missing – the result of an accident with an electric saw at work. He quickly gathered us together in a taxi and we drove to the tiny house in the equipment yard of New West Construction, which was to be our home for two years.

CHAPTER 3

Settling

Our first home in Edmonton was one-half of a tiny wooden duplex in the New West Construction equipment yards on 113 Street near the CN railway tracks. Our first night in Edmonton, I remember my parents putting my sister, brother and me to bed in a small double bed with a brown metal frame. Papa read us English fairy tales, among them *Goldilocks and the Three Bears* and *Little Red Riding Hood*. He not only wanted us to learn to speak English as quickly as possible but he was also continuing a tradition established in Italy. He was a wonderful storyteller and this was a way of re-connecting with children he had left behind two years previously to seek adventure on the continent where many of his relatives had gone before.

My parents were absolute believers that only through education could we improve our prospects. Thus, Papa had registered us at St. John's school in the Oliver neighbourhood where we lived. For the first day, he arranged for a teenaged neighbour girl, Geraldine, to take us. It was only Rosa and I; Giuseppe at five years old stayed home with Mamma.

Because we did not speak English, Rosa was put back two years and I one year, so I started in grade two and Rosa in grade four. At lunch or after school, the nuns kept us back and, together with two Dutch boys of a similar age, we were taught English. The nuns used the repetition method: I can't remember how many times I said, "The book is on the table. The book is under the table!" We quickly became fluent and I don't remember any difficulties in learning the language.

Rosa and I were eager to share what we read with Mamma and I think this is how we taught her to read. By teaching, we reinforced our own learning. I loved picture books with lavish illustrations and remember learning to read with Dick and Jane. Not only did these picture books help me to learn English, they also gave me a model of a "normal" family that we should aspire to become.

Papa was already well-established in the Italian community: he was one of the first men to arrive in the post-war wave of immigration from Italy. I have his tiny Italian-English/English-Italian dictionary. It was part of the series of Hugo "pronouncing pocket-dictionaries" published by the David McKay Company of New York. It also includes a table of weights and measures. His name, the Anglicized "Ralph Albi," is written confidently on the flyleaf, a bold assertion that he had taken on a new identify in his new home.

Through English language classes, he learned not only to speak well but also to read and write. In Italy he had completed the seven years of compulsory schooling which included study of the classics and then been apprenticed. He helped new immigrants and treated friends from Grimaldi and from other parts of Italy alike. It was customary for newcomers to seek help from those who were already established to deal with officials, and for any paperwork required. There was an added bonus when Papa did oral or written translations: many men, who had few if any carpentry skills, got their trade ticket. This placed them in a higher earning bracket as skilled tradesmen rather than unskilled labourers. Papa was respected in the community and everyone referred to him as "Mastro Raffaele," based on his master carpenter qualification. The style of address was brought to the new land and also the class system in the homeland. Landowners and shop keepers were higher in the pecking order than agricultural workers and they were also likely better educated.

From the outset of our school days, we had "good" clothes that we wore to church and school and "older" or more casual clothes that we changed into once we got home. The Army & Navy Department Store on 97 Street and 103 Avenue was where we shopped along with other immigrants. Bargains could be got there including one piece snow-suits to prepare us for our first winter. I believe that mine was red, a colour I loved when I was a child. Dress suits and dresses could also be purchased for Holy Communions and Baptisms. A family's economic betterment could be seen when they stopped shopping at the A & N!

At that time my mother's sister, Zia Teresa and her husband, Zio Paolo, lived in the upstairs apartment above a corner store on 97 Street, across from today's Law Courts and just half a block from the A & N. They had come to Canada in 1949 and were established. We would visit them in the inner-city Boyle-McCauley neighbourhoods that had been a haven for newcomers since the early part of the twentieth century. As the merchant and professional classes prospered, they moved to other areas of the city including the Highlands, Oliver and Old Glenora. The working class including immigrants lived in cheap boarding houses in the inner city. Trolley buses still ran in the fifties in the inner city. Zio worked as a janitor at the nearby Immigration Hall located on the crest of the North Saskatchewan River Valley and was part of the informal network of people who greeted new immigrants and helped them find work.

The biggest employer of Italians was New West Construction established by brothers-in-law Felix Nigro and James (Jimmy) Anselmo, in the mid-1920s. Felix's Father, Antonio, had arrived in the US in 1885 and worked on railway building with his brother-in-law Giovanni Veltri (John Welch). Felix joined his father in 1897 when he was 15. Jimmy's father, Domenico, also worked for the Welches and had his son join him in Canada around 1914 when he was 14. Based on a strong work ethic, the partners prospered and with their gangs undertook roadworks and railway repairs in Alberta and BC.

Papa had obtained work with them on arrival in Edmonton in 1949. With their wives, they held court in their large, two-storey Craftsman Style house near St. Joseph's Cathedral. They were not only from our home town but there was also some family tie. We would visit them and bring a small gift, and they would serve my parents wine or a liqueur, and Italian cookies. I remember them as old people sitting upright in grand wooden chairs like thrones. We were expected to be on our best behaviour and, if we took too many cookies or were restless in our seats, Mamma would give us a stern look and we would freeze in place. Our parents were disciplinarians (as most were at the time) and the threat of a slap on the bottom when we got home kept us in-line. We were obedient but not cowed.

My parents were over-joyed when their best friends Attilio and Stella Gatto came to Edmonton from Vancouver, and moved into the other half of the duplex. They had left Italy in 1949 with their son Emilio, a year younger than me, and gone to join Stella's brother in

Vancouver. It didn't work out for them and they came to Edmonton and Compare Attilio joined Papa at New West. My mother was pleased to have a good friend nearby and I to have a playmate. Their second son, Pasqualino, was born shortly after their arrival in Canada. In the middle of the duplex was a shared bathroom and one had to remember to close the door on their side to avoid embarrassment.

A fence separated the duplex from the construction equipment yard but we climbed over it easily and used the equipment as fairway rides. One summer, we climbed a large conveyor-belt and, when we reached the top, it began to tilt and we had to hang on for dear life. We didn't tell Mamma and Papa that we had done this. I remember on a beautiful summer day when I was wearing thin sandals I stepped on a nail protruding from a two-by-four. It went through my shoe and into my foot. I didn't tell Mamma immediately because we weren't supposed to play in the yard. My foot swelled up and turned an angry red with white streaks. The pain was unbearable and I was forced to tell. I was taken to the doctor and had a tetanus shot and an antibiotic that did the trick. From that time onwards, I realized that happiness was fragile and I had to beware of being too happy because my luck could turn in an instant.

While my brother, as the only son, was the favourite, Papa also encouraged his daughters to pursue education. In some Italian families this was not the case and, when children reached their sixteenth birthdays, they were sent to work: the boys in their father's workplace in labouring jobs and the daughters in hospital kitchens and housekeeping departments. The luckier girls went to work at GWG and other garment factories located in the city or in retail, if they spoke good English. Parents would seek advantageous marriages whether with men already here or in the hometown. Later, my sister became a popular bridesmaid at these weddings.

I think that I was a natural student: I loved learning and the subject matter was of no importance. I seemed to learn effortlessly and my only problems were related to whether or not I got invitations to birthday parties. There, the well-dressed, popular "English" girls dominated and I knew that I had to become their friend. These included Judy and her older sister Josephine, Babs, Noella, Sheila and her sisters, and others. I was thrilled when my mother bought my sister and I fashionable matching dresses with green velvet tops and plaid taffeta skirts and we were able to wear them for a Christmas party at school. There was entertainment and I remember Josephine and Judy dressed like ballet dancers in frilly skirts called tutus doing a short dance number standing on their toes. I was incredibly jealous. Later, I realized that it must have been one of the children's numbers from "The Nutcracker." I wanted to be like them and take ballet and music lessons but, while we were not poor, my parents didn't have money for luxuries.

I also wanted to eat what the other kids ate: we soon stopped taking Italian food since our friends considered them "stinky." Mother's delicious home-made bread was replaced by white, sliced bread purchased at the corner store with Velveeta cheese or Spam fillings. I never acquired a taste for peanut butter.

The divide between the "English" children and the immigrant children was enormous. Thankfully, Mamma was a clever seamstress and, when Giuseppe went to school in 1952, she began to work at GWG and earned money to supplement the household income. She took pride in dressing us well, cheaply, and she and Papa saved to buy their first house.

From the beginning of my schooling, I felt that I had to be not just as good as everyone else but better. We didn't want to disappoint our parents who we knew made great sacrifices for us. Mamma would come home from GWG with bleeding hands. The dye in the heavy jean fabric caused an eczema-type rash on her hands and they would crack. I remember her rubbing Vaseline on them and wearing white cotton gloves to bed at night. Rosa and I did the dishes to spare her having to put her hands in water, which always made it worse. But there was no getting around this because all housework involved water in some way from doing laundry in the wringer washing machine and then hanging it outside on the line to dry, even in winter, to washing floors, cleaning bathrooms and the whole range of housework.

Around 1953, we moved into a small bungalow in the Westmount neighbourhood in the west end and my parents made it into a cozy home. There was a living room/dining room combination, a small kitchen, a narrow bathroom, and two bedrooms. My parents had the front bedroom and the three of us had the one next to it. Rosa and I shared a small double bed and Giuseppe had a cot at the foot of our bed. It was a lovely neighbourhood, parts of which dated back to the 1930s and there were grand three-storey houses as well as more modest cottages like our own. Every yard had its apple trees and, in the fall, with other children, we would go for crab-apple raids.

Initially, we made do with second-hand furniture that Papa purchased from Podersky's, which was located at the time on 98 Street and Jasper Avenue (the store later moved to the south side). The store had a bargain basement and also introduced "easy credit terms." I remember the heavy, dark blue velvet sofa with the wooden arms and companion arm chair. In the creases, we found a pair of scissors, which my father sharpened and which we used for years. Another beloved piece of furniture was a large mahogany dining table, which stayed with us for years until it was replaced by a modern teak dining set in the 1960s. My parents didn't want to get into debt (the mortgage was their only loan) and they saved to buy furniture from Podersky's and, later, Woodward's at Westmount Shopping Centre, for cash.

Westmount was where my mother discovered that she had inherited her own mother's green thumb and we had a traditional Italian garden in the back and side yards. Papa did the digging and, in the fall, when the peas, beans, potatoes and other vegetables were finished, he would dig the plants into the soil to enrich it. We lived on this fresh produce (including asparagus) throughout the summer, and Mamma also canned vegetables in glass Mason jars for the winter.

Our first car was a used blue, 1953 Chevy which was the source of many pleasures. The Sunday drive to the country during the summer became a ritual and I remember going to Edson where a fellow *paesano* owned a hotel and restaurant, and Elk Island where we dipped our toes in the water. Summer and winter, we visited my mother's younger sister, Zia Livia, and her husband, Zio Sestilio, and our younger cousins, Vincent and Mary, in Wainwright. One spring day when we went out for the weekend, there was still snow on the road and Papa slid off the road and my sister and brother were thrown against me hard causing a massive bruise on my side. Papa had to walk to the local farm and the farmer pulled us out with his tractor. Zia was very kind and wrapped a sling around my arm to prevent me from moving it and also gave me aspirin.

The car was also useful for shopping trips downtown. Every Saturday we went to the City Market and shopped for fresh meat and vegetables. The building was an unattractive concrete structure but inside it was a feast for the senses. Fruits and vegetables as well as meats, cheeses and other edibles filled the counters. Much of the produce was grown on local farms on the outskirts of the city. I remember the honey counter: the stall holder frequently gave me a square of honeycomb from which the honey dripped. It was the best honey that I had ever had and reminded me of the bees that Papa had kept in Grimaldi.

On Saturdays my parents drove down 127 Street until it became a country road surrounded by farmland. This ritual was to ensure that we had the best fresh chicken bought from Ukrainian farmers. Rosa and I helped Mamma pick the feathers off it, and we always watched avidly as she cut into it carefully to remove the stomach and other innards being careful not to break the bile sack attached to the liver. She told us that, if that happened, it would ruin the meat making it very bitter. Roast chicken was our favourite Sunday meal. Mamma made a stuffing of minced beef, breadcrumbs and chopped hard-boiled eggs bound together by several raw eggs. The chicken was delicious with mashed potatoes and rich gravy made from the drippings. Mamma also learned to make pickles from the farm wives, which were garlicky, tart and crisp.

Every weekend we hosted *paesani* from our home town, Grimaldi, in particular, the men who were either single or were saving for their wives to join them. Some worked up north in the mines and only came to town occasionally. Mamma cooked all of her home-town specialties including home-made pasta and ravioli, and Rosa and I were expected to clean up. With Mamma working, Rosa soon became responsible for re-heating dishes she had made the previous evening so that we didn't keep Papa waiting when he returned from a long day at work. Eventually, I would share this task with her. We both learned to cook traditional Italian dishes at a very young age and assisted Mamma in pasta making.

A major occurrence in our life was when Papa began to work for Imperial Oil. My parents, their friends the Gattos, and others talked in whispers about this. It was only later that I learned that they discovered that Nigro and Anselmo were not paying them the full amount that they were receiving from Imperial Oil, which had subcontracted New West to do some construction work for the new Imperial Oil refinery and, later, for plant maintenance.

Papa had become friends with one of the bosses, an American called Joe Grey, and his girl-friend Helen, who was the company nurse. He took this up with them and Joe arranged for him to become an Imperial employee as well as his best friend and best man, Attilio Gatto.

For us children this provided unexpected benefits: there was the employee summer picnic usually at Borden Park and the Christmas

Party at the Macdonald Hotel. At the summer party, we played all sorts of games including baseball and there were small prizes. We ate hotdogs and pie and ice cream. But it was the Christmas Party that was a marvel. Not only was there a huge Christmas tree but underneath were presents for all of the children appropriate to their age group. I got my first Canadian doll with a cloth body and plastic head, hands and legs. My mother helped me to make clothes for it. Though I was almost too old to play with dolls, it was a treasured gift. We continued to socialize with Joe and Helen throughout my growing up until they retired and left Edmonton.

The Westmount house became a project for the entire family. My parents excavated the shallow basement and created a proper laundry room and larder. The rest was our playground where Giuseppe and I tossed balls, played pirates, and cowboys and Indians. Papa also extended the house at the back to create a bedroom for Giuseppe and a new bathroom. The old bathroom became a storage room.

From grade three to grade six, I attended St. Andrew's School at 126 Street and 114 Avenue. The school was located across the street from the Charles Camsell Hospital, which was where Indigenous People from northern Alberta came for tuberculosis treatment. From my first day, I was aware of the children looking at us through the chain link fence that separated the hospital grounds from the neighbourhood.

Since I spoke English perfectly (I was in grade four), there was nothing to distinguish me from the other students and I didn't think I had to prove myself. However, for the first time in my life, I encountered racism. As a dark, southern Italian child, I was taunted with the term "half breed" by some students. In fact, there were Indigenous and Métis children at the school and I became friends with them, in particular, the members of the L'Hirondelle family – Diane, Sharon and, Donnie, who was in my class.

The other awareness I took away from the school was an interest in football. Papa and Giuseppe were avid fans of the Eskimos. Con Kelly, whose mother taught at St. Andrews, was part of the 1956 Grey Cup winning team. A student in my class, George Matsuba, was a water boy for the team. We knew that football hero Rollie Miles and his wife Marianne both taught for the Edmonton Catholic School Board. We were, thus, close to greatness.

While school was sometimes problematical, summers were blissful. It seemed that the sun shone through all of July and August. Because Mamma was at work, we were left to our own devices. Virtually every day, we made French fries. While some parents would be horrified by this today, I think Mamma felt secure because she had taught us to do some basic cooking. We didn't deep fry the potatoes; we shallow-fried them. I remember that the best were the ones at the Edmonton exhibition. The potatoes were extra-large and each fry would be five to six inches long. We couldn't beat them but we came close. We loved to eat outside and dip our fries in ketchup. We would then go to the park behind Westglen High School where the city had a summer student teach crafts to the local children. We didn't get a regular allowance but sometimes we would get a dime or a quarter. For treats, we went to the Eccleston's Confectionery, a few doors away from our house. It had large display cases full of candy as well as a soda fountain with high seats. It was frequented by teenagers from the high school (the Eccleston boys attended Westglen). It was always a struggle for me to choose, and Mr. and Mrs. Eccleston waited patiently while I made up my mind. Inevitably, I chose a chocolate ice cream cone.

On Saturdays with our friends we walked to the Roxy Theatre on 124 Street near 107 Avenue for the matinee. We were each given 25 cents and I believe that the entrance fee was 15 cents leaving the rest for a treat: for me, usually an ice cream bar or an all-day sucker. I learned to love films and followed the lives of movie stars of the era. I was also an avid reader of comics and we traded those with friends including the Canton boys who lived across the street. I read Classic Comics, *Little Lulu* and *Archie* and the gang.

Around 1953 my maternal grandmother came from Italy and she shared her time among her three daughters: my mother, her older sister Teresa and younger sister Livia. Nonna Assunta was a kind, gentle woman who in Italy had managed several properties but who in Edmonton had nothing to do but help with the cooking and housework, and help with the children. She mostly stayed with Zia Teresa in the boarding house she and Zio Paolo had bought in Oliver. When she stayed with us, she shared a bed with me and Rosa.

I remember clearly the polio outbreak of the early 1950s when swimming pools and cinemas were closed in the summer. Pictures in the newspapers of the "iron lung" in which paralyzed children spent their days terrified me. I confided this fear to Nonna and she told me not to be afraid because only old people died. I accepted this with complete faith in her and it comforted me enormously so that I was not afraid to go to sleep. I've since discovered that between 1949 and 1954 more than 11,000 Canadians were left paralyzed: the worst year was 1953 when cases peaked at 9,000 with 500 deaths. In Alberta cases shot up from less than 100 in previous years to 1,472 that year.[1]

Nonna got ill with breast cancer and, although she had surgery, she died in 1955, the first close family member to do so. I knew that she was old but her death stunned me and I didn't know how to grieve her. My sister was very angry with me the day of the funeral when we were left at home to look after Zia Livia's young children while our parents and aunts and uncles went for the burial at St. Joachim's Cemetery. My sister accused me of having a heart of stone. Ultimately, this led to a revelation: I realized that I was an intensely private person who kept my feelings and opinions to myself, and was not comfortable sharing confidences with others.

As with other immigrants, improvement in economic circumstances resulted in a move to a bigger and better house. This occurred for us in 1956. My parents bought a brand-new house on 139 Street and 107 Avenue in North Glenora near Coronation School. On 142 Street there were still remnants of war-time Quonset huts and Papa obtained some scrap lumber that we used to build our garage. I'm sure that our neighbours marveled at the fact that all three children (Rosa, aged 16, myself, 13, and Giuseppe, 10), all were wielding hammers and helping to carry lumber and tools. Papa's progressively longer cars were housed there with the other half being a workshop where he spent many happy hours.

At nearby St. Vincent's Junior High School, I became passionate about literature. We had a teacher from England, who when I later saw the film *The Prime of Miss Jean Brodie*, became clear as a type of 1950s feminist. She had glossy, coloured and permed red hair as well as a fur coat and had an air of mystery about her. The fact that she had

1   University of Alberta, Faculty of Medicine and Dentistry, "Lessons from polio epidemic more relevant now than ever," retrieved September 9, 2020, URL: https://www.ualberta.ca/medicine/news/2018/march/lessons-from-polio-epidemic-more-relevant-now-than-ever.html?platform=hootsuite.

come from afar intrigued me and I fell in love with the English poetry that she made us read. She taught us figures of speech and rhyme, and opened to me the world of imagination and music captured in words.

While up to this point, I had excelled at the dash, relay, broad jump and other athletic pursuits, academics and, in particular, literature became the areas where I truly shone. My parents kept the small gold cup with my name engraved in the base: "Adriana Teresa Albi, Honours Grade Nine 1959." I had chosen "Teresa" as my confirmation name and continued to use it rejecting my actual middle name "Alba," which in Italian means "Dawn." Just too much alliteration (too many "a's"). In fact, at St. Andrew's School, I was known as "Audrey." It seemed that nobody could pronounce Italian names at that time. I re-captured my real name after the kind, elderly neighbour woman in Westmount heard my mother calling me and said to me, "It's a beautiful name and you should use it."

The year 1958 was incredibly important for the Italian community. Two priests came to establish Santa Maria Goretti Parish. The church was built near Clarke Stadium in Edmonton's inner city and became the gathering place for most of the city's Italian families. Prior to that, my family worshipped at St. Joseph's Cathedral and, later, St. Andrew's Church. Youth club events and feast days meant that boys and girls could freely mingle. Many marriages resulted from these encounters. The church hall hosted these gatherings as well as marriages. The youth and wedding dances enabled most of us to become good dancers and I still remember the thrill of the tango, rhumba and cha-cha-cha with a handsome partner, usually a paesano from our home town. We also gathered in the basement rumpus room of the Vecchio family near St. Joe's to dance and socialize. While the older brothers (Sam, Fiore and Tony) were busy at work, Silvano and Rita were still in school and enjoyed hosting on weekends. Fiore was a talented musician who played in a band, besides working as a real estate agent.

The other joy of Italian community life was soccer games at Clarke Stadium. While Papa and my brother, Giuseppe, actually were thrilled by the sport as were the other Italian men, we girls went to see and be seen. Soccer players such as Fidenzio Pasqua were local heroes. Rosa and I took particular care with our appearance when we accompanied Papa to games. It was truly an age of innocence and, though I am certain that bad things happened to people, the care and nurture that we received from our parents and their friends made us feel safe.

After Mass or a soccer game, the family went to the local Italian grocery familiarly known as Spinelli's on 95 Street across from Princess Patricia Park (later Giovanni Caboto Park when a Little Italy was formally established in McCauley). Again, this was a place to see and be seen and not solely to stock up on Italian goodies. Mamma was very conscious about not giving anyone the opportunity to gossip about her girls, so we were always strictly supervised whether by her or her friends, Commare Stella Gatto (she was Rosa's godmother) or her sister Maria Teresa Vecchio.

Zia Teresa and Zio Paolo were an important part of our circle. Zia ran a boarding house and also, for a short time, a restaurant and taught Mamma to make roast beef and delicious desserts including apple, lemon and Boston cream pies, and cream puffs. The famous chicken stuffing was her recipe as well as the rich gravies. After selling the boarding house, they bought a huge two-storey duplex dating back to the 1920s on 123 Street and Stony Plain Road near Robertson-Wesley United Church. They lived on the ground floor of one side and rented out the other rooms. When their daughter, my cousin Franca, came to Edmonton with her sons, Rudy and Paul, they lived in the attic. The house came with grand oak furniture and paintings and photographs including a framed wedding photo of Princess Elizabeth surrounded by bridesmaids, and a coronation photo of the young Queen. These were the possessions of the previous English owners but became a part of this very Italian household. Zio Paolo was a skilled winemaker and the cement basement housed his wine press and demijohns full of new wine. This was before it became legal to make wine.

While the passage from elementary to junior high was important, that from junior high to high school was life changing. At the time, there were two Catholic high schools in Edmonton: St. Joseph's on the North side of the river and St. Mary's on the South side. The schools were segregated between the "boys" half and the "girls" half. Priests and sisters, respectively, taught at each as well as some lay teachers. Next to the school, there was a chapel and we could attend Mass at lunch time as well as for special events.

I started high school in September 1959 and finished in 1962, the same year as the Second Vatican Council that would result in a spiritual renewal for the Catholic Church as well as challenging the established order. Religion dominated St. Joe's and extended beyond the formal religion class. The nuns, members of the Faithful

Companions of Jesus, believed it was their duty to promote vocations. This pressure was felt by all of us and, among my friends, at least half a dozen entered convents.

One felt a struggle for one's soul on a daily basis with, on one side, the devil, boys, dances and other temptations and, on the other side, the Blessed Virgin Mary, chastity, prayer and abnegation. To avoid temptation, teenage boys and girls, personified by their budding libidos, had to be kept separate. We only mingled in certain corridors as we changed classes, in the cafeteria, at dances and sporting events, and in two classes (I believe just drama and physics since the numbers didn't justify separate classes).

Most of the nuns were elderly and set in their ways: one or two were cruel. I remember fearing typing class because the nun who taught it would strike our fingers with a ruler if we made a mistake. I became a terrific typist as a consequence and this aided me in finding summer jobs during university and throughout my later life. The nun who taught home economics and helped us in finishing our assignments (I remember making a paisley blouse and a pink coral suit for Easter) warned us against garments with bare backs. She stated categorically that the back was the least attractive part of the chicken. The youngest nun was Mother Mary Kevin, who was around 30, and taught chemistry. One could talk about dating and other issues and she would giggle with us. In 1967, she left the order and married.

I was not one of the popular girls who wore tight sweaters and skinny skirts, used makeup and had boyfriends. I wore glasses. (I was convinced that this was due to the excessive amount of reading that I did.) My studiousness evidenced by my having my homework done all the time and my high marks in all subject areas marked me as a "brain." Add to this the fact that my parents did not allow us to date; even had I wanted to have anything to do with the opposite sex, I couldn't. I thus had a series of crushes on attractive boys who wouldn't have given me the time of day. At school dances, I was one of the wall flowers who stood around the edges of the room seeing others laughing and having fun. In order to participate, some brave souls danced in groups and that's how I learned to jive and eventually do the twist. I listened to popular music on the radio at home after finishing my homework.

To counter-balance my nerdiness, I took a drama course in grade 10. It was taught by well-known Edmonton actor and director John

Rivet, who also taught English in the boy's school. He was prominent at both the Walterdale and Studio theatres, respectively, in Old Strathcona and at the University of Alberta. I remember the improv aspects of the class some of which we did alone and others with a partner, sometimes one of the boys. This helped me to build confidence and has stood me in good stead not only in any teaching that I've done but also work meetings and dealings with the media. I had modest roles in year plays in grade 10 (Thornton Wilder, *Our Town*) and grade 11 (John Patrick, *The Curious Savage*). The performances, towards the end of the school year, gave us enormous visibility. There were popular kids, nerds and jocks. Theatre people somehow had an "edge" and this somewhat compensated for me being a nerd.

Not being able to date was ok for most of high school but became a problem for the graduation dance. I needed a date and it had to be someone in the family who would not threaten my virginity, or my reputation as a "good" girl in any way. My older cousin Pasquale Falcone took not only my sister Rosa to graduation but also me. He was a handsome man with a full head of hair, which he slicked back. He worked in the hospitality industry as a bartender and looked fabulous in a tuxedo. I was the envy of almost everyone at the school. (I didn't tell anyone that I was related to him.) I wore a lovely dress in a floral satin fabric the skirt of which looked like tulip petals. Pasquale was an excellent dancer and, from the Italian weddings and youth club dances, I had acquired good skills so we danced circles around the others. I'm not certain but I think that local band Barry Allen and the Rebels played.

I had a number of favourite teachers but the two who were most influential in determining where I would go next were Miss Maria Biamonte, who taught me Social Studies, and Miss Marie Louise Brugeyroux, who taught me French. Maria was the daughter of an Italian pioneer who arrived in Edmonton around 1905 and worked in local mines. She and her two sisters never married but all were well-educated. She taught me in grade 10 and the curriculum dealt with the ancient civilizations. She travelled to Europe and Egypt and showed us slides of her travels in class. In grade 12, she encouraged us to do term papers to prepare us for university. I remember that I read Tolstoy's *Anna Karenina* and decided to do a paper on the Russian Revolution. The school library was a treasure trove of exotic books gifted by parents or former students.

Miss Brugeyroux instilled in me a love of the French language. In grade 12, I obtained the highest mark in the Catholic system and the prize was attendance at a French summer school. I could have gone to Trois-Pistoles in Québec, which was the site of the University of Western Ontario's annual French immersion program (Canada's oldest such program established in 1932). Since I had only been away to my aunt and uncle in Wainwright for a month one summer, I was not comfortable enough to go that far. I chose instead to go to the Banff School of Fine Arts for the summer of 1962. The University of Alberta introductory French course, French 200, had an enrolment of about 15 girls and 15 boys, who lived in separate houses supervised by Francophone teachers. They ensured that we spoke French at all times for a complete "immersion" experience. Of course, we cheated but the methodology worked and made me a fluent French speaker.

Every day was spent in French language and literature instruction by top-notch professors attracted from different parts of Canada by the opportunity to spend a summer in the mountains. The rest of the time, we were free to sit in on rehearsals and also to attend performances. I couldn't get enough of this and saw everything that I could including ballet, orchestral, opera and chamber music performances. This experience shaped my love for all of the arts.

Everywhere we would see students and adults sketching the mountain scenery, which also captivated me. Every day, I woke up in the upstairs bedroom I shared in the little house on Bear Street and would draw the curtains and see how high the mist was on the mountain. We walked in small groups up a narrow trail on Tunnel Mountain to the top where the school was located in several buildings as well as dormitories and residence chalets. We did this in all weathers. I was frightened to do this walk on my own, not because of the danger of bears (this didn't even enter my mind at the time). It was the eerie music made by the pine trees rubbing against each other that raised goose bumps on my flesh. The whole air was filled with this sound.

A student dance brought another discovery. Young trainee soldiers from Québec were on an exercise near Johnson's Canyon and, when off duty, came up to the school to socialize. I met Michel, a handsome young man, at a dance. All the practising of the jive and twist in high school paid off and he was impressed with me. We had a lovely time and I saw him again at dances but refused to leave the building to go out into the woods and make out. We had all been warned about the danger of summer romances and I took this to heart.

My attendance at St. Joe's high school not only helped to shape my interest in drama, it also prepared me for attendance at university. In September 1962, I entered the Faculty of Arts at the University of Alberta, and family friend Silvano Vecchio entered the Faculty of Science. We were the first "immigrant children" of our generation in Edmonton to go to university. Through the grapevine, we heard that the infamous Mr. Anselmo had been heard to say that the children of immigrants should not go to university.

CHAPTER 4

University

I LEFT ST. JOSEPH'S HIGH SCHOOL in late June 1962. An Honours graduate, I don't remember having any fear about the academic courses facing me. I was thrilled to be going to the University of Alberta, beginning in early September, and starting the next chapter of my life. The campus at that time had only a few new buildings (for example, the Math-Physics complex and Engineering Building) and the traditional facades of the Arts Building, Medicine and Dentistry, St. Stephen's and St. Joseph's colleges and the Craftsman houses that formed a "ring" around one side of the university gave it a historic air. The campus was beautiful in the fall with the trees changing colour and the flowerbeds still showing their summer finery.

Well-dressed students were everywhere, purposefully striding towards classes or other activities. I was very conscious that I needed to look as good as they did. I had learned as a child immigrant the lesson of the importance of clothes in helping to project the image that one aspired to. I had purchased and read *Mademoiselle* magazine avidly, and knew what was fashionable on American campuses. Young women wore twin-set sweaters in lovely, pale-wool colours (cashmere if you could afford it) and pencil skirts or, for the more adventurous, plaid skirts. Simple pearls with matching earrings and an heirloom ring were the norm in adornment. Nylon-encased feet in penny loafers or other flats completed the outfit. While other girls straightened their hair to have smooth bobs, I was cursed, or blessed, with naturally curly hair and whatever I did, it did just that. So I left it short and let it curl around my face.

Dressing well on a budget was not a problem. My sister had obtained a job at the age of 16 at the Jack and Jill children's wear store at the Westmount Shopping Centre, one of the first malls in Canada. When Rosa finished high school and got a job with the Bank of Nova Scotia, I inherited the job working Thursday evenings and Saturdays. I was thus able to save money for clothes, bus fares and treats. I also occasionally babysat. My parents paid my university tuition fees for my first and second years.

I aspired to look like Rosa, who dressed beautifully in all of the current classy fashions. In spring 1962, she had married a kind, young German man, Rudy Fuerderer, who was a bar manager. They were living in my parents' basement saving to buy a house. I still remember the hot pink, wool, shift dress with a short boxy jacket (with a black leather purse and high-heeled shoes) that she wore to go away to their honeymoon in Vancouver. Rudy encouraged my sister to dress well and sometimes she would pass on sweaters or dresses to me. Since she was two and-a-half inches taller, and slightly heavier, the clothes would have to be fitted to my more diminutive figure. Mamma helped me do this on her trusty sewing machine. She had moved from GWG where she made work wear to ladies wear manufacturers White Stag and Toni Lynn, and was a skilled seamstress.

The bane of my life was the glasses I had to wear – in high school I had gold-rimmed granny classes but by university I was wearing ones with dark plastic rims with fake jewels encrusted on the pointy ends. I looked slightly less nerdy but I wanted more; therefore, I saved so that I could buy contact lenses. Dr. Rowand, at the Optometrist's Clinic at the bend of 124 Street and Jasper Avenue, helped me through this process, and drilled me about proper care of the glass lenses. I was not to wear them for more than 12 hours because I could wear away layers of cornea. This was a worry and I narrowly avoided this danger on a number of occasions because, if I was out late at the library or some event, I had to keep them on for longer. As a result, my eyes would be red, sore and achy, the next day. But the discomfort was worth it.

I remember once complaining to my sister about having to wear a girdle (we all did this at the time even if we were thin) and her response was, "We must be prepared to suffer for beauty!" The minor suffering that I experienced while wearing contact lenses was well worth the price of the transformation from ugly duckling to swan.

While other girls joined sororities, I didn't feel that I could either ask my parents for the money or raise it myself through work. I was, thus, not part of the monied elite of girls who wore clothing from Holt Renfrew and Johnstone Walkers, and had gold pins on their perky bosoms. The studious girls gathered in the Wauneita Lounge upstairs in the Student's Union Building. It had a large fireplace, comfortable sofas and chairs, and a lovely mural by H.G. Glyde titled "When All the World Burned." At the centre on a small island stand an idealized, Indigenous couple. Behind them is a tepee and they are surrounded by a number of animals including rabbits, squirrels, horses, deer and a moose. It comprises an Eden-like garden before the fall of Man. The work was completed around 1952 and was a companion to a larger mural that Glyde completed in spring 1951 and gifted to the University for the Rutherford Library Reading Room. Titled "Alberta History," it represented the successive transformations of Alberta from an Indigenous wilderness to an agricultural paradise and, finally, an oil-rich province. Roman Catholic priests and nuns are among the settlers depicted.

The Wauneita Lounge was a quiet place to go between classes and also to have lunch if one didn't want to go to the snack bar in the basement, or Hot Caf in the quad surrounded by the halls of residence (Pembina, Athabasca and Assiniboia) on one side, and the Engineering and Maths-Physics Buildings on the other side. The Collegiate Gothic buildings constructed of red brick with sandstone trim gave the campus an established look that underscored the importance of university learning in the City of Edmonton and Province of Alberta. The Students' Union Building was newer but was also red brick and sandstone. It housed the offices of *The Gateway* student newspaper, the *Evergreen and Gold* yearbook, the Radio Society and Photography Club.

Having English as a major and French as a minor, the English Department and Romance Languages Department housed in the old Arts Building were the two poles of my student life. I spent most of my time there except for excursions to other buildings to do the science and other options required for a general BA. My English 200 professor was Rowland McMaster, a Dickens scholar, who had recently completed his PhD at the University of Toronto. He and friend Frank

Bessai, whose specialty was Old English, decided that they would do once-a-week tutorials with their best students (half a dozen in each) and occasionally the two groups would meet together.

Rowland's best students were all girls and we got to know each other well. He would set a special reading for us and we would discuss it in a seminar room where we met around 6 pm. It was all very civilized and we felt proud that someone so clever had thought us worthy of these extra learning opportunities. I think that Rowland and Frank were incredibly generous in doing this and certainly had our best intentions at heart. They strongly believed that they were helping to shape the next generation of women academics.

Rowland was a thin, intense man in his thirties who was much troubled by the dropping of the atom bomb on Hiroshima and Nagasaki. He assigned us Robert Jungk's book *Brighter than a Thousand Suns: A Personal History of the Atomic Scientists*, which was published in 1956. He quoted Oppenheimer's famous line from the Indian holy book *The Bhagavad-Gita*: "Now I am become Death, the destroyer of worlds." He could certainly be described as "anti-American" as were a number of my professors and this became a part of my own political thinking.

Another memorable assignment was to read Katherine Mansfield's short story "Bliss." This was an introduction to symbolism for me – the pear tree was a phallic symbol admired by the central female character who was a virgin. I was fascinated by Mansfield, who had left her native New Zealand at the age of 19 to make a literary career in London, England. She died tragically young from tuberculosis at the age of 34 in 1923. She was part of the artistic circle that included authors D.H. Lawrence and Virginia Woolf (and other members of the Bloomsbury Group); literary patron Lady Ottoline Morrell; philosopher Bertrand Russell; and artist Augustus John.

While there were professors committed to the teaching of Canadian literature, at this point, this did not interest me. I was lucky to take the Twentieth Century English Literature course with Department Chair and author Henry Kreisel. I think that in all of my classes I was taught to be a critical thinker but it was Henry who refined my analytical skills with respect to poetry so that I could deconstruct figures of speech, layers of symbolism and appreciate the musicality of language in poetic utterances. I loved poetry though at the time I had no desire to write it. I particularly enjoyed the work of W.B. Yeats, Gerard Manley Hopkins and T.S. Eliot.

The Modern Languages Department also had some gifted professors; it was split into three sections: Romance, Germanic and Slavonic Languages. Because of having completed French 200 at Banff the summer of 1962, I went straight into senior courses. I remember, in particular, the Twentieth Century French Literature course that was team taught. While professors Ed Greene and Charles Moore were excellent, I was particularly drawn to Manoel Faucher and Danièle Billion du Plan because of their direct connections to France. It was said that Faucher had been a secretary to author André Malraux, Minister of Information for Charles de Gaulle and, later, Minister of Cultural Affairs. Faucher was confined to a wheel chair and gossip had it that this was a result of a deep-sea diving accident that nudged him towards academe. I never discovered whether this was true or not. Danièle was a recent arrival and probably one of my youngest professors. She was very thin with a cutting-edge Parisian style reminiscent of Coco Chanel. She became a close friend and later married my Italian 100 professor, Enrico Musacchio. While I enjoyed studying Italian and learning the structure of the language, I was not enticed to change my major or minor. I felt a greater kinship with British and French writers.

Most of my courses dealt with British writers but I did take one American Lit course taught by Ed Rose, who had a reputation as a "shit disturber." He did his PhD on William Blake, poet and revolutionary, with Northrop Frye at the U of T and did not get on with him. According to Ed, he had to start publishing chapters from his thesis to force Frye's hand into getting it approved. I studied "American Lit: 1850 to 1900" with Rose and marveled as he interpreted every work as an attack on contemporary American society. The symbolic vision of Blake that Ed explored in his thesis and various publications was applied to the works of Emerson, Hawthorne, Melville, Poe and others.

For Ed, the US was a fallen world that was focused on materialism and militarism. He introduced political commentary into all of his lectures. He was against the American government's attack on Cuba that culminated in the Bay of Pigs fiasco in April 1961 but it would be the assassination of President Kennedy on November 22, 1963 that brought out the Old Testament prophet in him. I heard about the event when I was sitting in the Wauneita Lounge between classes and rushed to my American Lit Class. We were reading Herman Melville's *Moby Dick* and I remember Ed throwing the book down on the table in front of him and shouting, "Those who live by the sword; die by the sword." This was totally out of keeping with what the media and other professors were saying. Most of the students that I associated with were enamored of the vision of Washington as Camelot reigned over by the glamorous power couple: John and Jackie (who was also my fashion icon). Ed was also against American militarism in Southeast Asia: what became the Viet Nam war.

Though I did not become a campus activist, I certainly was aware of political issues and my values were shaped not only by my professors but also my colleagues at the campus newspaper. Sometime during high school I had decided that I wanted to be a journalist so I joined *The Gateway* on my arrival on campus to get some writing experience. I spent my first year as a cub reporter doing whatever interviews the news editor assigned me. The Editor-in-Chief was Bentley Le Baron, a blond Greek God with an interesting past (the gossip had it that he had been banned from the Hutterite Colony where he grew up because he didn't want to toe the line). While he was on the left of the political arena, other youth journalists such as John Barr supported Barry Goldwater, a Republican and right winger, who ran for the presidency in 1964. One of the older students who came in to write occasional editorials was Joe Clark. The news editor was Bill Winship, an education student.

It was *The Gateway* that connected me to student politics and the greater world. Besides reporting on serious issues, it thumbed its nose at the administration and Student's Council, and teased the sororities and fraternities. The editorial team took a tongue-in-cheek approach to serious subjects and generally thought it was more clever than it actually was. A favourite ploy, though, on reflection, a childish and misogynistic one, was to place ads for the blood drive below photos of sorority events with the headline "Bleed your bloody veins dry: letting coming soon." Sexual innuendo permeated everything though I don't remember young women who were part of the volunteer staff being targeted or embarrassed. By and large, the guys were protective. Another somewhat playful issue related to the very strict laws with respect to where liquor could be consumed. Some of the editors had travelled to the UK and been impressed by the pub culture. When a new Student's Union building was proposed, the slogans "A Pub in Sub" and "No Man is a Camel" became banners used to fill gaps in columns of text.

With respect to provincial politics, we were mostly opponents of the Social Credit government. The association of founder William

Aberhart and current leader Ernest Manning with the religious and political right went against the paper's left-of-centre leanings. Again, John Barr was the exception: he supported the Socred Party and after graduation would be a part of the Peter Lougheed team that brought the Conservative party to power establishing another political dynasty in Alberta.

On occasion, municipal politics also became a target. Long-term mayor William Hawrelak was accused by Council member Ed Leger of using his position for the benefit of himself, his family and his business associates, many of whom were prominent builders. This was a serious charge since, with the coming in of the Leduc No. 1 oil well in 1947, the province achieved a heady new wealth as did many establishment figures. Oil money also fueled a large number of infra-structure projects that changed Edmonton's skyline and benefited the university. Hawrelak was twice found guilty of misconduct and forced to resign but narrowly won the 1963 mayoral election. Student pro-testers clashed with his supporters in front of City Hall. *The Gateway* gleefully reported on the doings of the "Four Horsemen of the Apoc-alypse," the individuals who led the protest. They were professors of philosophy Colwyn Williamson and David Murray, and Department of English profs Robin Matthews and Henry Beissel.

In 1963, Williamson and Beissel were among the group of young professors who published a small, literary/political magazine called *Edge*, which among other causes attacked the Social Credit govern-ment of Alberta as autocratic and anti-democratic. Matthews also attacked American foreign policy as colonial and accused Canadian universities of giving preference to American and British professors at the expense of home-grown academics, and also of neglecting Cana-dian literature. He was a strong believer that Can Lit should be taught in the school system.

The opposition to the Socreds came to a head in 1965 and *The Gateway* provided blow-by-blow descriptions of the clash of values devoting many pages to interviews with the ring leaders, and publish-ing many letters espousing a range of views. In the January 26, 1965 issue, an article by Wayne Poley appeared with the headline "Pam-phlet Turns Rotunda Into Political Arena." It mentions that 10,000 copies of a four-page political pamphlet titled *Commonsense*, edited by Williamson, were distributed by the group. While 1,500 were dis-tributed at the university including at the event at the Arts building that prompted the article, the remainder were delivered door-to-door in Edmonton, and sent to other Alberta cities including Calgary, Red Deer and Forestburg. The pamphlet attacked Socred's "Bible Belt" views and the stranglehold that the party had on the political life of Alberta. It referenced specifically a radio sermon delivered by the Premier on December 6, 1965.

Not everyone agreed with the position presented including President Walter Johns, who felt that the pamphlet brought disrepute to the university and could threaten provincial funding, which was generous. He asked Williamson to stop publishing *Commonsense*. This instruction was rejected. Department of Philosophy chair Tony Mardiros detested the divisive influence of Williamson and Murray within the department and ultimately had to deal with this.

The tension escalated and culminated in the National Student-Day Teach-in held at the university on October 27. The subject chosen for discussion was "the university's role in the community," and the panelists in the first of four panels were Premier Manning; Basil Dean, publisher of *The Edmonton Journal*; Williamson; and Dan Thachuk, a law student.

An article by Alan Hustad in the October 29, 1965 issue of *The Gateway* titled "Premier, professor tangle during teach-in" provided an overview of the debate. Manning observed that the role of the university was "the contribution of a supply of trained personnel to keep that society going," and noted that the university should be non-sectarian and non-partisan. Dean noted that there was growing unrest among academic staff and students who wanted to see change. He believed that universities should be a place for generating "unpopular" ideas that challenged dogma. Williamson noted that universities were a bastion for the "defence of reason" and that students should be encouraged to express their own views. Thachuk observed that "A university exists because society must obtain new ideas and knowledge to survive." In the November 5 issue, transcripts based on recordings made of the two-hour panel discussion by the Radio Society were printed in their entirety.

It was perhaps timely that assistant professors Williamson and Murray were undergoing tenure review in December 1965. Murray had completed five years and Williamson four years at the university; the normal tenure review occurred after four years. They were notified in January, 1966 that tenure had been rejected and that August

31, 1966 was determined as the end of their employment. The two appealed to the Welfare Committee of the Association of the Academic Staff of the U of A and it recommended that a new tenure committee be struck with different members. The university accepted the recommendation but chose not to change the membership of the committee. The outcome was the same though Williamson and Murray were offered an extension of employment to August 31, 1967.

The Gateway devoted a page to letters pro and con in the February 9, 1966 edition and the February 23 issue devoted a full page to "An interview with Colwyn Williamson or: let them call off their Dogs." Don Sellar, News Editor, and Ralph Melnychuk, did a joint interview. This continued to air dirty laundry that was not flattering to Department Chair Mardiros and his supporters, and revealed a severe fracture in the department.

Williamson and Murray did not accept the denial of tenure and, in March 1966, appealed to the Academic Freedom and Tenure Committee of the Canadian Association of University Teachers. This entity produced a report, after reviewing the matter, and stated that they could not deal with the specifics of the case but could make recommendations to make the process and rights and responsibilities of the university, and the two professors, clearer.

The issue then exploded into the national arena. In a May 2, 1966 article titled "The Thorn In Socred's Flesh" in *Macleans*, R.A. Fenn, a professor in the Department of Political Science at the U of T, championed Williamson's cause. Fenn referred to Williamson as "a brilliant young philosopher from Oxford" and asserted that he had been treated badly by the university. *Macleans*, in the July 2, 1966 issue, under the banner headline "The Williamson affair: is freedom in danger at the University of Alberta?" published a series of letters mostly pro. With no recourse, Williamson and Murray left the university and continued their careers in the UK. Beissel and Matthews also left the university.

In the end, whether Williamson published enough or not, or whether his classes were well attended or not (some of the grounds for the rejection of tenure), is immaterial. The dispute marked a clear divide between the authority of the university establishment, and professors and students who questioned their values. The establishment won in this instance but the later sixties and seventies would be marked by campus unrest galvanized by the Viet Nam War not only on American campuses but also campuses throughout the world.

Universities became catalysts for change and we were fortunate to be part of that generation.

While for Williamson and Murray, the Socreds' fundamentalist Christianity threatened campus life, in my experience, the university wasn't at all a religious place. St. Stephen's and St. Joseph's colleges though part of the campus were not central to campus life. As a practicing Catholic, I went through periods of going to Mass daily at St. Joe's at lunch time. There were a number of interesting seminarians who lived there, among them Fergal Nolan, who was doing his Master's in the English Department. It was an exciting time as the Second Vatican Council (October 11, 1962 to December 8, 1965) almost perfectly coincided with the period of my undergraduate studies. The clergy and students at St. Joe's implemented recommendations as they were made, including the use of English in the Mass. The chapel in the historic college building was also transformed: the wooden pews were removed and a lime green carpet installed so that worshippers could sit cross-legged on the floor. The beams were painted a kind of hot pink. Later in life when I worked in the museum field, I had a much less positive take on the defacing of a historic structure! While I went to Mass, I did not discuss religion with any of my friends feeling that it might be considered old-fashioned.

I certainly would not have discussed my Catholicism with members of *The Gateway* staff who considered themselves "freethinkers" and religion as inimical to that. I'm not suggesting that they were serious all of the time. In fact, much fun was had on press nights as we struggled to get each edition of the paper completed. Coffee get-togethers and regular parties took place and many friendships developed. I counted the one with Helene Chomiak particularly important (at the time, she used Helene rather than her actual name, Halyna). Though I was several years older, we bonded and even shared a memorable double date: she with Don Freeland, the man she would marry, and me with Barry Chivers. Don and Barry pursued legal studies. Helene was a child of a Ukrainian family committed to championing Ukraine in the face of Soviet oppression. This was the case for all Ukrainian settlers in Alberta whether they came before or after the 1917 Revolution. When Ukraine obtained its independence from the Soviet Union on August 24, 1991, as a law expert, Helene was brought in as a consultant to advise on the establishment of local governments.

The Gateway was part of the Canadian University Press (CUP) association, established in 1938. It was the oldest student wire service in the world and the oldest national student organization in North America. In my third year at the paper, I served as the CUP Editor and my duties were to read all the student papers from across the country and prepare a column of highlights of hot issues. It served as a snapshot of critical thinking at universities and was challenging to produce.

It was considered a great honour to be asked by the Editor-in-Chief to attend the CUP annual conference. The first I attended was hosted by The Gateway and took place at the Banff School of Fine Arts (in 1963 or '64). We stayed in the chalets on Tunnel Mountain and, besides the more serious issue-based sessions, much hard drinking occurred (not on my part since I was almost teetotal). I remember one evening someone ran into the room where we were congregating and said that the campus security was doing a check of residences and told us to leave (we were not supposed to have liquor in our rooms). Together with cartoonist William Salter, who like me was under twenty, we ran to hide in the trees along the Tunnel Mountain road. I heard a shriek as Bill went tumbling down the slope. I had to stop an oncoming car, which turned out to be the dreaded campus security, and tell them about the accident. Thankfully, they had large flashlights and were able to spot Bill, get him up the slope and take him to hospital. He had a broken collar bone and was incredibly lucky – at the bottom of the scree slope was a barrier to prevent landslides made up of giant logs nailed together by huge spikes only about a foot apart. He could have impaled himself on one of them. When the others drove back to Edmonton, I stayed with Bill to help and we returned to Edmonton by train.

The other big gathering was the CUP conference in Hamilton. I remember a tour of the Steel Company of Canada mill. It was difficult to climb up and down metal ladders that gave a view of various types of smelting equipment including the blast furnace in a tight skirt and high heels. At one of the evening parties in the hotel, I remember a handsome editor from an Ontario university referring to me as an "ice queen." Perhaps this was fitting: I was not only wearing a white lace dress but also probably had a look of boredom on my face as a result of the juvenile antics of the young, very drunk, mostly male, journalists. I also continued to be "my parents' daughter," that is, a good Catholic girl (not that I wasn't tempted but, somehow, I was able to resist).

I particularly enjoyed socializing with the student journalists from Québec so that I could improve my French. Besides holding their liquor better than their English counterparts, they seemed more politically serious. They were all Separatists and wanted to see the English establishment that dominated their province in business and government overthrown. I could understand their frustrations and sympathized with their cause. They would be part of the next generation of teachers and politicians who would almost lead Québec out of Canada.

To help pay for my fees and other costs, in summer of 1963, I took advantage of the long summer break (May through early September) and got a job at the University of Alberta administration department. The excellent typing skills I learned at St. Joe's in grade 10 made this possible. My bosses were happy with my work and hired me back for the summers of '65 and '66. Our duties involved assisting the staff with all aspects of registration and students records. Three to five students were hired each year and we were teamed up with a member of staff. We were expected to dress well: the men in suits and the women in classic shift dresses, suits, or skirts and sweaters. Having excelled at students records, in 1965 and '66, I was involved in the computerization of registration and records and am proud to say that I developed the abbreviations for faculties, departments and course codes that were typed into the old punch cards used by the mainframe computers located in the basement of the Administration Building.

Again, because of my seniority and accuracy, I was added to the team that evaluated foreign educational credentials and recommended credits to be assigned. This involved sometimes lengthy correspondence with students and universities all over the world. The office had calendars from these universities and we had to compare the content of our courses with those claimed by foreign students for equivalencies. I loved doing these and found that it added to my knowledge of the larger world.

The end result of this analysis was writing a letter that stated which courses would be given credit and which would not, and whether the student was eligible for admission to the U of A. This was a painstaking process and the letter was first drafted in a hand-written format and then typed with multiple copies made using carbon paper. The head of that section was a man who enjoyed very much the privileges of university senior staff including long lunches at the Faculty Club and attendance at various events on and off campus. Piles of these letters sat on his desk in the in-box for weeks waiting for signature. Eventually, he would get to them but being embarrassed to have them sent out with a date so long in the past, he would add a few commas or change a word or two so that we would have to retype them. It was infuriating and I think for the first time I began to question the power of "male" bosses.

In order to test my commitment to my proposed profession of journalist, in spring 1964 I applied for a summer internship at *The Edmonton Journal*. Basil Dean was the publisher; Andrew Snaddon, editor; Bill Newbigging, news editor; and Eddie Keene was on the news desk. At the beginning, I did all the menial stuff such as writing obituaries; sometimes this involved calling families to get additional information. They were always gratified for the interest in their deceased loved one and willingly provided information and photos.

As a woman, I also had to do a stint in the Woman's Department headed by Ruth Bowen, the daughter of former Lieutenant Governor John C. Bowen. She was a "society lady" and the women's pages were a mix of fashion articles; features on prominent women and the events that they hosted; stories about society weddings; and a calendar of women's events in the city. I worked on all of these. The story I remember best was one that I wrote on a couple of severely handicapped individuals who were defying their families and doctors by marrying, and setting up their own home. I remember that, in my story, I mentioned that the woman could get "in and out of bed." Ruth edited that out to avoid affronting anyone's sensibilities.

I was glad when I was assigned to the news desk. There are two stories that I particularly remember. The first was on Winnifred Stewart, a trained registered nurse, who championed children with mental and physical disabilities. In 1953, she started the Edmonton Association for the Mentally Handicapped and the school that bore her name. The school was the first of its kind in Canada and she headed it until her retirement in January 1973. At the outset, there were 25 students and 18 teachers who volunteered their services. She was motivated to do this because her son, Parker, was disabled and she wanted him to have a full and meaningful life. She devoted her time to developing new teaching methods and, at the time I interviewed her, she was promoting repetitive manipulation of the limbs of handicapped children to improve mobility. She felt that the "patterning" was crucial.

On a regular rotation, summer interns were also responsible for weekend duty that involved writing of a photo essay that appeared as a double-page spread in the Sunday paper. One weekend, my assignment was to go to a northern reserve on Saturday with the staff photographer, Dave, and report on a meeting of Indigenous People. Dave drove and we arrived at a community like none I had ever seen before where the housing was mostly shacks. We made our way to the largest building, which was like a community hall, and went in. The room was thick with smoke and filled with men. We introduced ourselves and were welcomed. I listened politely and with increasing interest and Dave took photographs. The men, chiefs and elders, were discussing treaty rights, in particular, hunting and fishing rights. I knew nothing about this and was captivated and convinced by their arguments that the Government of Canada and Province of Alberta had to respect those rights.

We drove back late afternoon and worked until after midnight, myself writing the story and Dave developing and printing the photographs to accompany it. We made the photo selection together and passed the text and images to the night production crew. I was thrilled with the way the spread turned out and was stunned at the weekly editorial meeting when Andrew Snaddon attacked me for my lack of objectivity, and accused me of having only represented the Indigenous position. His diatribe went on and on and, to stop myself from crying and embarrassing myself, I clenched my hands and later noticed that the nails had penetrated the flesh and I was bleeding. After the meeting ended, the business editor quietly came up and congratulated me and told me that I had done a good job. No-one else supported me.

The other nail in the coffin of my journalistic aspirations was when I found out that there was a bet as to who on staff would succeed in seducing me. The men hung out at the Greenbrier Hotel at 102 Street and 100 Avenue (across the street from *The Journal* building) weekdays after work and some also on the weekend. I realized that journalism was a male-dominated profession run by individuals many of whom had questionable values. This was not the world of the truth-seeking journalist that I had dreamed about since I was in junior high.

While I continued to work at *The Gateway*, the return to university in September 1964 marked a shift. I decided that I wanted to be an academic and follow in the footsteps of the many professors who had inspired me. I didn't know, as yet, what the subject area would be but knew that I had to undertake Master's and Doctoral work. This renewed my commitment to doing my best in my course work

not just English and French but also the science options that I had
to study to get my BA. In my first year I had done the introductory
botany course and got the highest mark in all sections. The course was
team taught and I was approached by Department Chair Dr. Harold
Brodie, who invited me to change my specialization. I thanked him
and said, no, with regret. I then took Genetics 351 which had all sorts
of interesting lab work some of which involved breeding fruit flies to
determine dominant and recessive genes. The lab assistant had worked
with David Suzuki, who in the 1962-63 academic year had been an
assistant prof at the U of A and had done leading-edge research on
fruit flies. I was fascinated and was almost tempted to change majors.
My final science course was Statistics, which I didn't care for but felt
might prove useful.

With renewed vigour, I completed the course work required for
my BA and, in 1965-66 completed a "makeup" year comprising only
English courses before taking graduate courses and beginning work on
a Master's thesis. I looked first at American Lit and considered Ernest
Hemingway, William Faulkner and John Steinbeck and read all of
their works. In the end, I didn't find them challenging enough so I
approached Rowland McMaster and he suggested I consider Dickens
and recommended the late novels since new scholarship was, in his
opinion, necessary.

I read them and also the works of the leading Dickens scholars
and racked my brains about what approach I could take that would
both interest me and result in new scholarship. One evening sitting in
a carrel in the new Cameron Library, I was reading "Songs of Experience" and "Songs of Innocence" for one of my graduate courses and
it struck me that William Blake was dealing with transformation.
With industrialization, child labour had become ubiquitous and the
small boys who worked as chimney sweeps frequently died from tes-
ticular cancer from exposure to carbon on a daily basis. In the poems
in "Songs of Innocence," the children are free to play unrestricted.
I thought of the possibility of exploring this theme in Dickens' last
four novels. In all of them, a character assumed the role of a fairy, who
waved a magic wand to change the dreadful circumstances of the pro-
tagonists. I discussed this with Rowland and we agreed that my thesis
topic would be "fairy tale transformation" in Dickens' last novels.

I knew that to complete three graduate courses, and undertake the research and writing of my thesis in a tight timeframe (one

academic year), would require hard work and discipline. Up to this point, I had been taking a bus in to the university and, if I stayed late, my father would pick me up at 10 pm when the library closed. Pointing out that this was a burden for him after a full-day's work, I convinced my parents to let me live at Pembina Hall. This was an amazing experience. The building retained all of its historic features and the rooms were spacious with a single bed, a desk and bookcase. I quickly went to the bookstore and purchased a poster of a Venetian scene with a gondola and two others with illustrations from Aubrey Beardsley's *Salome* series to personalize my room.

Pembina Hall housed mostly female graduate students and we took our meals in the large cafeteria in Athabasca Hall. The Dean of Women, Mrs. Sparling, still resided in the residence and greeted each new resident formally at a tea in her suite when you first moved in. I remember her rooms on one of the upper floors with their rich oak paneling and antiques. The suite had an excellent view of the quad.

Social events such as dances took place at Athabasca Hall, which was the male student residence. I remember the Halloween event when one of the boys dressed as Hugh Hefner. He looked remarkably like him and none of us were particularly attracted to him. I had a crush on Andy, a doctoral student in Physics from the UK who resembled Mick Jagger. We dated but, when I wouldn't "put out," he found someone else who would. In any case, I was too busy with my three grad courses and initial research on my thesis to worry about my romantic life.

When the academic year ended the last week of April, seven of us in Grad Studies jointly rented an old house in the enclave that former *Edmonton Journal* columnist Todd Babiak described as "The Garneau Block." There were rooms for all of us in the two-storey Craftsman house and we shared the housekeeping duties in rotation. We took turns shopping, cooking and cleaning the common areas. The house was the former residence of a high school art teacher and the basement, besides the giant, octopus-like gas furnace, had rooms filled with his paintings. One storage room had large glass jars full of baby clothing. I spent the day either at the Cameron Library doing research or at my typewriter in my second floor bedroom doing drafts of chapters. Again, my excellent typing skills stood me in good stead.

I returned home on Sunday for a home-cooked meal but the rest of the time I was my own woman, for the first time in my life. But while not directly under my parents' control, I was still their daughter and though friends had started to sleep with their boyfriends, I could not. Thus, my emotional development was stunted and involvements with the opposite sex always ended when the subject of sex came up. My lovers were imaginary and romantic and I listened repeatedly to songs of longing including those of Richie Valens, Joan Baez, Judy Collins, Tom Paxton and José Feliciano. Fortunately, I didn't have much time to brood about this because of the research and writing and the parties held by friends who were living in houses near ours. Party central was the house that Philosophy prof David Murray rented across the street from ours. My friend Patricia Hughes, who was also majoring in English, lived there and provided invitations to any happenings.

I loved living in the old house. We had formal meals in the dining room that accommodated all of us plus a guest or two. On the weeks I had cooking duties, everyone always wanted me to cook Italian, which I was happy to do. I made not only pasta Bolognaise but also pasta with meatballs, stuffed green peppers and lasagna. In the evening, if we were home, the fire would be lit in the old fireplace and we would talk about our work: three of the women were grad students in the sciences (the oldest was doing a doctorate and the others were doing Master's degrees); another was in Math, I believe; and another was a graduate student from Hong Kong. I was pleased to help her by editing her essays. She was so appreciative that, at the end of the summer, she took me to dinner at the Ling Yang. While I had eaten there before, I had never had Chinese food ordered by a Chinese person speaking the language. The food was delicious and I never forgot Lana's instruction to sip tea between bites to cleanse my palate. I wrote some poetry about the house, which are lost in the mists of time. I remained friends with three of the women for many years, mostly through the annual Christmas letter, as we scattered to different parts of the world for further study or to find jobs.

I remember one evening that we played with an Ouija board and the message spelled out for me was "Queen City." This would prove remarkably perceptive. Having decided that I wanted a career in academe, I had written to established Dickens scholars at the University of Oxford to see about doing a doctorate. I was accepted but was told that I could not begin until 1969. I think it was Henry Kreisel who suggested King's College, University of London. The Chair of the English Department, George Kane, was Canadian. I applied and was accepted for fall 1968. I also applied for grants and initially obtained an Imperial Order Daughters of the Empire scholarship, which I accepted. Shortly after, I was awarded a Canada Council Scholarship, which was much more generous and accepted that and turned down the IODE offer. Things were falling into place but I needed to fill a "bridge" year, 1967-68. My Chaucer prof, Don Chapin, who was going to teach at the University of Western Ontario, suggested that I apply for a sessional and I was chosen.

All I had to do was complete my thesis, which I did by August. Because Rowland was away, a colleague in the English Department, Alison White, helped me by reviewing my thesis and suggesting some refinements. She also shepherded me through the thesis defence. She had developed the Children's Literature course at the university and genuinely appreciated my exploration of fairy tale in Dickens' work.

I obtained my Master's degree and, in order to celebrate, Rowland and his partner Juliet (later his second wife) suggested that I join them and some friends on a hike on Mount Edith Cavell, Jasper National Park. It was about a five-hour drive from Edmonton and, when we got there, everything was organized and the skilled hikers (I was not) loaded their backpacks with supplies, and we began the ascent to the Cavell Meadows Summit. It was a steep but well-developed trail and, on parts of it, horses and riders had gone before, the horses leaving a trail of excrement in spots that had to be avoided. We also had to be careful because of the changes in terrain including a boulder field. We continued to climb above the treeline until we reached the sub-alpine, and then alpine, terrain. I believe that we hiked 14 miles and spent the night in a cabin that was shared with other hikers. I was exhausted and my feet and legs ached so between the pain and the snoring of one of the other occupants (not one of our group, I might add), I didn't get much sleep.

The next day we continued our climb and reached the Summit Meadow and I was amazed by the 360 degree views. I felt like a child filled with joy; this may have been the effect of lack of oxygen at such a high level making me light headed. I spun around in circles in exhilaration. The experienced campers in our group had put bottles of white wine to chill in one of the streams so we had a marvelous lunch and then began the descent.

I thought that climbing up was difficult but soon realized that climbing down was worse. The pressure on my toes and knees was almost unbearable and, at one point, I got cramps in both legs. I was told to lie down on the rocky ground and a member of our group, who was incredibly fit and also fenced, vigorously massaged my legs. It was painful but it worked and I was able to finish the hike. I had Rowland to thank not only for helping me to complete my Master's degree but also for making my last days in Alberta so special.

I felt that my years at the U of A were idyllic but I was not a total Pollyanna who saw only positive things. Some terrible things happened and I was fortunate that they did not happen to me. The girl living next to me in Pembina hall was in her third year and I remember one morning in the cafeteria being told that she was in hospital. With another young woman, I went to visit her in the U of A Hospital. She told us that she tried to commit suicide by overdosing on prescription medicine and drinking a bottle of liquor that one of the older girls had bought for her. I visited her on several occasions and she eventually told me that her older brother had raped her when she was in her mid-teens. She couldn't tell her parents that she hated going home because he would do it again. I encouraged her to talk to her counselor because her parents needed to know. I hope that she got the help that she needed.

Another terrible incident was the result of the heavy drinking that some students, both male and female, indulged in. One of the young women in the circle I partied with got very drunk and fell asleep under a tree near the Old Rutherford Library. She awoke to discover that one of the male graduate students was trying to have sex with her. I don't know whether she succeeded in stopping him or not but the next day, she went to the Campus Cops and he was arrested.

The third incident that affected me deeply was when the younger brother of one of my circle of friends came up to campus from rural Alberta, and decided to stay and drop out. He was only 16. I still think of this sensitive soul who never got to grow up and how fortunate I was. In comparison to these three individuals, I knew that I was blessed and felt that my life had a magical quality.

In early September 1967, I took a flight to Montreal to see Expo, Canada's grand celebration of its centenary. From April to October the International and Universal Exposition titled "Man and His World" (from Antoine de Saint-Exupéry's *Terres des Hommes*) provided access to pavilions from 62 countries.

I was anxious to see Montreal not only because of the World's Fair but also because, in November 1966, I had met Leonard Cohen at readings at the university and was anxious to visit his birth city. I had a week there seeing all of the pavilions and was particularly inspired by the Canadian Pavilion. I became an unashamed patriot and this has remained with me throughout my life. I then took the train to London, Ontario to begin my duties as a sessional instructor at the University of Western Ontario. I was responsible for two sections of the tutorials for the first year English course, and was privileged to teach a Shakespeare course because the professor scheduled to do it couldn't.

I made three excellent friends who were graduate students in the department: Doris, an Ontario girl; Tina from London, England; and Penny, from Manitoba. Doris, Tina and I had bedsit apartments in the Jack Tar building, a former hotel in the downtown. We cooked for each other once a week and every evening met in Doris' apartment (the coziest) to watch the 10 o'clock news. The news was grim at the time, in particular, the famine in Uganda. In spring 1968, I accompanied Doris to Barrie where she was interviewed for a position at the newly-developed Georgian College. The offices were housed in a strip mall. She was successful and would spend her entire academic career there culminating as chair of the department.

In late May, 1968 I returned to Edmonton to visit my parents and pack up my trunk for my sea voyage to England. I returned to Montreal towards the end of June and met my brother Giuseppe, who was to begin studies at the École des Beaux Arts in September. We toured Expo together and I helped him find a cheap basement apartment to live in. We took a taxi to the docks and I boarded. I waved to him as the ship began to move out of the harbor heading for Liverpool.

This was 17 years after my arrival in Canada at Halifax's Pier 21 as a child immigrant. A Canada Council grant would pay for my studies in London so all I needed to do was find a thesis topic, do the research and complete the thesis. That was only the academic side; on the personal side, I would be living life on my own terms for the first time without any family support.

CHAPTER 5

My Encounter
with Leonard Cohen

A S A STUDENT AT THE UNIVERSITY of Alberta in Edmonton, I had a very interesting companion on my bus journeys from the Westmount neighbourhood, where my family lived, to the University and back. I don't know when this began exactly but, likely, what led to a friendship developing was an empty seat, and either Eli Mandel or I sitting in it. The bus was always full around 8 am or between 5 or 6 pm when I did my daily journeys. I got on the bus at the stop on 139 Street and 107 Avenue (just a three minute walk from my house) and Eli would be on it, coming from further in the west end where he lived. At the University, I would get on at one of the stops near St. Stephen's College, the United Church College at 88 Avenue and 112 Street.

Eli would have been in his early forties at the time: a short, compact man with a moustache, which was unusual at the time. We introduced ourselves and found that we had much in common beginning with the fact that he was a professor in the Department of English, and I was a student in the same department. I think that we started to talk about literature at first and, specifically Can Lit, since this was one of the courses that he taught in addition to creative writing, and then about our personal lives. I think that we bonded over the fact that his parents were Russian Jewish immigrants from the Ukraine who settled in Estevan, Saskatchewan where he was born, and I was a child immigrant.

I learned that Eli was a poet, as was his wife Miriam, and that they had two children, Charles and Evie. He cared passionately about teaching and also his writing, not just poetry but also literary criticism promoting other Canadian poets. We also bonded because we both had highly developed social consciences. In fact, I think that all of the professors that I was close to did. We discussed the Holocaust: not only Eli but also Henry Kreisel, the Department of English Chair, and Ed Rose, who taught me American Lit, were Jews. Genealogists among my Spokane relatives had connected our family with Joseph Albo (this was the spelling of our name before immigration), who was a fifteenth century Jewish philosopher who lived in Spain. Though Catholic, I was fascinated by the idea that the family had converted as a result of the Spanish Inquisition. My International Politics professor, Neville Linton, showed us documentaries shot by troops as they entered concentration camps at the end of the war.

It was this friendship with Eli that prompted me to choose to take his Victorian Poetry graduate course in the 1966-67 academic year. At that time, I was living in the graduate women's residence, Pembina Hall. I was a short (five foot one inch), dark, curly-haired, brown-eyed girl and, further, a perfect romantic who believed in the power of "LOVE."

At the same time, as an avid reader, I had fallen in love with the study of literature. I had as models, not only Eli but also Rowland McMaster, my English 200 prof; Henry Kreisel, who taught me Twentieth Century English Lit; Frank Bessai, who taught me Old English; and Hank Hargreaves, who taught me Shakespeare. A number of the professors had PhD's from the University of Toronto including Rowland, Henry, Frank, Eli, Ed Rose and Wilfred Watson. They were well-connected to the academic intelligentsia of that university – Ed's PhD supervisor was Northrop Frye and Wilfred was a colleague of Marshall McLuhan and, according to him, had helped to formulate theories such as "the medium is the message." Wilfred was an avant-garde poet and playwright with a strong following among some students. Ed taught me American Lit and I took Wilfred's graduate course on Metaphysical Poetry.

The Department of English at the time was a powerhouse with Kreisel as chair. As an established Canadian author, he not only nurtured students' understanding of the greats of English literature but also encouraged writers in the department to publish. I felt part of this flourishing of creativity. Professors encouraged us to test our intellects through discourse that sometimes degenerated into argument (albeit civil). We were expected to take different points of view and defend them thereby honing our intellectual skills. These debates would continue in the Quonset-style "Hot Caf" in the centre of campus, or the "Tuck Shop" where poet Jon Whyte held court. Most of my closest friends were fellow students in the English Department, or writers and photographers at the campus newspaper, *The Gateway*, for which I wrote.

While I did not take a Can Lit course (my interests were in traditional English literature), through Eli, I began to know of the "greats" of Can Lit most of whom he knew, at least the poets. The University of Alberta had a wonderful Canadian poetry reading series and I attended each avidly (some likely with Eli), particularly in the period 1965-67. I remember hearing Earle Birney, bpNichol and the memorable Irving Layton. Although a small man, he had a great aura and wore a dark woolen cape that flowed around him as he walked. I remember his very lustful verses.

In spite of my traditional Italian upbringing, I was not a prude and had read D.H. Lawrence and cult writers of the period including Ernest Hemingway, John Barth, John Updike, Lawrence Durrell, Henry Miller, Irving Stone, Anthony Burgess, Edward Albee, Vladimir Nabokov, Mary McCarthy, Anaïs Nin, Gore Vidal, Frank Herbert and many others. This was my "free" reading and not my academic life, which was quite separate.

Eli, during the year that I took his graduate course, separated from his wife Miriam. He did not talk about the cause of the separation with me but, from department gossip, I heard that Miriam was high-strung and suffered from depression. I think that Eli had also fallen in love with Ann Hardy, one of the graduate students in the department. She was an exotic and unusual young woman in her mid-twenties. She had an hour glass figure and bleached blond hair, and was taller than him. I believe that her father was a professor but didn't know the family. Ann seemed very sophisticated and cosmo- politan in comparison to the other female students. I think that she loved the fact that Eli was an established poet and enjoyed being part of the Can Lit scene.

Eli moved into an apartment downtown and it became a ritual that, after the graduate class ended, five or six of the students would gather at his apartment to talk about Tennyson and Browning, the subjects of the course, and also Can Lit. Beer and wine were consumed though not much by me since having grown up with wine at the table for festivities, I didn't consider it taboo and, therefore, had no great desire to drink. I didn't like the fact that it made me light-headed and not in control. Eli took great pleasure in discovering culinary treats (one was pickles from a Jewish deli) and sharing them with us. Some evenings we called poets whom Eli knew, and I remember a failed attempt to contact Lawrence Ferlinghetti in the US.

We did succeed in reaching Leonard Cohen one evening and we all spoke to him. Eli had mentioned that he was on a grants jury (I believe Canada Council) that had given Leonard funding and knew him well. Perhaps it was their "Jewishness" that also drew them together, as it did with Irving Layton. (In 1969, Eli wrote an essay on his work.) We invited Leonard to come to Edmonton and he mentioned that his publishers, McClelland and Stewart, were sending him on a book tour to publicize his new book, *Beautiful Losers*.

To prepare for Leonard's visit, I purchased and read his earlier novel, *The Favorite Game*, published in 1963, and also his books of poetry: *The Spice Box of Earth* (1961); *Flowers for Hitler* (1964); *Let Us Compare Mythologies*, which was first published in 1956 and reprinted in 1966; and *Parasites of Heaven* (1966).

I also remember in this period seeing the documentary "Ladies and Gentlemen ... Mr. Leonard Cohen" on CBC. I watched it with my mother and was utterly captivated by him. On the weekends, I would leave my residence at the University and spend time at home with my parents. I don't know what my mother made of it. She was a typical Italian housewife whose interests did not extend to poetry but she loved me and was proud that I was excelling at my studies, and I think did it to humour me. In the documentary, Leonard is teasing and controlling, and plays the part of the poet as *enfant terrible*. I think this is what attracted the documentarians – he was not only handsome but he also dominated a room with his clever repartee.

With a minor in French, I knew well the poetry of Charles Baudelaire and Arthur Rimbaud. Living at the beginning of the drug culture of marijuana and LSD, I was intrigued by Baudelaire's notion that beauty could be evil, and his exploration of "artificial paradises" fueled by drugs; however, not enough to induce me to try drugs, at that time. I also loved Rimbaud's free-spiritedness and exploration of symbolism and anti-establishment behaviours (such as his affair with fellow poet Paul Verlaine). From my readings of his works, Leonard fit into the mold of a poet as challenging authority. I saw the sacred and profane in his works and admired the way that he used myth and mythic personalities in a contemporary context. He also embraced the persona of the poet as outcast.

The Gateway offices were abuzz with Leonard's upcoming visit. The November 18, 1966 edition of the paper had a review titled "Cohen's pornographic novel comes out a beautiful winner." The November 25 issue had a photo of Leonard and his lover Marianne posed with a strange puppet figure with the headline "Cohen is coming."

Eli had booked Leonard to read at one of his Canadian Lit classes and also to perform at the Yardbird Suite, a performance venue renowned for its live jazz. Wilfred Watson had been one of the founders and occasional poetry readings took place there. Eli had read his own poetry there about a week before Leonard arrived. He also "stage-managed" the tour activities in Edmonton beginning with an interview with Leonard on Monday, November 29th at the historic Macdonald Hotel where he was staying. This was a group effort led by Jon Whyte, who edited an occasional poetry magazine inserted in *The Gateway* titled *Inside*. He was accompanied by English undergrads Patricia Hughes, Terry Donnelly and John Thompson. I knew all of them. The newspaper came out on Friday and we were all anxiously awaiting what they would say.

The day of the readings, Tuesday, November 29, was cold. In mid-afternoon, I rushed from a class in the Education Building to the Tory Lecture Theatre, known familiarly as the "Tory Turtle" for its shape. The winter wind stung my face as it swept along Saskatchewan Drive on the south crest of the River Valley. I was afraid I was going to be late and rushed into the entrance where I saw Eli talking to Leonard who was lounging against the rock wall of the entry dressed in black slacks and black, rolled-neck polo sweater.

I greeted Eli and he introduced me to Leonard referring to me as one of his brightest graduate students. I was already out-of-breath but the beauty of the slim man with his dark, curly hair and fine-boned hands stunned me. I mumbled something about loving his poetry and comparing it to the poetry of Baudelaire and Rimbaud. He said that he was pleased to meet me and was flattered to have his poetry compared to that of these great poets. We then entered the bowl-shaped lecture theatre which was full of students.

Eli introduced Leonard and I remember him doing various readings from his poetry books and novels. When he switched to reading excerpts from *Beautiful Losers* there was a stir in the room and a sense of unease. Having read the book, I knew how outrageous it was with its explicit eroticism (both hetero- and homosexual). I was captivated by his voice and watched as more and more students left as the material he read affronted their sensibilities, religious beliefs or both. While a strict Catholic, somehow I could accept all types of behavior in literature perhaps, literally, undergoing a "suspension of disbelief."

At the end of the lecture, I arranged with Eli to go to the reading that was to take place that evening at the Yardbird. In 1965, it was located on the southside of the North Saskatchewan River in Old Strathcona at the corner of 81 Avenue and 102 Street, and not far from the bars on Whyte Avenue, popular student haunts.

The venue had wooden, bleacher-type seating in a warehouse space. Leonard came out all dressed in black, and carrying a guitar, and began to sing. The dim spotlights illuminated his expressive face and he was embraced by darkness. His deep, sonorous voice gave the impression that what he said was of utmost importance, and the simple accompaniment on the guitar drew you further into the world that he presented. He sang "Suzanne" and "So Long, Marianne," but I don't remember what else. For the rest of my life, I've had a passion for "tea and oranges," whether they came from China or not. I sat on the top tier of seats with an excellent view of the small stage next to Miriam Mandel, who had come to the reading with the children. I had the strange sensation, or delusion, that he was singing directly to me and that he had "touched my perfect body with his mind" as he sang in "Suzanne." I walked out of the Yardbird on a romantic high.

Eli had invited the half dozen grad students from his course to join Leonard at the Macdonald Hotel. His suite was a gracious living room with a separate bedroom and bathroom. Leonard greeted us and mentioned that his publishers were paying for everything and proceeded to order champagne and oysters for us, since most of us had never had them.

Shortly after, he made his way to me and we began to talk. Eli had told us that Leonard was studying Buddhism in California and was celibate, and that he also had given up drinking and drugs. So, from the outset, I did not view this as a pickup. I was wearing a tight skirt and a high-necked sweater. A simple gold cross that my grandmother in Italy had sent me hung around my neck. I didn't consider myself a great beauty but I felt that I looked good. I believe that I had a bloom of innocence about me, which I knew had intrigued other young men who I had met during my university days.

In person, Leonard was unlike the ironic and satirical figure in the NFB documentary. He was quiet and thoughtful, and interested in my life and beliefs. He encouraged confidences. I told him about my immigrant family and that I had attended St. Joseph's High School in Edmonton where most of the teachers on the girl's side were Faithful Companions of Jesus. Sisters of Charity had also been teachers in the Edmonton Catholic schools. Many of my friends had joined religious orders; I had not, feeling that my life was somehow bigger than that. I told him that I loved university and wanted to continue my studies in Europe. I also mentioned that I felt like a fish out of water since most of my Italian girl friends were married, or finishing university and becoming school teachers. He encouraged me to do whatever I felt that I needed to do with my life and not let others, or fear, restrict me. I confessed to him that I had had the strange sensation that he had been singing to me at the Yardbird and he said that he had, and that I had beautiful eyes.

At some point, he noticed my cross and excused himself for a moment to go to the bedroom. He returned with a tiny locket with a glass back and tin cover with an image of St. Joseph holding the baby Jesus impressed on it. He lifted the lid and showed me the tiny rosary inside made of red and white ceramic beads. He told me that he got it at St. Joseph's Oratory in Montreal and that he kept it with him always. I expressed surprise that he would be interested in Catholic religious imagery but he told me that he studied Catholicism and was drawn to the religion. He believed in the existence of sin and the need for forgiveness and redemption. I told him of my interest in comparative religion and that I took a graduate course in "Victorian Thought." The principal course text was *Sir James Frazer's The Golden Bough: A Study in Magic and Religion* but we also read Joseph Campbell's *The Hero with a Thousand Faces*. I mentioned the crucified god, a part of many Middle Eastern religions. It was clear that we had similar interests and points of view with respect to not only literature but also religion. I think that Leonard also mentioned an interest in the cloistered life and I suppose that was a part of what appealed to him about Buddhism.

I believe that we talked for at least an hour and during our conversation the room filled with people. I don't remember who ended the conversation but was aware that a new group of people had arrived including a couple of undergraduates in the English Department, Barbara and Lorraine. I felt that the magic time between Leonard and me was over and said he should probably talk to some of his other guests. I handed him back the locket and he said, no, I was to keep it. I clutched it in my hand like a precious relic and decided to leave.

It was around midnight and I went down to the lobby and asked for a cab. As the cab travelled through the downtown and across the High Level Bridge to the University, I began to cry. The driver stopped near St. Stephen's College; I paid him and started to walk across the quad to Pembina Hall. It was so cold that I felt the tears freezing on my cheeks.

I knew that something special had happened to me and I didn't talk about it with anyone. In the Friday, December 2 edition of *The Gateway*, the article "A session with Poet Cohen" appeared. It was a double-page, centre-spread and was a Q & A. With Eli in the background (he only makes one observation), Jon Whyte, Patricia Hughes, Terry Donnelly and John Thompson quizzed Leonard about the nature of his poetic creativity, sources, the role of poetry (and the poet) in society, and also his move from poet to singer/songwriter. They are respectful and deferential but challenging and wanting somehow to catch him out. The unasked question was – "Are you a talented novelist and poet, or a fraud?" The article was accompanied by three photographs and it was easy for me, as a Gateway writer, to get copies from photographer Al Scarfe.

Jon, Patricia, Terry, John, Barbara and Lorraine were friends and I heard that Leonard had stayed on in Edmonton for several weeks in a room at the Alberta Hotel downtown. Situated virtually across the street from the Macdonald, it had begun its life in the 1880s as a grand hotel but, by the 1960s, was down-at-heels and its bar was a hangout for inner-city drunks and some brave students. Leonard attended parties in the old Garneau house rented by philosophy professor David Murray and which also housed students such as Patricia whose bedroom was the front porch (a cold proposition in the winter).

The visit to Edmonton has become part of Leonard Cohen lore. Early in 1967, he would be in New York talking about recording with Judy Collins, meeting Bob Dylan and members of The Band; in fact, anyone who was anyone in the folk and rock music scene. But I believe that Edmonton was not only the testing ground for his career in music but he also found a congenial circle of young poets and lovers of poetry that fueled his next generation of songs. Wilfred Watson, in a poem titled "lines 1966" that focuses on the lack of an appreciation or audience for Canadian poets writes:

> What more did they want
> DID THEY EXPECT HIM TO LOOK LIKE LEONARD
> COHEN AND STAND BEFORE THEM NODDING
> A SILKEN UNICORN'S MANE?

It is intriguing that Watson chose to represent Leonard as a unicorn. His reputation as a lover was well established and he could have referred to him as a satyr. But the image of the unicorn is compelling not only because they are magical, fabled beings but also because they could only be captured by virgins.

After the magical encounter with Leonard, I completed my thesis and got a job as a sessional lecturer at the University of Western Ontario in London. In early September, I flew to Montreal to see Expo '67 and contacted my friend Nat Bernstein. We had met when he was doing his Masters at the U of A on a Jacobean playwright. He was part of the Montreal Jewish community (his parents were in the clothing industry) and I told him about my encounter with Leonard. He kindly took me to various Cohen haunts including Notre-Dame-de-Bonsecours, "Our lady of the harbor." I fell in love with the city and the Church and have carried this in my heart to the present.

In September 1967, I settled in my bedsit in the Jack Tar building in downtown London, Ontario and began teaching at the university and made friends. On weekends I would go to Toronto on the bus and stay with my friend Catherine Siemens, who lived in an old brick house the rooms of which were rented out individually. She worked at the U of T library. I also saw Eli and Ann, who had married and moved to a high rise apartment in Toronto so that Eli could begin teaching at York University. I was at the launch party held in a Rosedale Mansion for his book of poetry, *An Idiot Joy*, for which he received the Governor General's Award in 1968. Through him I met poet Phyllis Webb and authors and staff of The Coach House Press. Eli with Phyllis and Gael Turnbull had published a book of poetry tiled *Trio* in 1954.

On one of my visits, I arrived at Eli and Ann's apartment for dinner with a candle and Eli was delighted to tell me that it was the Feast of Hanukkah, the Festival of Lights, which commemorated the re-dedication of the Second Temple in Jerusalem. I was also among the first people to know about Ann's pregnancy with their daughter Sara.

In my Jack Tar apartment I waited anxiously for Leonard's first record to come out. There was a record store in a downtown mall near my apartment and I would go there every couple of days to see whether the LP had arrived. It was finally released on December 27, 1967 and I bought one of the first copies sold in London. It was a bad pressing and skipped so I had to return it on several occasions until I got one that worked. There were both familiar and new songs on it and I came to love it though initially I was put off by the backing singers and the "country and western" flavour, though Leonard had told *The Gateway* interviewers that he had always played the guitar and played in a barn dance group called the Buckskin Boys. I memorized every song and loved, in particular, "The Sisters of Mercy," written for Barbara and Lorraine. I've always felt that the conversation about religion and faith that Leonard and I had had that magical evening had somehow influenced his creativity at the time.

On Election Day in June, 1968, I boarded a ship in Montreal harbor to go to England to begin doctoral studies at King's College, University of London. I brought with me one trunk, perhaps an homage to the trunk that my mother had placed all of our belongings in when we left the Port of Naples for Halifax in 1951. I gently placed inside the portable record player I had bought in London so that I could listen to Leonard's LP and the collection of classical music that I began to acquire. At midnight, with the Plains of Abraham behind us, election results began to come in and Pierre-Elliott Trudeau was announced Prime Minister.

I found an apartment in an old brick house in the North London neighbourhood of Willesden Green and fell in love with the owner, David. I introduced him to Leonard's writing and songs. In the large living room which occupied almost the entire ground floor of the house, I would put on *Songs of Leonard Cohen* and dance and spin around like a dervish. When the relationship ended and I moved out, David kept all of my Cohen books. I couldn't bear to go back to retrieve them because he was my first lover and it hurt too much.

Leonard had mentioned in *The Gateway* article that Judy Collins was working on an LP that would include some of his songs. I purchased *wildflowers*, which was published in 1967, in England. I was delighted to hear "Sisters of Mercy" and "Hey, That's No Way To Say Goodbye" but I was stunned by "Priests." It is nearly five minutes in length and is a lament on the part of the poet for the loss of virginity of the woman he writes about. I was convinced that he wrote it for me; perhaps another delusion. It begins as follows:

> And who will write love songs for you
> When I am Lord at last
> And your body is the little highway shrine
> That all my priests have passed
> That all my priests have passed?

In the poem, the poet/priest, though he has written love songs for her, has not taken her virginity. I believe that this is an intentional act: he describes himself as being "Lord at last" and also "Lord of memories" unable to take on the role of physical lover. He presents her body as a sacred shrine frequented by other priests, who treat it with disrespect and "wear away the little window." As a lover of many women, it is significant that Leonard in his priest persona chose not to love this woman in a physical way.

Over the years, I have continued to believe that he wrote this song for me and, if he didn't, I reflect that, as he says, in "The Sisters of Mercy," "we weren't lovers like that and besides it would still be all right." This poem presents a poet who is in need of shelter and comfort. In "Calm, Alone the Cedar Guitar," another Edmonton poem, Leonard names the woman that inspired it – Patricia, one of his interviewers with whom he connected. There is a stillness created by the snow that blankets the roofs of cars and he is inside soothed by the scent of sandalwood and Patricia's pomander. "Winter Lady," states:

> Trav'ling lady, stay a while
> Until the night is over
> I'm just a station on your way
> I know I'm not your lover.

Another poem titled "Edmonton, Alberta December 1966, 4 a.m."
again references the scent of sandalwood as well as the snow and the
ice of the North Saskatchewan River. He observes, "It all keeps us such
sweet company." These poems are distanced from the sexual wars that
are the frequent themes of his work and, I think that they are reflective
of the celibacy that Eli had mentioned that Leonard had espoused,
at least for a time. None of the women that he connected with in
Edmonton have written about the experience, until now.

My staff at the Alberta Museums Association and one of my
board members (Catherine Luck) knew that I loved Cohen's work – it
was a habit for me to have his tapes on in the car when we travelled
out of town for museum site visits, or other travels. In October 1999,
when the board of the association established the Heritage Community Foundation and I was to leave to head up the new entity, a "roast"
was arranged for me. The highlight was when a member of my staff,
Kate Gunn, handed me what looked to be a framed poem which she
asked me to read. It was an email, dated Wednesday, October 27,
1999 1:50 am. It said:

Dear Adriana,
Our paths have crossed again. How pleasant that is. This is a little
song I wrote a few weeks ago. I send it from Bombay with my
warm greetings.
Love,
Leonard

YOU HAVE LOVED ENOUGH
I came to you with flowers –
You said, Come to me with bread
I could not make a living –
You employed me with the dead
I swept the marble chambers
You sent me down below
You kept me from believing
until You let me know
I am not the one who loves
Loving seizes me
When hatred with his package comes
You forbid delivery

And when the hunger for Your touch
rises from the hunger
You whisper, You have loved enough,
now let me be the Lover.

Hydra
September 1999

Kate had contacted him and told him who I was and he had immediately responded.

In February or March, 2002 I saw the production of *Doing Leonard Cohen* at Edmonton's Citadel Theatre. The production was a creation of Calgary's One Yellow Rabbit Company. At the beginning, the audience was warned about the nudity and foul language. The first part dealt with interpretations of about 50 poems drawn from various volumes. The second part was a stylized re-enactment of sections of *Beautiful Losers*. The narrator anti-hero (it is implied that it is a version of Leonard) is nude and, as the scene unfolded, people began to leave the theatre. For some, a nude male figure was enough to cause an affront. For others, the scenes suggesting hetero- and homosexual sex acts were too much. It brought back memories of Eli's classroom in the Tory Turtle 36 years before.

I saw Leonard perform at a concert in Edmonton on April 25, 2009. I didn't go back stage.

CHAPTER 6

Queen City

To recapture the romance of my transatlantic voyage from Italy as a seven-year-old child, I chose to go to the UK by boat to begin my doctoral studies. My brother Giuseppe, who had arrived in Montreal to attend l'École des Beaux-Arts, saw me off on this grand adventure. All my worldly goods, at least those that were transportable, were packed in a brand-new, dark blue trunk with brass trim.

The port of Montreal was an incredibly busy place because, in 1967, it had become a container port and, in 1968, Manchester Liners began weekly shipping services to the UK. The Canadian Pacific Montreal to Liverpool and return passenger service was provided by liners such as the *Empress of England*, which carried about 900 passengers (first class and tourist) with a crew of nearly 500. The ship was air conditioned and tourist class cabins had their own small bathrooms with showers. I didn't realize at the time that the romance of the transatlantic voyage was ending and, in 1970, Canadian Pacific would sell the *Empress*. My voyage was thus historic in many ways.

I don't know what I expected when I boarded but was surprised to discover that the majority of the passengers were British seniors returning home for a visit after a life-time spent in Canada. There was an excited buzz in the air and they treated the voyage as a cruise. The only person my own age among the passengers was a young man but, after several stilted conversations, it became clear that I wasn't interested in him nor he in me. I remember eating too much: there was nothing else to do other than eat and read since I was not into board games, or other types of official entertainment. This meant not only the three normal meals but also morning coffee with biscuits and afternoon high tea with sandwiches and pastries.

I shared my tourist cabin with two women, one of whom was the mother of Canadian dancer Veronica Tennant, going to visit her daughter who was performing with the Royal Ballet in London. Doris Tennant was a very attractive middle-aged woman, who had been widowed in 1964 and worked as a researcher and script writer at the CBC. She was born in England in 1921 and thus my mother's age but totally unlike her. The elderly men buzzed around her like bees around a honeypot and she enjoyed the attention enormously, and asked me to help her choose who she should focus on, and what clothing to wear for dinner. It was actually very sweet. Her life was certainly more interesting than mine: the only romance I was getting was through the novels I borrowed from the ship's library, which I consumed voraciously. I read my way through Jean Plaidy's fictionalized histories of European royals as well as the Gothic romances of Victoria Holt. I didn't know at the time that they were both pen names for English author Eleanor Alice Hibbert. I also read Nikos Kazantzakis's *Zorba the Greek*.

The journey across the north Atlantic seemed endless but, eventually, we arrived at Liverpool and I debarked and boarded the train for London with my trunk. We sped south through the English countryside and I was captivated by the large brick houses on both sides of the tracks. I loved the beautiful gardens and the various types of climbing roses that appeared to be a feature. When we reached Euston Station I was overwhelmed by the crowds but managed to find a taxi driver willing to take me, and my trunk, to the nearby YWCA where I had a booking. It was an old building and my metal-framed bed was in a large dormitory occupied by only a few girls, who had left their homes in other parts of the UK to find work in London. I knew that I had to find a place to live and one of the girls told me about agencies on Oxford Street that would help you to do this.

While the countryside had been beautiful, the area around the station was a nightmare, particularly at night. The air was thick with the fumes of cheap booze and one had to be careful not to step on the bodies of drunken men, who lived rough in the square and used the amenities of the station. I had an irrational fear that one might grab me. My friend Nat, who was doing his PhD at University College and who had been in London for a year, told me that they were unemployed meths drinkers. (While today the word "meth" refers to the drug "methamphetamine," at the time, the word was short for "methylated spirits," which was used for cleaning products or paint thinner.) I had never before encountered such misery.

London was the largest city that I had ever visited and I had to adjust to the grandeur of the royal palaces, Houses of Parliament, the British Museum, Westminster Abbey and St. Paul's, and the squalor that I encountered sometimes when I diverged from the well-trodden paths. There were still ruined buildings enclosed in high fences, the casualties of Second World War bombing raids. Since I had no idea where to live, the only criterion was that the flat be attractive and relatively close to King's College on the Strand. My visits to possible flats to rent took me to some unsavory places including the working class East End of London. The class system that I had encountered in Dickens' novels still seemed to be prevalent.

Eventually, I found a place in North London at Willesden Green then on the Bakerloo Line. I got off the train and walked up to ground level to discover a village main street. I walked down Walm Lane and about ten minutes later reached a gorgeous, three-storey red brick house. I rang the bell and was shown inside by a young woman in her thirties accompanied by a little boy, three or four years of age. She told me that the house was owned by her brother David and that the flat was in the attic. The house was in process of being restored. The ground floor entry had stained glass windows surrounding the door, floral tiles on the floor and a grand staircase leading upstairs. The flat comprised two rooms under the eaves: one a bedroom with a lovely bed with a floral quilt, and the other a sitting room with a tiny kitchen located in a cupboard. I fell in love with it; rented it immediately; and moved in. I wasn't bothered about the fact that I had to share the bath on the second floor with Paula and another tenant.

Paula befriended me and I spent many happy hours drinking instant coffee and strong tea with milk, both cloyingly sweetened with multiple cubes of sugar. Her apartment comprised two large rooms on the second floor and she lived there with her son, Charles. She was a chain smoker with a deep, throaty voice and the face of a Renaissance angel. She was divorced and unemployed but had various boyfriends. Her two best friends were Maureen, a young, unmarried woman with a baby who cleaned the house, and Ann, an older, bleached blond who dated men from the Middle East with flats in the St. John's Wood area. She liked to party and drink, and may have been a call girl.

All of the rooms in the house appeared to have been designed by a decorator. There were some lovely old, stripped-pine pieces of furniture including tables and chairs, as well as wicker furniture with large cushions covered with William Morris fabrics. The same fabric was used for curtains that spanned the large windows from floor to ceiling. Paula told me a great deal about her brother, who was on holiday in Greece. He was a former art student. (There were some of his paintings in the house as well as a clay sculpture bust of a man with a scythe.) He owned a wicker furniture manufacturing company in the East End of London and was doing extremely well since that type of furniture was experiencing a revival. She mentioned that he was gay.

Having settled into my flat, I took the tube train to Trafalgar Square and visited the Canadian Embassy. A street photographer snapped a photo of me feeding the pigeons, which I still have. I felt like Alice in Wonderland. Things were both familiar and strange. Because of my extensive readings in British literature, everywhere I went I found streets with familiar names and I loved the blue plaques on historic buildings where famous people (mostly men) had lived or worked. I always stopped to read them and was thrilled when I knew their works.

I felt adrift and used the Canadian Embassy as a surrogate home and went there frequently to read the newspapers and magazines to remind me of who I was. I registered as a student abroad and was invited to a talk and reception to be given by Pierre-Elliott Trudeau, on his first visit to the UK as Prime Minister. In my International Politics class at the University of Alberta, I had read an essay by Trudeau on the European Common Market and viewed him as a respected academic. However, like other young women of my generation, I was caught up in "Trudeaumania" and, before leaving Canada, I had my friend Doris take a photograph of me in front of an election poster in the window of the small grocery store in the Jack Tar building in London, Ontario where we lived. His talk was inspirational and reinforced my sense of how wonderful it was to be Canadian, young and in London at this important time in world history.

Since university would not begin until early October, I had planned a six-week trip around Western Europe with my friend Sydney.

She didn't finish her Master's thesis on Wilfred Watson in time so I had to travel alone. I was young enough to still have that sense of being "immortal" and, fortunately, had not had any dangerous experiences to deter me. In mid-July I took the boat train to France and began my travels around Europe using my Eurail Pass.

Nothing could have prepared me for the lines of Parisian police in riot gear that I encountered in public places including the picturesque St. Saint-Germain-des-Prés area where, besides the book stalls along the Seine embankment, were located l'École des Beaux-Arts, the School for Advanced Studies in the Social Sciences, numerous cafés and fashionable shops with designer clothing. I had heard about the student protests that had begun in May of that year throughout France but it was different seeing the streets where cobblestones had been ripped up and used to attack police. The protesters championed the rights of workers and challenged the existing political order. These protests were so severe that the government of Charles de Gaulle feared civil war until some accommodations were negotiated. While these were similar to the protests at the U of A against American imperialism, capitalism and consumerism, the scale was like nothing I could ever have imagined.

Like all tourists, I saw the Louvre and other museums, Notre-Dame Cathedral, the Eiffel Tower and royal palaces. I made pilgrimages to Montmartre and took the Metro to the Père Lachaise Cemetery, which opened in 1804 and was one of the world's first "garden cemeteries." There I visited the tomb of Oscar Wilde; I also went to the Montparnasse Cemetery to see the grave of Charles Baudelaire. I was going to write about both in my doctoral thesis. I also took the train to see the royal court at Versailles and was overwhelmed by all of the gold in the décor. The expansive gardens with their careful plantings, fountains and surrounding countryside offered a relief from the density of Paris.

When I was ready to move on after about a week, I decided to go to Grenoble because of the 1968 Winter Olympics. I felt more at home: the mountains reminded me of Jasper and Banff though they were less grand. I visited the Olympic venues and also took the cable car up to the summit of La Bastille Hill that housed a historic fortress. I chose other destinations for their historic significance, or on a whim. This worked, by and large. Sometimes I would spend just a day at a location – the Eurail Pass gave me enormous freedom to travel. All I had to do was book and I got preferential treatment.

In Lyons, I wandered around the huge *Parc de la Tête d'or* and found myself in late afternoon being followed by a man in a trench coat. As I sped up my walking, he also sped up leaving no doubt that he was following me. There were few people around and I began to get desperate. Fortunately, I eventually found a gate out of the park and a few hundred yards away an outdoor café. I went to the only table occupied and spoke to the older man and young woman enjoying a glass of wine. I told them who I was and that I was being followed, and they invited me to join them. They loved my "Canadian" French (I was frequently referred to as "la petite Canadienne" during my travels in France) and we shared life stories. He was a journalist and was very interested in what was happening in Quebec. I ended up having supper with them and they walked me to my hotel near the railway station and I felt safe.

I chose my hotels from Erich Fromm's bible: *Europe on Five Dollars a Day*. While this was convenient, I soon came to realize that the areas around railway stations that were the cheapest were also frequently the locations of "red light" districts. This was certainly true in Rome where I found lodging in an old palace located in the inner city. I remember walking the first evening to find a restaurant and having a line of prostitutes wearing low-cut blouses, short, tight skirts and high boots taunt me. They wanted me off their turf and reminded me of Federico Fellini's *La Dolce Vita* in which journalist Marcello Mastroianni wandered the streets of Rome searching for love. It was released in 1960 and I believe I saw it as a Film Society feature at the U of A. This and other films such as Michelangelo Antonioni's *Il deserto rosso* released in 1964 had shaped my view of contemporary Italian society, or at least the way in which trendy film-makers viewed it.

But that was not the worst of it. As I was walking back to my lodgings after supper, I discovered a man was following me. He was talking to himself and, because I spoke Italian, I was able to understand him. He wanted to pick me up and eventually caught up to me and enquired whether I wanted to have a drink with him. I said nothing and, after persevering for a few minutes and my not responding, he assumed that I was deaf. This somehow changed his intent. By this point, I was feeling dazed and confused, and lost my way. He asked me if I was staying at a near-by convent and I pulled out the piece of paper on which the address of my lodging was written. He very kindly took me there and said goodbye. I began to feel a bit like the central character, Candide, in Voltaire's novel of the same name: naïve and innocent and always averting disaster by the skin of the teeth.

I realized then that I had to be much more careful in my travels and avoid being out late at night on my own, or in places where there were few people. I headed south to Naples where I had another dangerous encounter. The cheap hotel where I stayed was frequented by what I assumed to be drunken sailors. The night I stayed there someone kept knocking at my door to be let in. He was ranting and accused me of being a heartless bitch. The next day, I moved to another hotel.

I then headed south to Calabria to visit my Nonna Alessandra, my father's mother. I arrived at a tiny railway station where I was to get a bus for Grimaldi. I had some time to kill and sat at a café and ordered something to eat. At the neighbouring table, the group of men enjoying espressos and cigarettes quickly identified me as an "American" and theorized about what they would like to do to me, and how much I would enjoy it. For them, all foreign women were "whores" and were "begging for it," which was evidenced by their sleeveless dresses and short skirts.

I tried not to bolt my food but finished quickly and went to sit on the bench where the bus would stop, and where there were elderly people and mothers with children to keep me company. They struck up a conversation with me and, when they heard I was from Canada and visiting family, they made me feel welcome and shared their food. All seemed to have relatives in Canada and wondered whether I had met them. I had to explain the great size of Canada and how far Toronto was from Edmonton.

Grimaldi is situated in a hilly area and the town winds down a hill: at the top is a church and convent, at the bottom, a large stone piazza worn away by generations of oxen grinding grain. My grandmother's house was towards the bottom end of the town and, while the house itself was three-storeys high and quite lovely, she lived in the gloomy basement area. The upstairs was rented. The walls had been white-washed but the furniture was ancient. Framed family photos were in every nook and cranny. I remember the large spacious rooms upstairs where we had lived when I was a tiny child.

I stayed there for one night and didn't know whether I could do it again. Fortunately, we went to visit the Albo family: the mother, Sandra, was my grandmother's niece and a member of the Falcone family. They took me in and welcomed me, and convinced my grandmother to let me stay with them. Pietro, a school teacher, and Sandra had four children: the oldest, Maria, lived in Cosenza with her husband, Tonino, and baby daughter, Pasqualina. The remaining children from oldest to youngest were Wanda, Clara and Achille. All were students. They had me join them for all of their visits to the provincial capital, Cosenza, beaches and other student locales and we became life-long friends. Through them I discovered Italian pop music and the San Remo music festival.

Soon it was time to head north. I travelled to Florence, Pisa, Sienna and Venice and visited the wonderful museums and historic sites. I admired these structures that reflected Italy from Roman times through the Middle Ages to the Renaissance. However, my heart was untouched. Throughout my travels in Italy, though I spoke the language, I felt more and more alien. Though it was the country of my birth, it did not feel like home. It was too crowded, too down-at-heels and too arid. My childhood memories of Italy were of a village surrounded by small farms with fruit trees and grapevines. The river flooded annually. In the 27 years since I had left, public waterworks had been built and every house had indoor plumbing. This meant that the water table had dropped dramatically and the surface waters, rivers and streams, were shallow or non-existent. As I travelled around the country, I found that the landscape was shaped by the absence or abundance of water.

The city of Venice suffered from extremely high and low tides and, in summer, the smell from the canals was over-powering; some days there was a palpable sense of decay. In 1966, floodwaters reached almost two-metres high and Piazza San Marco was covered. My bedroom in the *pensione* where I stayed was tiny (because I was travelling alone, I had to rent single rooms and these were always more expensive and inferior), and I felt alone and depressed. I was haunted by scenes from Thomas Mann's novella *A Death in Venice* in which the elderly protagonist, author Gustav von Aschenbach, becomes enamored of a young boy and ultimately dies as his traditional values are swept away by sexual longing.

In this frame of mind, it's not surprising that one of my most traumatic experiences occurred in Venice. I saw all of the sites including a visit to the ghetto and the Murano glass works, and then booked a train to go north to Germany. At the station, I saw a man having an epileptic seizure and instinctively ran to help him, and placed my hand in his mouth to stop him biting through his tongue. He bit down on my fingers and eventually calmed down. I was surrounded by a group of three young women and a mother and daughter.

After station officials took over the care of the epileptic man, the women took me for coffee and bandaged my hand. I discovered that the young women were Americans and the mother and teen-aged daughter were from Edmonton. I exchanged information with the young women who were going to be in London in late September and linked my fate with the mother and daughter, and we travelled north to Munich. They both spoke German and invited me to stay at the place where they had booked. Their story was fascinating: the mother was Jewish and had spent time as a young woman in a concentration camp (she showed me the numbers tattooed on her arm). Because of her aptitude for languages, she was used by the Germans as a translator and survived the war, and ultimately made her way to Edmonton. She was in Germany because the government was making reparations to victims of the Holocaust, and she was there to arrange this. I did a lot of sight-seeing with them and was happy for the guidance and the company.

Also staying at the pension was a young petroleum engineer from Canada who was making his way to work in the Middle East. He invited me to go to a local *bierkeller*. He was older than me (in his thirties) but seemed very nice and I agreed. I didn't realize that beer was served in litre or half-litre glass mugs. I had half a litre, the most I had ever drunk, and he had several at least. The music was lively and we danced and generally got on very well. When we started to walk back to the pension, I was distinctly light headed. He had his arm around my shoulders and began his seduction patter. The upshot was that he promised that, if I slept with him, he would come to England to visit me and that it would not be a one-night-stand. I refused and he turned out to be a gentleman and let me stagger to my room.

I went on to visit Switzerland and finally returned to London in late August to my attic flat. Towards the end of September, I re-connected with the American girls whom I had met in Venice. We went to see the Broadway musical *Hair*, which opened at the Shaftesbury Theatre on September 27, 1968. We were captivated by the music and the story of the hippies living in New York, practicing "free love" and opposing the Viet Nam War. The nudity did not bother us and we even got up to dance in the aisles. I think that it was then that I decided to let my hair grow and do what it wanted to do. I can still sing "Age of Aquarius."

We also went to see *2001: A Space Odyssey*. The simulation of space flight and the classical music accompaniment was uplifting. The evolution scenes, in particular, the naked ape that grabbed a thigh bone to use as a weapon reminded me of Konrad Lorenz's *On Aggression*, which I had read at the U of A. It seemed that the rise in militarism throughout the world was the fulfillment of Lorenz's view of human beings as natural aggressors.

Because university was still about a month away, I was effectively alone. This was not a happy period – I had never been alone for so long. I went out every day and got to know all of the shops in central London including Selfridges and Harrods though I favoured more trendy ones such as the Top Shop on Oxford Street. I wasn't interested in buying stuff: I just wanted to be around people.

I found that I no longer cared for my flat. I gave Paula my notice and went to an agency to find another. This one was also at the top of an old house but was located in the much trendier Swiss Cottage area of south Hampstead, just north of St. John's Wood. The house was on Langland Gardens and had the fashionable NW3 postal code. The underground stop was Finchley Road and, then, a brisk 10-minute walk past restaurants and trendy shops before I started the climb up to the house. The housing stock on the hill was much grander than in Willesden Green: mostly large, brick mansions some of which had been subdivided into multiple, one- or two-bedroom flats. My flat had central heating and was also cleaned weekly.

Around September 17, my birthday, I decided to go to Walm Lane to pick up any mail that had arrived for me. As I walked up to the house, I saw a beautiful man, tanned and shirtless, washing a bottle-green MGB convertible in the gravel driveway. He was over six feet tall with dark-blond hair and hazel eyes. He greeted me and I explained who I was, and my purpose in coming over. He introduced himself as David, the owner of the house, and invited me in for coffee. He checked to see if there was post for me and I don't remember whether there was and we, then, went into the kitchen where we sat at a stripped pine table. He made fresh coffee and served it in Swedish blue and white china cups. We began to talk and he told me about his month in Greece with friends. Paula had told him a little about me and described me as the "mad American girl." I think that had intrigued him.

I think that I was looking my best – in Montreal I had bought a two-piece Nehru-type trouser suit in a golden paisley pattern and my hair was short and curly. My brother Giuseppe had taken a picture of me in front of the Thai Pavilion at Expo and I had tangible evidence of me in my prime. There was a sexual spark between us and, perhaps, after a very long time, I was ready to lose my virginity.

It all happened very quickly. David invited me to his bedroom. I told him I was a virgin and he told me not to worry and it happened. It was pleasant but not as earth-shattering as the literary accounts that I had read but I was happy. Afterwards we went to the large living room with its brown leather couches and listened to music and he gave me some wine and snacks. He then drove me home in the convertible. I was elated: as I turned twenty-five, I was no longer a virgin. David was 32.

A few days later, David visited me at my place in Swiss Cottage. I was dressed in a wool-knit mini-dress that had stripes of orange and yellow on it. He said that I looked like an Art Deco lamp and we made love again. This time it was very special. He asked me if I wanted to return to the house because one of the tenants had left and I could have the two-room apartment on the second floor next to Paula's. Without hesitation, I agreed.

The beautiful apartment (formerly occupied by the call girl) had a bedroom in which the panelled walls were painted deep blue and an old, decorative desk was placed in front of a large window that over-looked the back garden. I could imagine my portable typewriter on it and me at work on my thesis. The combined kitchen/living/dining room had floor-to-ceiling drapes in a red and blue Chintz floral pattern and a neo-classical style white fireplace. David had made the wooden oblong sofa that was painted red and had a covered single-bed mattress on it with lots of lovely cushions. I put up my Salome and Venetian posters that I had brought from Edmonton and set up my record player.

Because the rooms were heated only by the gas fires in the fire places, I went to bed at night with a hot-water bottle and a long flannel night dress. In the morning, I would light the fire and warm each one of my under-garments before putting it on. I singed the bottom of my full-length bathrobe on several occasions and had to cut the burned part off and re-hem it. Bathing in the hall bathroom was an adventure. The room was unheated and one would have to light the geyser (a huge hot water tank). The water was dangerously hot so one avoided showers and just had long baths with steam coming off the surface of the water. I mastered reaching for a towel and quickly wrapping it around me to avoid freezing.

I introduced David to the music and poetry of Leonard Cohen and he introduced me to fashionable London life, which seemed to be classless with the only criteria for joining being beauty, talent or wealth. Though I continued to live in David's house for two years (I paid rent), the relationship didn't last beyond six months. Our lives did not "merge" as I had hoped and the place did not become my home. We did do some amazing things including going to hear Frank Zappa and the Mothers of Invention at the Royal Festival Hall on October 25, 1968. The performance was recorded and would later be issued as an album. The air was pungent with the smell of marijuana. I had to accept the fact that David was bisexual and part of the gay scene in London (his friends included the Queen's physician and curators from the Victoria and Albert Museum), and while I enjoyed the parties and other activities that we did, I wanted an ordinary life.

More importantly, I wanted to be his only lover. While I initially convinced myself to tolerate the boyfriends; I could never deal with the occasional woman. Our times together were thus infrequent. After a rowdy party in his place when I smoked marijuana and inhaled, I went up to my bedroom. In the middle of the night, David joined me in bed and we made love. It seemed like there were not just the two of us in bed but other limbs belonging to three or four other men. The next morning I realized that, when we made love, I was also doing this with all his sexual partners and I no longer could.

As things settled in my personal life, towards the end of September 1968, I turned my attention to my studies and got acquainted with the University of London starting with the University College buildings in Gower Street near the British Museum. They are located in Bloomsbury where some members of the Bloomsbury group lived or worked as evidenced by many blue plaques. I would periodically take the tube in to Trafalgar Square and walk along the embankment to King's College. It was not at all a grand place like Somerset House, the Registry Office next door, or the University College buildings. There were lots of narrow stairwells leading to classrooms, libraries and

professors' offices. The basement cafeteria reeked of boiled cabbage or
Brussels sprouts and the tea and coffee steeped all-day in giant urns,
but the food was cheap and I frequently ate there.

One day, I spotted a notice on a bulletin board that the vicar of
St. Anne's Parish, located at 55 Dean Street in Soho, was looking for
student volunteers to man a telephone line to help at risk youth. The
Reverend Kenneth Leech, who was 29 at the time, set up the Soho
Drug Group in 1967 to rehab the "rent boys" – young homeless men
who sold their bodies for sex and who lived rough in the region of
Piccadilly Circus. This was the centre of "swinging London" in all of
its many meanings. Ken had a connection with Kings: in 1961, he
completed a BA in History there and then went up to Trinity College
and was ordained an Anglican minister in 1965. He initially served
at Holy Trinity Church in the East End of London and, in 1967, was
moved to St. Anne's where he began his youth work. In his mid-teens,
he had heard Trevor Huddleston speak and was inspired by his Christian socialism and anti-apartheid stance.

I called and made an appointment for an interview and was
surprised when I discovered that there was no proper church. In September 1940, St. Anne's had been bombed during the blitz and only
the tower remained. It was restored and used for the parish offices
and worship. Ken and I got on very well and I agreed to go in one
day a week, and answer the telephone. We were warned not to give
any advice to the young people who called; rather, we were to talk to
them and then direct them to the agencies that could best serve their
needs. Ken believed that youth talking to youth would work in drawing them out, which I believe to be true. In order to volunteer, I had
to attend some workshops that provided information about youth
homelessness, drug abuse, sex abuse, venereal diseases, etc. I believe
that Lord Longford, a British politician and social reformer, helped to
fund these and he actually spoke at one of the sessions.

Besides the telephone work, on some occasions, Ken would take
me on his rounds around the Piccadilly Circus area with its famous
winged statue of Eros atop a memorial fountain. This seemed somehow fitting since many strip clubs were located in the area and love was
for sale any time, day or night. I later found out that the winged figure
was not Eros but, rather, Anteros, the Greek god of requited love. The
fountain was dedicated to Lord Shaftesbury, politician, philanthropist
and reformer who pushed for the education of children, as was the

main thoroughfare Shaftesbury Avenue that led from Piccadilly Circus to New Oxford Street.

Ken, dressed in a long, black cape and wearing clergymen's clothing with a white collar, would stride down the street and speak to any young people (mostly boys) who were loitering. Most had accents that I had difficulty understanding and told the same story of trouble at home and running away to London for a better life. He would ask them whether they had eaten and, depending on the answer, we would take them out for coffee or lunch. The intent was to get them off the streets and into some kind of sheltered accommodation. In 1969, Ken set up Centrepoint, the UK's leading charity tackling youth homelessness.

This volunteer work grounded me and gave me a sense of purpose and I continued to do it until 1971 when Ken left St. Anne's to become chaplain and tutor in pastoral studies at St. Augustine's College in Canterbury. In 1974, he became pastor at St. Matthew's in Bethnal Green, a working class area of London, and continued to serve the poor and oppose the National Front and its racist policies.

With other King's College students, in the fall of 1968, I went to see Gillo Pontecorvo's *The Battle of Algiers* in a small cinema in the King's Cross area. The film was not only about the Algerian people's desire to get rid of their colonial masters, the French, but also about the racism that inevitably went hand-in-hand with colonialism. The establishment in the Western democracies viewed the film as a training-ground for terrorists and this may or may not have been true. I know that, that evening, the largely student audience cheered on the Algerian freedom fighters and the new world order that might emerge if similar battles were won around the world. While I did not join picket lines, my allegiance was with other students of my generation who believed in "making love and not war."

By mid-October, it was time for me to focus on my academic work. While some Canadians studying in the UK at that time had difficulties with their supervisors, I was blessed with Leonée Ormond. She was only three years older than me and had received her BA from Oxford, in 1962, and her Master's from Birmingham University in 1965. She had joined the English Department at King's College in 1965 and was in the process of publishing her thesis on the artist and author George Du Maurier (this came out in 1969). She had a genuine love of literature and life. I met her every week and we discussed books that I had read pertinent to the topic that I had chosen: the art for art's sake and decadent movements in nineteenth century English and French literature. The focus became Tennyson, Walter Pater, George Moore and Oscar Wilde on the English side, and Théophile Gauthier, Charles Baudelaire and J.K. Huysmans on the French side. She provided gentle guidance and I would present my findings knowing that she would give them a fair hearing and provide useful feedback.

I did an enormous amount of reading using the resources of not only the King's College Library (not just the main library but also the tiny specialist French library) but also those of the University of London Library, and the British Library at the British Museum. I loved to think of the famous people who had held some of the old books that I consulted. It was a thrill to be in the Reading Room under the large dome.

Leonée and husband, Richard, who is an art historian and was then the Assistant Director of the National Portrait Gallery, became good friends. Shortly after meeting at King's, she invited me to their lovely flat above a photographer's studio in Highgate. There were stunning views of all of London from the heights of this historic village, which I came to love. I was also invited to their first party at the old house in Holly Terrace, nearly at the summit of Highgate West Hill, which they purchased and renovated. It was Christmas 1969 and it began to snow as I entered the brick walkway topped by a wrought-iron arch and walked to the end to discover a late eighteenth century, three-storey historic property.

I believe I met Roy Strong, who had become the Director of the National Portrait Gallery in 1967 at the young age of 32 and who was Richard's boss. He had begun curating a series of shows that challenged the traditionally "stuffy" image of this institution. In 1968, the featured exhibit consisted of 600 Cecil Beaton portraits including images of the Queen Mother and the young princesses – Elizabeth and Margaret. He presented them beautifully dressed and posed as romantic figures. His photographs made them accessible as Queen Victoria and Queen Alexandra were not, and began the obsession with young royals that we still see today.

Besides working hard on my thesis, I embraced the rich cultural life of London. I went to exhibits not only at the National Portrait Gallery but also the National Gallery, the Victoria and Albert Museum, the Tate, the Hayward Gallery and other smaller galleries. With friends from college, I also attended concerts at the Royal Festival and Albert Halls, and performances at the various theatres in central London. All had student rates so they were accessible and, in some facilities, there were seats in "the Gods," which were steeply raked and meant for the resilient bodies of students. I had an insatiable appetite for "culture" and, because of the generous Canada Council grant, I could indulge it.

I remember two memorable performances. One was Bertolt Brecht's *Resistible Rise of Arturo Ui* at the Saville Theatre in 1969. The play, written in 1941, is a satirical allegory set in Chicago. Leonard Rossiter played the grotesque, Hitler-like grocer who takes over the cauliflower racket by killing other grocers. The other was The National Theatre Company's *As You Like It* with men playing women's roles as in Shakespeare's time. It had an all-star cast that included Ronald Pickup as Rosalind, Anthony Hopkins as Audrey, and Derek Jacobi as Touchstone.

To avoid ever being lonely again, I established a circle of friends, who became my substitute family. The performances that we attended were treats since most of them did not have grants. Mostly, we entertained each other in our flats and consulted cook books to create delicious and interesting meals. My Italian cooking was very popular and we also enjoyed French, Spanish and Greek cuisine. We were mostly single, and in the process of finding ourselves and shaping our lives.

My first London friend was Nat Bernstein from Montreal, who had completed a Master's degree in English at the U of A. He went to London in 1967 to begin a PhD at University College and, when I arrived, had a basement flat in a 1930s block on Tavistock Square. He was my cultural guide and particularly loved classical music and theatre so we saw a number of productions together. He was a very handsome young man and had many girlfriends.

I also made friends with a young couple from Australia. Peter was doing his Master's at King's and I would visit their flat, the second storey of a house on Hammersmith Road near Barnes. They had very little money but Elizabeth was an excellent cook, and they also loved music and theatre. I remember the smell of the paraffin heaters that used to heat whatever room they were using in the flat. Although they had fireplaces with gas inserts, these had meters that gobbled up coins and were never used. Peter was fiercely anti-establishment and did not want to return to his homeland, which was extremely conservative and had a terrible record of abusing its Indigenous People.

My circle of new friends was completed when Terry Bagg arrived from the US in 1969 with his girlfriend Andrea to begin a Master's degree at King's. He was slight with bright blue eyes, framed by gold-rimmed "granny" glasses, and curly blond hair. He wore the most fashionable hippy clothes including silk shirts, velvet pants and leather boots. He was like a diminutive Mick Jagger. In contrast, Andrea was not particularly keen on fashion and was dark-haired and serious, and wanted to be a journalist like her father who had completed a ground-breaking book on the Mafia in the US.

Terry was the son of a wealthy New England couple and had gone to private schools and university (I think it was Princeton) and eventually ended up in New York in Greenwich Village where he wrote poetry and smoked marijuana. Happily, he met Andrea who was much more materially astute and they moved in together. He quickly immersed himself in the drug subculture and took too much LSD and ended up in Bellevue Hospital. He survived without harm and this gave him material for his poetry. To escape the draft, he registered to do a Master's in English literature but really he just wanted to be a poet living in London.

Terry was also an excellent keyboardist and loved the harpsichord and the works of Handel, including obscure oratorios. He discovered that Fenton House, a late seventeenth-century historic property in Hampstead near the Heath, had a marvelous collection of musical instruments and music students could play them. Andrea was working as a writer and editor whereas Terry and I were graduate students and our time was our own. We would leave King's and take a series of tubes and buses to Fenton House. I listened to Terry play these incredible instruments and was jealous of his musicality. We would end our afternoon outing at a pub either in Hampstead or Highgate with glass mugs of cider. Among our favourites were the historic Spaniard's Inn and the Flask. These were not student haunts but served mostly tourists or the wealthy people who lived in these posh areas of London.

Terry would play all afternoon and, when I had had enough, I wandered around the rooms in the house admiring the antique furniture, paintings and knick-knacks. I imagined myself living in the house in its heyday. The house had received its name from Philip Fenton, a merchant who made a fortune in exporting Russian goods to London, shipping them from Riga in Latvia. He bought the 100-year-old property in 1793 and lived there until his death. The collections in the house were not his but belonged to the last owner, Lady Katherine Binning, who purchased the house in 1936 and bequeathed it to the

National Trust on her death in 1952. The collection of early keyboard instruments was amassed by Major George Fletcher in the first part of the twentieth century and includes virginals, clavichords, harpsichords, spinets and early pianos. All were kept in perfect working order by the National Trust.

Another favourite was Kenwood House located in extensive grounds bordering on the northern portion of Hampstead Heath. The original house was built in the seventeenth century but, in 1764, the owner, the Earl of Mansfield commissioned neo-classical architect Robert Adam to renovate it. I went there so frequently that I could give a guided tour, which I frequently did when friends from Canada visited.

In the period 1968-70, several of my U of A professors came to the UK on sabbatical. My Shakespeare professor, Hank Hargreaves, came to London with his family and did research. He loved the theatre and I attended some plays with them. I was invited to dinner at their large rental house in Ealing, which was used by many professors over the years. The bus went past the iconic Art Deco Hoover building. Rowland McMaster and wife Juliet spent a sabbatical year in Oxford and their son, Rawdon, was born there. I had some lovely visits with them and explored the various colleges.

My most unusual visit to Oxford happened with a group of friends from Rhodesia, one of whom, Jill, was a student at the University of London. Her grandfather was a younger son of an aristocratic family who had gone to Rhodesia to make a living, and had become a very successful farmer. Jill arranged to visit a friend doing graduate work at one of the Oxford colleges. She, her friend Tessa, and I took the train to Oxford. Tessa's father was a judge and opposed the apartheid government of Ian Smith, head of the Rhodesian Front Party, who in 1965 declared Rhodesian independence unilaterally from the UK. We were met by a group of young men and Jill decided that she wanted to go punting. We rented a punt and Jill was in high good spirits and, at one point, stood up in the boat and fell into the water. The boys quickly pulled her out and we went to their room where she got out of her sodden clothes and borrowed dry ones from her friend. We then took a bus out into the countryside to see her relatives. She had visited them before but somehow got off at the wrong stop and we had to trek across a muddy field. We arrived dirty and bedraggled at a wonderful Elizabethan country house with a thatched roof. Her kind aunt and uncle welcomed us, allowed us to clean up in their washroom and served us high tea.

An even more memorable visit to a Cambridge college would occur indirectly through a U of A friend, Gordon Carnegie, who moved to London in 1969 and registered to do a PhD. The real purpose for his coming to England was because his ex-wife Becky had moved there with their young son. They were the first among my group of friends to marry and, after completing his Master's degree, he had accepted a job teaching English Literature at the Red Deer College. With alimony payments, he did not have much money so he ended up sharing a flat in a house in North London with a young Frenchman, Michel. Unlike my beautifully furnished apartment in Walm Lane, their place was down-at-heel and downright ugly. I made a bedspread for him to improve the looks of the living room, which served as his bedroom and study. Michel had the bedroom and went out to work. While Gordon had little in common with him, Michel was a good cook. I remember that he went home to France for Easter and brought us back snails stuffed with butter, parsley and garlic prepared by his mother. We all loved French food.

Gordon, Michel and his friend Chantal and I socialized and I remember some memorable walks on Hampstead Heath ending in pub lunches. We also went to the Highgate Cemetery and visited the tomb of Karl Marx. The cemetery was huge and overgrown with more than 50,000 graves, many topped by statuary. It was a fashionable place to be buried from the mid-nineteenth century on and there were many Gothic-style tombs. The statues were of angels, young women, children and lambs and, on occasion, *memento mori* skeletons. To reach it, we had to take the tube to the Archway station and walk up the hill to Highgate. There was an entrance at Swain's Lane.

I took Gordon to a party in the flat shared by friends of Tina Day, the graduate student who I had met in London, Ontario, and who had returned to the UK with her twin brother Roger, who had done his degree at the University of Toronto. Ghita, an architect, and her sister Jo lived in a mansion block of flats near the Tottenham Court Road area of London. It had multiple bedrooms and was very different from the housing of most students. Gordon and Tina met for the first time and dated for a while. The one relationship that lasted was that of Penny Christoffersen, whom I had met in Ontario, and the architect that she met at the party, Len Clarke. They married and, surprisingly, he accepted a job in Edmonton and they moved there around 1971.

Gordon's relationship with his ex-wife was very fraught and they fought over their son. I was in the unfortunate position of being a friend of each of them and would hear their mutual complaints. Becky was living with another man. Their tiny row house in south London had an outside toilet but I enjoyed visiting them. It was there that I met a handsome young West Indian man, Michael, who was studying at Cambridge (either medicine or law). He was several years younger than me but took a shine to me and invited me to the Spring Ball. I couldn't refuse – this was an experience I didn't want to pass up. I took the train to Cambridge and he met me and we drove to the King's Mill, a historic mill on the grounds of King's College. The mill had been converted into a residence many, many years before and, although the mill wheel no longer turned, you could hear the water flowing under the living room in the converted structure.

Michael shared the house with a fellow student, who was also going to the ball and was dating Michael's sister. By this point, I had stopped cutting my hair and I wore it in the Pre-Raphaelite style with curls flowing all around my head down to my shoulders. I also dressed the part and for that evening I wore a lovely spring-green tunic over wide-legged black silk pants. My fingers were covered with rings – I had begun this affectation in London and was acquiring special rings at markets and antique shops.

The spring ball period in late May/early June in Cambridge was amazing. Students in evening dress were everywhere going from college to college, a kind of moveable feast of parties. Large tents were set up on the grounds to create dance floors and spaces to dine. The ball at King's College, though referred to as the May Ball, took place on Wednesday June 12 and Pink Floyd was the live band that performed. (They had performed earlier in the evening at a ball at Homerton College.) We went from venue to venue enjoying the music and I remember at one college seeing Marsha Hunt, an American singer who had appeared in *Hair* and was one of Mick Jagger's girlfriends. She had an impressive Afro.

We were all happy and glad to be alive. The parties lasted all night long and ended with breakfast being served around six am. We returned to the house where Michael slept in his room and I slept on the sofa above the mill run, lulled to sleep by the flow of water. We woke up around noon and had lunch in the house. Michael asked me to see him again but I felt that he was too young for me but I think that I lacked courage. He was black. Though I could see him as a friend and even a temporary boyfriend, I am ashamed to say that at the time I could not see him as a husband. He took off all of my rings and kept them hoping to entice me to see him again but I never did.

Playwright David Hare would immortalize college balls in his 1975 musical *Teeth 'n' Smiles*, which featured Helen Mirren as the lead. The ball he describes took place at Jesus College, where he studied, in 1969, and the central character was an out-of-control rock singer called Maggie, who was modeled on Janis Joplin. When I saw it at the Royal Court Theatre in September 1975 when it premiered, it reminded me of Michael.

In July 1970, I moved to a new flat on St. Gabriel's Road, which was parallel to Walm Lane. It was in a huge, three-storey, red brick house built in the1930s. My flat was under the eaves and would have been a gathering place for the artistic family that had built the house. My bedsit comprised the entire top floor under the eaves and there was a large, raised platform in the bay window, which would have served as a stage. The windows had stained glass and the room was panelled in a light oak. There was an old gas stove and the kitchen cupboard and sink were located in a closet. I fell in love with it and made friends with a couple of young school teachers who had a bed-sit on the ground floor. They taught in the East end of London and showed me how to shop at East Indian grocers and to make curry. They had learned from their students' mothers.

One Saturday evening, Terry and Andrea were to come over for dinner and we were to go to a friend's party in south London. They called in the afternoon and said that their downstairs neighbor, Hugh Davies, had his older brother's car on loan for the weekend, and would pick us up and take us to the party. This was huge because most under-ground trains stopped around midnight when many student parties were at their best, and there would be a struggle to get a late-night bus home. I agreed. During dinner, they told me that Hugh had moved into the downstairs flat and shared it with Thomas Rochford and his girlfriend Pamela. Terry admired him because he was a violinist who practiced all the time. Shortly after dinner, my door-bell rang. We quickly got ready and went down stairs and Terry made introductions.

We got into the car and headed for south London. By the time we arrived, it must have been around 8 pm. The wine, beer and the Strongbow cider were flowing, and the music was loud.

Hugh was six foot tall and had longish, dark-blond hair. He was fashionably dressed in a dark, silk, patterned shirt with tight black, bell-bottomed trousers. He wore gold-rimmed glasses. I was wearing a peach-coloured, two-piece, knit outfit that skimmed over my hips and had tiny buttons down the front. There was an instant attraction and he asked me to dance. It was The Doors and Jim Morrison was moaning "Come on baby, light my fire." Hugh was not a particularly good dancer but we continued to dance and talk, and get to know each other.

He invited me to a party the following day that his younger brother Humphrey, who was studying Arabic at Cambridge, was hosting and I agreed to go. It was a lovely afternoon and Hugh and I continued to get to know each other. He told me that, later that afternoon, he was leaving to take part in an early music festival in Haslemere and mentioned that the festival had been started by Arnold Dolmetsch in 1925. Arnold collected early instruments and then began fabricating them, in particular, recorders. Arnold's son, Carl, who played the violin and viol, had succeeded his father. Hugh said that he would be away for most of the next week and invited me for a date the following Saturday.

I made time in my research schedule to go to Oxford Street to find something to wear for this special date and ended up buying a full-length, tight, T-shirt dress in a metallic pale-green. Hugh picked me up at St. Gabriel's Road and took me to an Italian restaurant in Soho. I ordered pasta and was astounded at how badly it had been cooked – the strings of spaghetti stuck together. Hugh went to pour me some more wine and struck my glass with the bottle and it toppled over spilling the red wine in my lap. While the mechanics of the date went badly, we did go back to my place and made love. I also succeeded in getting the red wine stain out of my iconic dress which I still have.

I was enamored of the fact that Hugh was a musician and had played with the National Youth Orchestra. At University he had studied Law because he felt he could make a better living at it but, after completing his articles, he decided that he didn't want to practice law. He had made the decision to go to the Royal College of Music and, in September, was to start a one-year performance diploma program. He was two years younger than me. I told him that, in early August, I was going to Italy to visit my grandmother and some cousins in Calabria. He asked if he could come with me and I said, yes, but only to Rome. I had hitherto been mostly a cautious person and this was so out of character with me but perhaps I felt that the time was right to take a risk.

We had a wonderful week in Rome seeing all of the sights and it was a kind of honeymoon. There was a real meeting of minds and interests, and I felt that we had the chance at a future together. He returned to London and I took the train to Calabria where I had a happy reunion with Nonna Alessandra and the Albo family. But I was anxious to get back to London and see Hugh. I was flying to Heathrow and then taking the train to London arriving at King's Cross Station where Hugh was to pick me up. I waited and waited but Hugh did not arrive and I was distraught. I eventually took a taxi to St. Gabriel Road. Later that evening, the telephone rang downstairs (we didn't have our own telephones and there was a coin-operated phone on the ground floor) and I rushed to get it. It was Hugh and he was extremely apologetic about not having made it to pick me up and explained why. We agreed to meet the following evening.

After a happy reunion, we went to Terry and Andrea's for dinner. Terry was delighted to see that we were getting on well and suggested that Hugh and I move in together. We did, in September 1970. This was the academic year that I intended to finish my thesis. We found a one-bedroom flat with its own bathroom in the riverside community of Barnes in south London. It was a three-storey row house owned by a retired British civil servant, who had spent most of his working life in India. It was traditionally furnished and still had red velvet, fully-lined blackout curtains that not only kept the light out but also kept the heat in in the winter. It was also not too far from Peter and Elizabeth's place.

Since we were living together, Hugh decided that I needed to meet his parents, Phyllis and John Davies, and arranged for his mother to invite us to tea one weekend in late September. Their house in Muswell Hill, north London, was on a busy road, Colney Hatch Lane. It was a three-storey, semi-detached residence and, once you entered the large front door, you stepped back in time into an Art Nouveau Edwardian house filled with antiques. The spacious entry hall had a grand staircase leading upstairs. On the landing was an elaborate wooden pillar topped by a bronze statue of a young woman playing a flute. The elaborate plate rail high up the walls of the entry had lovely antique plates. The living room had a grand piano. The entire family was musical and on Thursdays, all day, Phyllis hosted the Strings Club, a group of north London amateur musicians. She provided food and the musicians filled almost every room in the house playing trios and quartets. The quintets were played in the living room with the grand piano.

We went out to the small garden where she sat at a circular garden table topped by an umbrella. She was an impressive woman, almost six-foot tall with white-blond hair that was braided in a twist at the top of her head like a crown. She served cakes and pastries that she baked herself and Lapsang souchong tea from a silver teapot. We made polite conversation and things seemed to go well.

We reciprocated by inviting them to our place in Barnes. John was the music librarian of the BBC and had received an OBE (Order of the British Empire) for services to the country. At one point, she took me aside in the kitchen while I was making preparations and said that, though she did not approve of my "living arrangements" with Hugh, she would welcome me into their family when we decided to "regularize" the situation. This was very gracious and unlike the response I would have received from my parents; though I wrote long, newsy weekly letters, I never mentioned my love life.

Hugh's older brother, Robin, and his wife Hilary also welcomed us into the family. Both were librarians like Hugh's mother and father, and had an 18-month-old son, Crispin. They lived in a small end-of-terrace house in Finchley in north London and invited us frequently for tea and dinner. Hugh's younger brother Humphrey, a friend of emerging playwright David Hare, also became a friend. At the time, he was about to go to the Middle East as an Oxford University Press sales representative.

To make our relationship known to everyone, shortly after we moved in together in September 1970, we had a party for our circle of friends. New attendees were Bill Beard and John Thompson, friends from the University of Alberta who were registered to do doctorates at the University of London, and who were sharing a flat. I introduced John to my English friend Ann Harris, who was doing her doctorate on Shakespeare at King's, and they immediately connected. They were both shy and studious and seemed made for each other. Thus, my friends were all pairing up and Terry and Andrea gave us the exciting news that she was expecting.

My Canada Council grant was going to run out and I had to complete my thesis in 1971. I was under pressure to finish and was completing the chapter on George Moore. He was an Irish poet and novelist who had lived in Paris in the 1870s and had met not only the visual artists of the time but also the writers. His poetry was influenced by Baudelaire and his novels by the French realists. His first novel, *A Modern Lover*, dealt with the hero's Bohemian lifestyle (including sexual adventures) and the book was banned in the UK. In his novel *Evelyn Innes*, Moore focused on the musical circle headed by Arnold Dolmetsch in London and the heroine, a talented opera singer, is torn between her art (and the decadent life style that it involved) and a religious calling. Thus, the literary and musical elements of my life were merging.

The final chapter of my thesis dealt with Oscar Wilde and this is when things began to unravel for me. I read all his works as well as *The Complete Letters of Oscar Wilde*, which were published in 1963 and edited by Rupert Hart-Davis. I found the details of his life as revealed in the letters depressing. His trial for buggery and conviction that resulted in time in Reading Gaol and exile to France, as well as his final days in France living on the charity of friends, was a sad end that he did not deserve.

Whether as a result of the pressure to complete my thesis or the uncertainly of what was to become of my relationship with Hugh if I returned to Canada, I began in spring 1971 to experience panic attacks. I remember a particularly severe one that occurred when I was at my bank near Canada House in Trafalgar Square. I struggled with the terror that paralyzed me and was able to get a black cab and went straight to my doctor in Barnes. I told him what was happening and he suggested that I share what I was experiencing with Hugh, rather than keeping it a secret, and also prescribed some tranquilizers. I took time off from work on the thesis and went in to the Royal College of Music with Hugh and attended the classes and performances with him for about a week. One particularly memorable evening, to enable a student orchestra performance to go ahead during a power outage, candles were placed all over the stage. It was magical.

Hugh and I were married on July 17, 1971 at the registry office in Wood Green. (I was Catholic and he was Church of England so a religious ceremony was not possible.) He wore his dark-blue solicitor's suit and I wore a cream-coloured, thin muslin dress with ruffles at the neckline and at the wrists. My brother Giuseppe had arrived from Montreal and he was one of Hugh's groomsmen; my friend Laurel was my maid of honour. Afterwards, we went to Hugh's parents' place where they hosted a lovely garden reception for us. That evening, Humphrey hosted a party of all of our friends in the mansion flat that he was living in at the top of a grand, terraced-house in Paddington. Everyone brought food and drink.

We took a student flight to New York and I introduced Hugh to life in North America. After a few days of sightseeing, we took the bus to Montreal and spent a few days there. While Hugh found the city fascinating, particularly the Francophone past, he was less interested in locations associated with Leonard Cohen (he never liked his work). We continued our bus journey to Toronto where we saw Hugh's cousin, Bridget, who was doing a doctorate in science at the U of T. We stayed in one of the university residences and visited museums, the hippie area centred around Yorkville, Little Italy and Chinatown, and other places of interest. One evening, Bridget took us to the fabled Horseshoe Tavern, a country bar that had opened in 1947, and we heard a rock and roll act. I also took him to Sam the Record Man where I had bought my earliest classical music LPs when I lived in London, Ontario. He was impressed. We took the train to Barrie to visit my friend Doris, who with her husband, Arthur, taught at Georgian College, and took us sightseeing in Thousand Islands country, which was breath-taking. We then headed West by train to Edmonton. While Hugh had been to France and other parts of Western Europe and, when he was 18 visited India, he was blown away by the breadth of the Canadian landscape.

My parents welcomed him into the family and gave us our third wedding reception, a formal one held in the Jewish Hall overlooking the River Valley in the west end. Hugh got to meet all of the Italian relatives and friends. He had been teaching himself Italian and was able to make appropriate remarks at the reception, which endeared him to everyone. The two weeks in Edmonton was a round of hospitality and Hugh bonded with my parents and extended family. My friend Catherine Siemens arranged for a memorable camping trip to Jasper and our time in Edmonton came to an end.

We flew back to New York and stayed in the apartment in Queens of a friend of the Davies family, Dorothy Roberts. Her husband Denis, a friend of Hugh's father, had been brought over from the UK, in 1946, to set up the UN library and Dorothy had begun to teach in the school for the children of the international staff. She continued to do so after her husband's death in the mid-1950s eventually becoming principal of the elementary school. We went to the museums but also enjoyed going to cafés and bars in Greenwich Village. Dorothy took us to a memorable New York City Opera performance of Janacek's *Makropulos Affair*. It made use of projections on screens and a range of other effects to tell the story of Emilia Marty, who had lived for over 300 years after taking a potion conferring immortality, and was looking for the formula to end her life. While some critics hailed the production, others felt the company was devoting too much time to "non-standard" works. Dorothy also took us to an outdoor classical concert that was magical. Towards the end of August, we flew back to London to begin our married and working lives.

CHAPTER 7

Marriage and Work

REALITY BIT AFTER OUR RETURN from our honeymoon in North America in late August 1971. Hugh had completed his Performance Diploma at the Royal College of Music in June and had to find an orchestral job in London, which was very difficult. I also had few prospects: I had obtained my PhD in Comparative Literature from the University of London in July at a time when virtually no academic hiring was happening in London. Had I chosen to return to Canada, I would still have been able to obtain a job in some English department. The cutbacks would not begin there until the mid-1970s.

All of my years of university education had not prepared me to find work; instead, I found that the typing skills that I had acquired at St. Joseph's High School, and had honed most recently working on my thesis, were a saleable commodity. I went to the Manpower temp agency to find clerical work. I had seen many of their ads in tube trains as I travelled around London. I got an impressive result in the typing skills test (I believe I typed 70 or 80 words per minute with no mistakes) and was sent to the Independent Broadcasting Authority (IBA), the regulatory agency for commercial television in the UK, where I was assigned to the engineering department that dealt with technical standards. My bosses were delighted with my ability to take technical data (they measured whether programs began and ended on time, whether there were any disruptions to services and a range of other technical matters) and turn them into readable reports. If I had chosen to stay, they would have made my job permanent but I aspired to something more: if not academic, then, in the arts.

The IBA offices were across the street from Harrods department store located on the Brompton Road in Knightsbridge, one of the wealthiest areas of London. It was the largest store that I had ever been in and sold what appeared to be everything that anyone with money could want. Besides being a beautiful building, all of the displays were set up to please the eye including the food department which had seasonal displays of produce. To save money, I brought in a packed lunch but, after eating a sandwich at my desk, I liked to leave the office and browse the aisles of Harrods admiring designer dresses and other fashionable items. Even on sale, the merchandise was expensive but I did buy a beautiful pair of knee-high leather boots when they made the final Christmas sale reductions.

In late fall and winter of 1971-72, the IRA were extremely active and several times a week a man with a thick Irish accent would call the IBA with a bomb threat. Whether it was genuine or not, the building had to be evacuated while the police searched the premises and this would take up to three hours. Thankfully, none proved real. (Major bombings in London would not begin until the following year.) Because it was cold outside, I spent the time wandering around Harrods and other pricey shops in the immediate vicinity. As a result, I came to resent the purchasing power of the wealthy.

Leonée Ormond, my former PhD supervisor, saved me from the IBA. In February 1972, she contacted me to let me know of a research job with three young men who had worked for art publisher George Rainbird Ltd. Among them, they had a range of design, layout and editing skills. They set up a small "boutique" publishing house – Carter Nash and Cameron – and were intending to publish an encyclopedia of antiques. They established an office in the East End of London in a former corner store on Upper Street not far from King's Cross, and hired contract staff. I was interviewed and immediately offered a job. I was assigned silver and gold artifacts (a huge section), carpets and tapestries, musical instruments, scientific instruments, jewellery and *objets de vertu* (small luxury objects that can't be described as jewellery). For the next eighteen months, I researched and wrote all of the entries in these fields based on stylistic guidelines and models provided to us.

I spent about six months in a grand room on the second floor of the Goldsmiths' Hall near St. Paul's Anglican Cathedral in central

London researching the gold and silver entries. The Hall is the head-quarters of the Worshipful Company of Goldsmiths, a livery company (guild) that has existed at this location – the junction of Foster Lane and Gresham Street – since the early fourteenth century. The current building occupies an entire block and was opened in 1835. It is a neoclassical style structure and the grandest of all of the guild halls in London, though the Plaisterers' Hall is larger. Its façade has elaborate pillars and inside there is a grand staircase. On the lower flight of steps, marble statues by Samuel Nixon of children representing the four seasons stand on pedestals. The staircase is clad in 10 different colours of marble. A gilded wooden statue of St. Dunstan, the company's patron, is found on the first floor landing. At my first meeting with the librarian, I indicated the scope of the project and she brought out a range of books for me to consult.

It was like walking into history taking the train and buses there every day and entering the "hallowed" hall. A warden would welcome me and tell me that the librarian was expecting me. Every day, depending on what I had researched, the librarian would show me the part of the collection relating to that type of silver and the production of a particular goldsmith including the pieces that gold and silversmiths made to get their certification. They had the largest collection of ceremonial plate and utilitarian ware in the country. Every morning, I would be served coffee and biscuits and every afternoon, tea and biscuits. It was the best research gig I have ever had. At lunch time, during the summer, I walked around the historic area and frequently popped into St. Paul's. Sometimes I would be lucky and hear music.

The remaining fields were researched at the Victoria and Albert Museum and specialized libraries such as the London Library in St. James Square, which had an extraordinary fine and decorative arts collection, which could only be consulted in situ. It was run by a charity and clients had to pay for a pass. The V&A was a treasure trove with myriad collections. It had an extensive specialized library and, after researching a particular field such as tapestries, I could walk around one of the permanent galleries and admire stuff that I had just researched. It was through this research that I became a lover of museums and gained some knowledge of the fine and decorative arts. The so-called "South Kensington Museums" included not only the V&A but also the Science and Natural History Museums and were a celebration of Victorian England and Empire.

Our entries were reviewed by the co-editors, Ian Cameron and Elizabeth Kingsley-Rowe, and then sent off to experts mostly at the V&A and auction houses Sotheby's and Christie's for final review and approval. The book was published in late 1973 as the *Collins Encyclopedia of Antiques* in the UK and as *The Random House Encyclopedia of Antiques* in North America. It had an introduction by Sir John Pope-Hennessy, art historian and director of the V&A. It was extremely successful.

Hugh was getting bits of freelance work through contacts and eventually got a three or four-month contract with the Royal Ballet touring company. The dancers, sets and orchestra travelled around the midlands and northern England and a typical performance involved two or three, one-act ballets. They were accessible and enormously popular and filled theatres wherever the company went. The musicians had a very basic living allowance, which meant they could only afford to stay in the cheapest rooming houses. These were late Victorian or Edwardian three-storey, terraced houses that frequently suffered from rising damp and smelled of stale, fatty bacon from the ubiquitous "English breakfast."

I joined Hugh every weekend and got to know various cities including Birmingham, Leeds, Manchester and Newcastle upon Tyne. There was always a rehearsal before a performance so I had time to kill and visited museums and shops. I also saw the performances and so frequently that I almost memorized them. Because these were virtually the same in every city, I eventually stopped going unless the weather prevented me from being out of doors. I remember, in particular, "Monotones," a one-act ballet for two men and one woman choreographed by Frederick Ashton to a piece titled "Gymnopédie," by Eric Satie. At the other extreme was "Pineapple Poll," which was inspired by Gilbert and Sullivan, and choreographed by John Cranko with music arranged by Sir Charles Mackerras. The first was starkly beautiful and the last was a comic pirate number.

As the tour was coming to an end, Hugh decided that he needed to bite the bullet and go for some auditions outside London. He called one of his teachers at the Royal College of Music, Tessa Robbins, for a few lessons to brush up on his technique. She had been a finalist in the 1955 sixth edition of the Queen Elizabeth Music Competition and had had a very successful career as a soloist. She had decided to teach so that she could settle down and have a family.

Hugh auditioned for the Bournemouth Sinfonietta and I went down with him for the day. I walked on the boardwalk and admired the ocean views. At the same time, he went for an audition with the BBC Concert Orchestra, which was a pops broadcast orchestra and had a regular program – Friday Night is Music Night. The program, comprising light classical and popular music, had been running since 1953 on the BBC Light Programme (later BBC2). It was recorded live at the Camden Theatre in Islington until 1972 and, then moved to the Hippodrome in Golders Green.

Hugh was successful in both auditions and had the unenviable task of deciding whether to play with a classical ensemble outside London or with a light music orchestra in London. The BBC won. The leader, Arthur Leavins, was extremely kind to Hugh and he began to make musical friends who sometimes invited him to do freelance gigs. These were mostly religious works in performances outside London, frequently in churches. I attended all of the live performances in the two years (1972 and 1973) that Hugh played with the Concert Orchestra, as well as the gigs he did as a freelancer.

On our return from our honeymoon, we had moved from Barnes to an upstairs flat in a house on Savernake Road in North London. The railway tracks were at the end of the back garden and the two stations were Hampstead Heath on the west and Gospel Oak to the East. The other side of the tracks was the south end of Parliament Hill Fields and, from our bedroom window we could watch people flying kites on windy days. The café where George Orwell played chess and wrote was a short walk away as was the historic home on East Heath Road where Katherine Mansfield had lived with her husband, the literary critic John Middleton Murry.

It was a lovely place to live but we left it about a year later to take up residence in the ground floor of the three-storey house belonging to Hugh's Uncle Geoffrey. The house was located in Highgate near St. Joseph's Roman Catholic Church on Highgate Hill; the nearest underground station was Archway at the bottom of the hill. Waterlow Park was a few hundred metres away and was part of the ribbon of green in North London that includes the Highgate Cemetery and Hampstead Heath. Literary references abounded here too: Andrew Marvell, John Keats and Samuel Taylor Coleridge are among famous literary figures associated with Highgate. I loved walking and looking for blue plaques on the historic frontages of charming old houses revealing their connection to famous authors or prominent public figures.

Uncle Geoff was a professional musician, who had met his future wife, Jane Vowles, while they were students at the Royal College of Music in the 1920s. She was a talented opera singer who had spent most of her adult life as a music teacher. (The large living room in the house had two grand pianos, his and hers.) Jane was the inspiration for 93 songs written by the Leicester composer, Benjamin Burrows, in the period 1927-29. Geoff and Jane became Communists during their student days and she was delivering copies of the *Morning Star* when she collapsed and died on Highgate Hill in January 1973.

Geoff's musical life had been more diverse and he conducted various orchestras (including the London Philharmonic) and also was a talented orchestrator. He was music director of the Ballet Rambert and the London Festival Ballet, and a professor and conductor with London's Trinity College of Music. In the period I knew him, he travelled abroad for most of the year as a music examiner. The reason we moved into the house was that he and Jane had separated in 1971 and she had bought a flat above a shop at the centre of Highgate village. While his friend Reg, a ballet administrator, lived in the first floor flat and some ballet dancers in the top flat of the house, the ground floor was empty and the rent very modest.

We entertained our friends on weekends and enjoyed taking them on literary walks and also for visits to Highgate Cemetery, which was terribly overgrown with huge holly bushes and ivy. These threatened to topple the various tomb monuments and were living proof of the transience of human endeavour. On Highgate Hill on the wall in front of Lauderdale House there is a plaque with the following information: "Four feet below this spot is the stone step, formerly the entrance to the cottage in which lived Andrew Marvell, poet, wit, and satirist; colleague with John Milton in the foreign or Latin secretaryship during the Commonwealth; and for about twenty years M.P. for Hull. Born at Winestead, Yorkshire, 31st March, 1621, died in London, 18th August, 1678, and buried in the church of St. Giles-in-the-fields. This memorial is placed here by the London County Council, December, 1898."

In August 1972, the Davies family was shaken by the death of Hugh's father. Shortly after I met him in September 1970, John was diagnosed with cancer of the esophagus and had major surgery.

He recovered and, although frail, took part in our wedding in July 1971. The cancer returned and the last six months of his life were very difficult as he suffered from constant pain. Wife Phyllis looked after him to the best of her ability with health care workers coming in daily, and he died at home. There was a tribute in *Brio* magazine for his contributions to music at home and abroad. Not only had he been the Music Librarian of the BBC, he had also been president of the international music librarians association and was considered a pioneer in the field. This had been acknowledged through the award of an Order of the British Empire.

Phyllis continued to be indomitable though she grieved her husband to the end of her life. At the time of his death, she was 67 and incredibly active: she not only played the viola and hosted the String's Club weekly in her home but also volunteered at an animal shelter, and for the local church. The Davies home was always full of people and she was a wonderful cook. Every Sunday we gathered at 1 pm for dinner beginning with a glass of dry sherry in the living room and then moved to the dining room for a lavish meal of roast beef, roast lamb or roast pork with crackling. There were also two or three desserts, all homemade. The table was beautifully set with crystal wine goblets and silver, and an arrangement of flowers from her garden or the local flower shop in The Broadway. There was always company, not only us but Hugh's older brother Robin, wife Hilary and son Crispin as well as her brothers Peter and Geoffrey and their wives, and friends, both old and new. She was incredibly hospitable and had a highly developed social conscience. During the war, when John had served with the code breakers at Bletchley Park (many librarians were part of the team because of their facility with words), Phyllis had hosted Jewish families fleeing Germany.

Hugh and I counted ourselves lucky to be employed and decided to buy a house with the assistance of my parents and his mother, who loaned us $5,000 each towards the down payment. In fall, 1972, we found a maisonette (second floor and attic) on Priory Road in Crouch End, just south of Muswell Hill. Priory Park stretched behind the house and to the side of the house were tennis courts. From the upper windows, we could see on the hill Alexandra Palace, an entertainment complex dating back to the mid-nineteenth century with a huge circular skating rink under a dome. We shared the garden with the owners of the ground floor flat, Colin and Sheila. He was an art teacher and she a textiles designer and we quickly became friends.

We proceeded to fix up the house as cheaply as we could and did most of the work ourselves. This is what all of our friends were doing. We removed the carpet from the living room, dining room, hallway and two bedrooms, and sanded and polyurethaned the floors. We painted the walls white in the living room and I made pale-yellow floor-to-ceiling curtains. My brother Giuseppe helped us build the wooden frame of a sofa, and I made the brown corduroy covers for the seat and cushions. Hugh's brother Robin put up the wallpaper in our dining room and bedroom (both William Morris-style prints). We found a good used gas stove in a shop in the Holloway Road as well as a pine table and an old stripped-pine dresser, which we put in our dining room. We bought a new fridge and washing machine. Hugh's parents had given us their small oak dining table and matching chairs when we moved to the house in Savernake Road and they looked wonderful in our new home, which was a mixture of old and new. I loved to go to junky antique shops in the area to see what I could find for our home and Hugh left the decoration to me. I've often wondered whether my love of antiques and used furniture was the result of having left everything behind when my family emigrated from Italy.

It was an exciting time: all of our friends were in a frenzy of pairing up, nesting and having children. My old friends from King's College, Peter and Elizabeth, were no longer interested in socializing with us because, according to them, we had become "too bourgeois." Whether that was true or not, we certainly had moved away from the relatively carefree student life into the serious world of adulthood. Among the first were Terry and Andrea, who had daughter Jennifer. They moved to a cheaper flat in south London and Terry abandoned his studies at King's College and got work at a private school teaching English. Their next move was to Tunbridge Wells to be closer to the school. Hugh's university friend Martin returned from Northern Ireland where he was teaching at the university in Belfast and he and wife Elizabeth and their two children became part of our circle.

Leonée and Richard were also expecting their first child and Augustus was born at a time when the National Union of Mineworkers was at war over pay with the Conservative government of Edward Heath. Since coal was used to generate electricity, there would be rolling strikes, which meant that the only heat in a home might be a gas stove or paraffin heaters. I remember Leonée, a staunch Tory, being furious with the miners, as she struggled to keep her newborn warm.

Our friends Laurel and Stephen Brake were in the same position – their son Simon was born in October 1972. Both were Labour supporters and used paraffin heaters in their house in East Ham without complaint. Our friendship had developed when I discovered that all of the books relating to Walter Pater, which I required for my doctoral research at the University of London, were in the possession of one person, Laurel. I got the librarian to recall them, and when I got notification that they were in, I went to the University Library to pick them up. The librarian told me that Mrs. Brake wanted to meet me. We hit it off immediately. She was from New York, the daughter of Jewish professionals. While at university she had espoused left-wing causes and had marched to protest anti-black racism before moving to the UK to do her doctorate. Stephen, the son of a clergyman, had worked with youth in the East End of London and was a student at the St. Martin's School of Art. My brother Giuseppe had found work there as a model for the live classes before going off to Amsterdam to paint.

In fall 1972, shortly after the move to the house in Priory Road, I had a miscarriage. This was painful and disappointing but my doctor was very encouraging and helped me to get over the inevitable depression. Happily, I became pregnant again in early 1973 and our son, Alexander John, was born on November 1st at University College Hospital in London. At that time, new mothers were kept in hospital for a week as we learned to breast feed and care for our infants. It was a gorgeous autumn day when Hugh took me home and there were still leaves on the trees. We were greeted by his mother who had commissioned a lovely teddy bear with moveable arms and legs for him, and had also crocheted some sweaters. My mother came from Canada and stayed with us for several weeks to help with the baby.

The year 1973 is memorable not only because of Alex's birth. In March, the Provisional Irish Republican Army began its campaign of bombings on British soil with the planting of four car bombs in London. The sites were near official buildings such as the Ministry of Agriculture off Whitehall, one of the March bombing sites. We were all gripped by fear. On August 23, a bomb was found in an abandoned bag in the Baker Street Station ticket hall and was defused. I worried about Hugh going in to central London for rehearsals, recording sessions and concerts since he used public transit during the day. On August 31, a bomb exploded on Old Quebec Street near Marble Arch and damaged two hotels. Two railway stations were targeted: Victoria

Station (September 8) and King's Cross (September 10). Both bombs exploded and five people were injured at King's Cross. Other bombings occurred on December 18 in Westminster at a building occupied by the Home Office, and injured at least 40 people. On December 24, a bomb went off on the Finchley Road at Swiss Cottage and injured six people.

Seeing these bombings in the city that I had come to love gave me cause to remember my attendance at the film, *The Battle of Algiers*, shortly after my arrival in London in 1968 when I had cheered the freedom-fighting bombers. I could not condone the IRA bombings, and remembered our friend Martin's observation when he left his university job in Belfast that it was better to be a clerical worker in London than a professor in "Hell." This was how he described their life there. His wife Elizabeth mentioned the daily searches of the baby carriage for bombs when she went to buy groceries.

In September 1972, I had started to teach two classes for the University of London Extramural Department (their faculty of extension) as part of the Diploma in English Literature program: one in East Ham, a working class area of London, and the other in Harlow, which was a new town north of London on the border with Hertfordshire. I got to East Ham by train via King's Cross so the bombings were a real concern for me. The train journey to Harlow was much more complicated and Hugh had to drive me. After Alex's birth, we had to take him with us and Hugh would sit with him in the staff room while I taught the three-hour class. In the break, I would go in and breast feed him. Most students were adult learners, many of whom were school teachers who wanted to upgrade their credentials by further study in their specialization. John Spence, a new friend who was working on a PhD on Jane Austen with Leonée as his supervisor, took over some classes for a couple of weeks while another friend, Pauline Honderich, took over the others to allow me to heal from childbirth.

I had never learned to drive in Canada as my brother and sister had when they were 16 so I had to learn in London. This was a daunting task not only because of the traffic volume but also because of the narrow streets with vehicles parked on either side. We had an old car that Hugh had purchased from his Uncle Paul and he began to teach me. I finished up with some lessons from a professional and got my driver's licence. For the last class in spring 1974, as a newly minted driver, I was able to set off for Harlow. I was terrified but Hugh had a musical engagement and I was on my own. The drive took more than an hour in rush hour traffic. I longed to get to the part of the route that went through Epping Forest because it was quieter. Another reason for driving was that I had to deliver to the students all of the books that they would need for the following year's class. I taught the two courses for a total of six years and a number of my students received their diplomas and university credits.

After about two years with the BBC Concert Orchestra, Hugh was successful in obtaining work with the New Philharmonia Orchestra, in fall 1974, and became part of the first violin section. Perfect sight-reading was required as well as superb musicianship. This was Hugh's dream job and all started well with the beginning of the orchestral season at the Royal Festival Hall in London but, when he checked the schedule, there was very little work in the New Year. Hugh discovered that the general manager had been fired for incompetence. The new manager, Gavin Henderson, who was hired in 1975, once he hit stride was incredibly successful and the orchestra had major concert bookings, tours and recording sessions but, for his first year in the orchestra, Hugh brought in relatively little and my earnings were necessary to make ends meets. We ate cheap cuts of meat and fish such as mackerel, and I also made my own bread. I have not eaten mackerel willingly since then.

To supplement our income, I began to look for freelance editorial work. I remember that I even filled in for my friend Janet, who worked at Stikeman Elliott, a Toronto legal firm with offices in London, for three weeks while she was on holidays. The money was good and the transactions they were dealing with related to high finance and were very interesting. Through Leonée's good graces, I obtained a contract to research the life of Mrs. Isabella Beeton, the author of *Mrs. Beeton's Book of Household Management*, and her publisher husband Sam Beeton. Sarah Freeman, a journalist who had worked for *Queen* Magazine, had become fascinated by Mrs. Beeton, whose influential book had gone through many editions since it was first published in 1861. Sarah was not an academic and also had two young children so she reached out to Leonée (they had been at Oxford together) for a recommendation for a professional researcher who could do this work for her. I found the topic really interesting and so I took it on.

I spent many happy hours in the reading room at the British Museum (BM) and at the national newspaper and magazine collection at Colindale near Hendon in North London. The BM, established in 1753, was the first public museum in the world and opened its doors in 1759. A huge circular reading room was located under a dome and galleries spread out in various directions and the collections from Egyptology to the Graeco-Roman world forward reflected British colonialism.

My research was beginning to take on a pattern: most took place in historic buildings many of which served as museums. The book was as much about Sam Beeton as it was about his wife Isabella though it was titled *Mrs. Beeton's Book of Household Management*. The story begins with him. Sam wanted to become a publisher and began work with C.H. Clarke & Co. He read Harriet Beecher Stowe's best-selling book, *Uncle Tom's Cabin* and convinced his boss to send him to the US to obtain the rights to publish the book in the UK. Stowe was much taken with the young man and the fact that he was willing to pay for the rights while other publishers simply disregarded her copyright, and a deal was struck. The first London edition appeared in May 1852 and immediately sold 200,000 copies. A luxe edition was produced that also sold well.

As a result, Sam had money to invest and set up his own publishing house. He began with the *Englishwoman's Domestic Magazine* in 1852 and the *Boy's Own Magazine* in 1855. Both were incredibly successful and, in 1856, Sam married Isabella Mayson. Her mother had been widowed young and had been left with three daughters so Isabella had to grow up fast. Her mother married again, a highly-successful widower who was the Clerk of the Epsom race course. Henry Dorling, who had four children, not only ran the course but also a massive entertainment complex that included lodgings and food preparation and service. Running the merged households was an enormous task and much was left to older daughter, Isabella, who rose to the challenge. The couple had an additional 13 children.

Sam and Isabella's marriage was a love match (he was 26 and she 20) and, for her, a welcome escape from her demanding family. She quickly became involved in writing columns for the *Englishwoman's Domestic Magazine*. Together they became a "power couple" leading the charge in terms of popular magazines and popular culture. The magazine had recipes, some of which were submitted by readers, a craft section as well as an advice column that included "letters from the lovelorn." But it was the fashion content, some directly from Paris, and the lavish illustrations (some in colour) that drew hordes of women readers. Isabella took that under her wing.

Mrs. Beeton's Book of Household Management, which appeared in 1861, was an offshoot of the magazine. With the emerging middle class, women were looking for advice on how to manage their households with minimal help; this was not unlike today's lifestyle television programs and blogs. The book provided very practical advice and much content was drawn from agricultural, scientific and technological publications of the time; for example, the sections on various domestic animals, butchering techniques, etc. Sam did this research at the British Museum and obtained the illustrations and materials required for these sections as well as doing some of the writing. As I sat in the Reading Room at the BM, I read the same books that he had over 100 years earlier. In 1861, the couple started Queen, a magazine that focused on British royals and aristocrats. They thus had all the bases covered in popular journalism.

Isabella, who had had a series of miscarriages, died from puerperal fever at the age of 28, in 1865, after the birth of her second son, Mayson Beeton. Sam felt very guilty because she had been working on the magazine and the proofs for The Dictionary of Every-Day Cookery, which was drawn from Mrs. Beeton's Book of Household Management. Her family felt that Sam had over-worked her. For many years after Isabella's death, Sam used the pages of the magazine to explore childbed deaths in the UK and provided statistics. He also championed sterilization of medical equipment to avoid sepsis and observed that you were better off with a drunken mid-wife than a society doctor whose gown and instruments were covered with the blood of previous surgeries. (This was not an uncommon practice.)

I read all of the magazines as well as Mrs. Beeton's Book of Household Management and found all the source materials for Sarah. I also undertook genealogical research on the families as well as researching the literature with respect to the role of women at the time, development of specialized fashion and cookery books, and other relevant contextual materials. Sarah drew on this research and wrote Isabella and Sam: The Story of Mrs. Beeton, which was published by Victor Gollancz in 1977. The acknowledgement of my work is limited but was the norm at the time, and many of my friends who did research for academics had much more to complain about.

The year 1975 was exciting because we went to Egypt on holidays in May and that summer my parents came to visit us in London and we travelled to Italy to visit Nonna Alessandra. At the time, Hugh's brother Humphrey was working in Cairo on a dictionary of colloquial Egyptian Arabic being developed by his professor at Cambridge, Martin Hinds (it would be published in 1986). Because we had Alex, who was then about 18 months old, Humphrey had arranged for us to stay with his friend, Dutch economist Deodaat Breebaart, and his young Palestinian wife, Nadia, and their baby daughter. Daat taught at the American University in Cairo and was a specialist in Middle Eastern economics. They had a very large apartment in a mansion block in Maadi and had servants. This was an affluent, suburban district of Cairo on the east bank of the Nile.

Daat and Nadia treated us extremely well and other than worrying about Alex, who refused to eat anything other than the delicious, small Egyptian bananas and dehydrated English baby food, we had a wonderful time. Humphrey had arranged various sightseeing tours and most of the time we had to take Alex with us because he refused to be left behind. Thus, he saw the pyramids, the tombs in the Valley of the Kings, and various museums. We visited markets and mosques and, because there was so much donkey and horse excrement about, Hugh always carried Alex on his shoulders. He was very popular with people we met in the streets who would rush up to touch his golden curls. Hugh had started to learn Arabic and would introduce him as "Iskander," Egyptian for Alexander. We did leave him behind when we took a small propeller-powered airplane to see the two rock temples at Abu Simbel surrounded by the waters of Lake Nasser. The temples to Pharaoh Ramesses II and his wife Nefertari were carved into a mountainside in the thirteenth century, BC, and with the creation of the Aswan High Dam reservoir were relocated in 1968 to an artificial hill high above the waters.

During my parents' stay in London, we not only showed them all of the sites including Buckingham Palace, my father also made time to build a cupboard in one of our bedrooms and do other handyman-type work. The trip to Italy was very emotional for them, particularly for my father who reunited with his mother, whom he had not seen since 1949. She was living in a home for seniors attached to a convent. She was delighted to meet Alex, who was named for her. We stayed with some old friends of the family and my parents enjoyed talking to friends who had not emigrated. They also met up with friends who had gone to Canada and were holidaying in Grimaldi, a practice that became very common for many immigrants at that time. Some even acquired ancestral lands that had been sold by their parents. My parents never desired to do that. They were happy with their lot in Canada. I think that they had a memorable holiday that was not repeated. It was during this visit to Italy, on a hillside that our second son, William Raphael Hasan, was conceived. His middle name was an Anglicized version of my Father's name, Raffaele, and Hasan was the name of Hugh's Arabic tutor. He had begun taking private lessons from an Egyptian doctoral student at the London School of Oriental and African Studies.

This summer of escape was followed by a return to ordinary life, which was oriented around Hugh and his work; I did the majority of housework and care of the children. He did what he could. When he was at home, he was also practising for the next performance and I had to keep the children quiet. We continued to see friends but, because of the concert schedule, Saturday nights were out for dinner parties and, most of the time, we entertained at Sunday dinner (served at 1 pm). Since most of our friends had young children, they would stay on for a walk to the park and tea.

One of my graduate student friends the year I lived in Pembina Hall, Cathie Brown, had married Chris Ashley, an English post-doctoral student who was visiting Canada, and we re-connected in 1970 when he was teaching at the University in Bristol. In 1976, he obtained a position at Corpus Christi College, Oxford. They would visit us in London and we went to their place in Oxford. Their three children – Andrew, Molly and Emily – had hedgehogs and Alex was particularly fond of them. Cathie called me in fall 1977, asking if she and the children could come to stay with us for a few days. She told me excitedly that Prime Minister Trudeau had passed an amendment to the *Citizenship Act* that allowed the Canadian mothers of children born abroad to sign them up for dual citizenship. Specifically, a child born to a Canadian citizen parent between 1947 and 1977 could acquire Canadian citizenship if his or her birth was registered at a Canadian embassy, consulate or high commission. The deadline was imminent and she wanted to get this done. Cathie came and with children in tow we took the tube to Trafalgar Square and went to Canada House to do this. I was delighted that my children would also be Canadian. While I was proud of my Italian ancestry, I was a Canadian patriot at heart.

These were full, happy years but also very stressful. Hugh began to suffer from platform nerves, which was common among the professional musicians in London, and took tranquilizers to get by. He would go for stretches of up to a month without a day off and, because of his early experience with having no work, he didn't dare take time off. It was a constant round of performances, recording sessions, run-outs to performances outside of London, and tours abroad. The orchestra at that time performed at an annual spring festival in Barcelona and a summer festival in Salzburg, and also travelled to Europe, Japan and Mexico. Hugh was a staunch Musician's Union member and, his entire time with the Orchestra, he was a musician's representative on the board of management. (The Orchestra was self-governing and the musicians were all freelance.) One of their most important duties was to negotiate contracts and pay scales as well as choosing the music director and principal conductor. He was devoted to this work and had an excellent relationship with Riccardo Muti and the musicians. One benefit of working so hard was that he was earning extremely well. This enabled him to buy an eighteenth century Italian violin made by Lorenzo Carcassi, one of a collection owned by his former teacher Tessa Robbins. The sound was exquisite.

The pressure of two careers and family began to weigh on our relationship. Neither of us had any time for ourselves nor to relax. I remember relating to Shirley Conran's book *Superwoman* when it came out in 1975. It was a reference book providing guidance on how to run a home, and save time and money (shades of Mrs. Beeton). In 1977, she published *Superwoman II*, a sequel, an indication of how popular the first book had been. Later, she claimed that she had suffered from PTSD. I suppose this was the down side of women's liberation: that we could have careers but we also had to excel at women's traditional roles as housewives and mothers. I certainly could relate, being a career woman and mother was a hard slog, and being a perfectionist to boot, made it even harder.

I was not interested in feminist theory though one of my friends, Laurel Brake, certainly was and we had some discussions about it. I was, however, living in the trenches; that is, I was trying to have it all: being wife/lover, mother and career woman. I had read Germaine Greer's *The Female Eunuch* in 1970 when it came out and was not convinced by her argument that women's traditional roles including the "nuclear" family repressed them sexually rendering them sexless eunuchs. The fact that she had never given birth and had to care for a family, I believe, skewed her thinking and explained her focus on sexuality. I hadn't read American feminist writers at that time but I felt that women had to work twice as hard as men and frequently earned less, and did not reach the upper echelons in their chosen career paths. This was certainly true in academe and the museum world, which I had experienced.

I felt that I was juggling a number of balls in the air and it kept getting harder and harder. That is why finding time to relax and do pleasurable activities was crucial. A major treat for me was to attend New Philharmonia performances at the Royal Festival Hall on the South Bank. Hugh got free tickets for me and all I had to do was find a babysitter. I looked forward to this all week and would have a bath and choose a nice dress. (In those days, women dressed up to go to concerts.) For a time, like Cinderella, I would cease to be "Mummy" and become the much more glamorous, Adriana, the woman who had developed an eccentric personal style (part Art Nouveau, part Art Deco, part hippie and part Mary Quant). On performance evenings, Friday or Saturday, we would drive down and park in the car park. In the block of seats set aside for the orchestra there would be other orchestral wives to talk to and, at intermission, because Hugh was on the Board, I could join him in the musician's bar back stage. It was a thrill to rub shoulders with famous conductors and soloists.

The New Philharmonia was at a performance peak at the time and this profile was enhanced by Riccardo Muti. He had begun to conduct the orchestra regularly, beginning in 1972, and, in 1973 had succeeded Otto Klemperer as principal conductor. Under his baton, the Orchestra became highly sought after for recordings and the sessions took place at various venues with good acoustics including the Fairfield Halls in Croydon North London. Under Muti, the orchestra recorded the following operas: *Aida* (1974), *Un Ballo in Maschera* (1975), *Nabucco* (1977), *I Puritani* (1979), *Cavalleria Rusticana* (1979) and *La Traviata* (1980). Other conductors brought other recording contracts and these were tied to live performances.

I attended one of the recording sessions and was amazed at how frequently the taping was stopped while the conductor pondered how to get a musical passage just right. He consulted with the concertmaster and soloists, and passages were repeated again and again. The seamless final product revealed none of that effort. One session involved Placido Domingo and one of the orchestral wives, who was also a professional violinist with one of the other London orchestras, mentioned that, when Placido was interested in a woman, he would offer her beautifully-made Spanish high heels.

The Orchestra also performed at the Edinburgh Festival. In August 1976, when Alex was two-and-a-half and William four-months old, as a treat for me, Hugh suggested that we go as a family. We drove up in our Renault 4, a small economy car, with Alex strapped in his car seat in the back and William in his cot, also strapped in. We stayed at various bed and breakfasts and I remember one particularly drafty old house in which the wind made a whistling noise as it moved past the double-glazed windows. Alex was frightened and we had to open the inner window to let a little bit of wind in to stop the disturbing noise.

I remember that the weather in Edinburgh was glorious. The musicians were booked rooms in university residences while the conductor and soloists stayed at posh hotels. Carlo Maria Giulini was the guest conductor at one of the performances at the Usher Hall. During the day I would go out with the boys, pushing William in a stroller and then I would meet Hugh at the back door of the Hall at the end of the morning's rehearsal, and we would go for lunch. One day, as I walked up, Giulini exited the Hall and, when he saw me, he paused, and raised his arms and said, "Madonna, bella, bella." Since I was still struggling to lose "baby weight," I was thrilled. Afterwards, we travelled through the highlands and we were relaxed and happy. Alex sitting in the back seat would sing "songs" and I remember, in particular, "the little tree song" that he composed. I sang Gordon Lightfoot songs as well as popular folk songs such as "This Land is Your Land," and the boys (and Hugh) were content.

When we reached home, we made the decision to move from our flat in Priory Road. It wasn't just the shortage of space, it was that our friends Colin and Sheila had divorced and an elderly woman had moved into the ground floor flat. She was fine but she had a grumpy boyfriend who didn't like children and complained about every sound we made; he also hated Hugh practising. We found a lovely old house on the "borders of Highgate" in estate agent language (it was across the street from the fashionable N6 postal code) and we could therefore afford it. It was a late nineteenth century, two-storey, semi-detached cottage with three bedrooms, two sitting rooms and one bath. It also had central heating.

We made an offer and got it but we had to take a bridging loan because we hadn't yet sold our flat. We had booked to go to Canada for Christmas so Hugh decided I should go ahead with the boys so that he could close on the house and the flat (thankfully, we had found a buyer) and move our stuff in. This would also allow him to do the Christmas concerts at the Royal Festival Hall, which finished around December 23.

I flew to Canada with the boys and they were well behaved on the plane. I remember that the air crew and other passengers in our vicinity were very kind. Alex was a very endearing three-year-old who carried his teddy bear, a gift from his Gran, and his tattered yellow "blankie" everywhere; William was a roly-poly eight-month-old. At the Edmonton International airport, the crew helped us off the aircraft and, in the hurry and confusion, Alex left Teddy and blankie behind. They would not be returned to us for about a week and this caused problems because Alex couldn't sleep without them and constantly sucked his thumb. Since he refused to wear mittens, the thumb got inflamed and red from the cold and the knuckle lines cracked so he was in a lot of pain. The good thing was that he had to stop sucking his thumb and didn't resume when his beloved objects were returned. The air crew had written a nice letter to Alex telling them about Teddy's adventures while away from him.

We were welcomed into the bosom of my extended Italian family and had a wonderful time. Hugh arrived, I believe, on Christmas Eve and we were caught up in a flurry of hospitality. There were Christmas and New Year's gatherings not only at my parents' home in North Glenora but also at my sister Rosa and brother-in-law Rudy's home in Castledowns. Our two boys fit in nicely after their four sons (Stephen, Ralph, James and Robert), who were older, and they had lots of toys to play with. My sister also habitually sent me parcels of clothes that her youngest Robert, about two years older than Alex, had outgrown. We also visited aunts and uncles and cousins and it was the Italian version of the Christmas card festivities celebrated in Hollywood films. Traditions merged and we had home-made ravioli for starters and then turkey with all the trimmings on Christmas Day.

We flew back to Heathrow in early January and arrived at our house in Highgate to find that it was stone cold – although London was warmer than Edmonton and there was no snow, it was still cold, particularly for children. The people from whom we had bought the house had kindly left a list of tradesmen including the electrician who had installed their new central heating gas-powered boiler. We found that he lived across the street and, when we called, he came over immediately and fixed the starter.

I had my classes to teach at East Ham and Harlow, and Hugh returned to work with the orchestra and we settled into the new home. My sister-in-law Hilary wanted to get rid of two loveseats covered in gold, floral-patterned linen and passed them on to us. They fit in the small living room that had sliding glass doors into the garden. The larger dining room, when not being used for dinners, became the domain where Hugh practised almost every day. In late spring, we got the builder who did work for Hugh's Mother to renovate our kitchen and bathroom. Our next-door-neighbour with whom we shared a partition wall was extremely nice and would babysit for us on occasion.

Our house had an interesting location. The backyard was huge and sloped down to the Archway Road and was a few hundred metres from Hornsey Lane, the road that linked Highgate to Crouch End. At the end of our terrace of houses (about four houses from our own) was the old bridge over the road that gave the road its "Archway" name. It was cast iron and had been erected in 1900 to replace the original. It was about a ten-minute walk to Waterlow Park, which had a playground and an aviary with a mynah bird called Charlie, whom the boys adored. During the rush hour at the beginning and end of the day, the roar of traffic was deafening and that's why we could afford the house. Thankfully, the local council paid for the double-glazing of the windows and skylight so when we were inside we didn't hear the noise. When we were outside we just got used to it. In any case, traffic was light on weekends when we used the garden the most.

At one time, the sloped garden was beautifully maintained with flagstone steps and rockeries. Hugh and I did some work but we were just too busy to become keen gardeners so it retained a wild air about it. We did, however, plant about a dozen rose bushes in a bed near the patio just outside the sliding glass doors in the living room. There were huge elm trees at the side and bottom of the garden but some succumbed to Dutch elm disease, and had to be cut down. When we had this done, we built a new fence, with a gate at the bottom onto the walkway that led down to the Archway tube station. This cut about ten minutes from the usual half-hour walk. It was easy walking down but going up the hill at the end of a working day was a hard slog.

We settled into a pleasant routine with Hugh being busy con-
tinually and away at least once a month on run-out concerts outside
London and every few months on a tour, some abroad. While the two
classes a week for the University of London Extramural Department
were manageable, in professional terms, I wanted more. This came
when Richard Ormond asked me if I was interested in becoming a
researcher on the project that he and Malcolm Rogers, a colleague at
the National Portrait Gallery, had designed. Since the NPG received
so many requests for portraits of eminent people from historians and
researchers, they decided that a companion to the multi-volume *Dictionary of National Biography* that focused on portraiture would be
highly desirable. They decided on a four-volume work that would
provide information on the portraiture of eminent people (known in
portraiture as "sitters") in a short-hand fashion including details as to
type of portrait, artist, medium, collection and location.

I started this work in fall 1978 initially working only four days a
week (Monday through Thursday) at the NPG near Trafalgar Square.
Alex was nearly four and William was 18-months old. When I gave
birth, the National Health Service had paid for a cleaning lady for a
few months and we became friends, and she continued to clean for
me occasionally. When I was offered the job, she agreed to look after
William and to take Alex to the Montessori play school where he
went mornings. She did this for about six months but then her new
husband asked that she quit. I found a young woman who had just
completed an early childhood education diploma through an agency,
and that worked very well for about another six months. She then quit
for a better job without giving notice and I was stuck. I looked at the
local Hornsey paper and saw a small ad from a woman, Sybil, who had
cared for a little boy from birth to six years of age. I interviewed her
and was immediately impressed. She was a mother and grandmother
in her own right and her daughter Lorraine and her husband Ollie
lived with their two young daughters in Germany where he was based
(a career soldier with the British Army). Sybil mentioned that she had
decided to quit her job because the boys' parents, who both worked
for the BBC, regularly came home late and she had to leave at 6 pm
to prepare supper for her husband, Bert. I hired her and she became
an invaluable addition to our household. She arrived at 8 am and left
promptly at 6 pm; since she drove, she was able to take the boys on
outings and, when her husband was home for lunch, she would take

the boys to her house and they would have lunch there. She became "Auntie Sybil" and he "Uncle Bert."

Because of this stability, I was able to concentrate on NPG work. Richard had also hired another of Leonée's former students, Elaine Kilmurray, and we shared the eras covered by the four volumes: I did the beginning of portraiture to 1600 ("The Middle Ages to the Early Georgians") and sitters born 1850 to 1900 ("The Twentieth Century"); and Elaine did sitters born in the middle period, 1601 to 1849 ("Later Georgians and Early Victorians" and "The Victorians").

We perched on stools in the library filled with banks of card catalogues and books on portraiture and other types of art, sales catalogues, books on stately homes and their collections, as well as a range of art magazines. There were two main types of card catalogues: some based on artists' names and others on sitters' names. The oldest had the spidery handwriting of the first director, George Scharf, and that of his secretary. The gallery was established in 1856 and was arguably the first in the world. It had been at the current location at St. Martin's Place off Trafalgar Square and adjoining the National Gallery since 1896.

Elaine and I researched each sitter in the *Dictionary of National Biography* and other sources, and then looked for portraits in the catalogues and print materials. We wrote this information down in a formulaic way for each volume. We identified portraits in various media (oil, watercolour, chalk, gouache, etc.) and mechanical reproductions such as etchings, lithographs, photographs, etc. If the portrait was in the collection of the NPG, we would go find it and examine it ourselves, whether on display or in the storage areas of the gallery (some onsite and some offsite). Occasionally, we were even allowed to visit several stately homes in the British countryside where famous portraits were hung in surroundings similar to those where the sitters had lived. Among these was Montacute House, a National Trust property which in 1975 became an outpost of the NPG and that displayed period-appropriate oil and watercolour paintings.

Malcolm Rogers supervised my work and Richard that of Elaine and they reviewed our entries every couple of weeks and looked for errors or omissions. We finished by typing out all of the entries for each volume. While many academics and other experts barely acknowledged their researchers, Richard generously insisted that Elaine and I be credited as the authors of the volumes. This was unheard of. I remember one day that the former director of the NPG, Roy Strong, who had moved on to the Victoria and Albert Museum, was in to do some research. When Richard re-introduced me to him (I had met him socially at the Ormond home when I was working on my doctorate) and told him what I was doing, he observed "that's not real research."

My area of responsibility included Tudor and Stuart royals (fifteenth to seventeenth centuries) and there were many stunning portraits in the collection. The best were on permanent display in galleries that were organized in a chronological fashion. Artists included Hans Holbein, Anthony Van Dyke and Sir Peter Lely. Historians would pay pilgrimages to see particularly famous portraits such as the "Chandos portrait" of William Shakespeare. It was lovely to walk through the galleries and listen to the whispered conversations. The portraits of Queen Elizabeth I, the daughter of Henry VIII and Anne Boylen, were particularly stunning and numerous (over 130 in all). She was at pains to create the image of a powerful queen who needed no man to support her. Thus, the portraits had objects that were symbolic of her power (globes, crowns, swords, etc.) and virginity (the moon, pearls, etc.). Other monarchs paled in comparison. I realized that to be the perfect monarch, she had to deny her womanhood.

The fascinating research was accompanied by the formation of some new friendships. My co-researcher Elaine and I became friends and frequently had lunch together eating food we brought from home in the basement coffee room. Once a week we treated ourselves to a meal at a reasonably priced restaurant in Soho, the area bordering on the NPG. While very junior in the pecking order of professional staff (there was a ranking going down from the director to curators to conservators and preparators, designers, warders and caretaking staff), we were treated extremely well, and we frequently discussed sitters with the curators responsible for that particular era, some of whom had written books on portraiture or specific sitters. We thus became part of the cycle of work on mounting exhibits for feature galleries, which was very exciting.

When I was working on the 1850-1900 volume, one of my sitters was the Queen Mother, who was born in 1900. For her eightieth birthday, the NPG mounted a birthday exhibit which included the best of her portraiture from babyhood to the present. I even consulted the Surveyor of the Queen's Pictures, Sir Oliver Millar, who had an office in St. James Palace. I showed him the outline of portraits for her, which was extensive, and he was very positive about it. Sir Oliver had published *The Queen's Pictures* in 1977 and also a catalogue for the NPG's exhibit on Sir Peter Lely in 1978. One of my last activities at the gallery was to attend the opening of the Queen Mother exhibit. Large pots of her favourite heirloom roses were placed in the feature gallery and I remember thinking how short the Queen Mother, Queen Elizabeth and Princess Margaret were (not much taller than my five-foot-one-inch frame) and how beautiful their complexions were.

The fourth volume of the *Dictionary of British Portraiture* dealing with the last half of the nineteenth and first half of the twentieth century included photographs. The first director had initiated photography of eminent figures, mostly men, and these head and shoulders and full-length photographs were mainstays of the collection. But it was the more exotic private collections that the gallery had purchased or had gifted to them that really interested me. Many of the early glass negatives were stored in old tea chests with some of the tea leaves still in the bottom of the box. There was a new photographic curator at the NPG, Terence Pepper, and he began to have prints made of some of the glass negatives. These included some belonging to the famous photographer Julia Margaret Cameron, who had taken formal and informal photographs of the family of Alfred Lord Tennyson and other Victorian greats. The family groupings had a "soft focus" quality about them that made them dream-like. There was also an extensive collection of members of the Bloomsbury Group pictured in their homes in London and the countryside.

I was particularly fascinated by the collection of photographs of Thomas Edward Lawrence, archaeologist, army officer, writer and diplomat who became known as "Lawrence of Arabia" for his role in the military campaign in the Sinai and Palestine against the Ottoman Empire and the Arab Revolt, both during the First World War. The collection included rare photographs of him as "Aircraftsman Shaw," when he was serving in India. To avoid his fame, in 1922, Lawrence had enlisted under a pseudonym, "T.E. Shaw" and served until his death in 1935, mostly in the Royal Air Force. In 1926, he published the work for which he is best known, *Seven Pillars of Wisdom*. There are also photographs of the cottage in the Dorset countryside where he was living when he had his fatal motorbike accident. Lawrence was a close friend of George Bernard Shaw and his wife, Constance, and had adopted his surname as his pseudonym. Constance gifted the photos to the NPG.

Because of my passion for my work, I came to live in two worlds. After an exciting day of research, I would arrive at home out of breath from climbing up Highgate Hill, and become "Mummy" again. Sybil greeted me at the door and the boys would rush to embrace me and immediately after would break out into squabbles. Sybil would observe, "But they've been as good as gold all day." Our lives were hectic. On weekends, we entertained and all of our friends were in the same position of juggling work and family. Some marriages failed at this time. Terry and Andrea divorced and the friendship lapsed though we would hear about him from mutual friends. He worked at Queen's College, an independent school for girls aged 11 to 18, and with composer David Bedford, wrote an opera titled *The Death of Baldur*, for youth voices. Some orchestral marriages also failed (the touring schedule meant that the temptation to have affairs was ever-present) and it was clear that marriages that involved juggling two careers and families were difficult to manage.

Attending orchestral performances was the highlight of my busy week but Hugh wanted to do other things and, when he had an evening off, we would sometimes go to see a play. I made sure that I had several babysitters to hand. As the boys got older, Hugh's mother sometimes babysat for us but she was profoundly hard of hearing (the result of a botched mastoid operation when she was young) and even with hearing aids did not always hear a baby crying. I remember one outing in 1979 that took us to the Roundhouse theatre in Kentish Town for a performance of Henrik Ibsen's *Lady from the Sea* with Vanessa Redgrave and Terrance Stamp. The set was stunning – a circular walled structure (like a shallow swimming pool) was created and flooded and the action took place on strategically placed boulders serving as islands with trees. There was also a working row boat that was used in the production.

A highlight of 1978-79 was seeing an old friend from University of Alberta days, Sydney Smith. She and her husband Ken Craig spent the academic year in Oxford with their children Kenneth and Alexandra. He was a clinical psychologist and, after completing her Masters' degree, Sydney had gone into education and completed her PhD at UBC. They visited us in London and we went to Oxford to see them. Our children were roughly the same ages and got on well together and, when they were occupied, we adults could compare our busy lives and how difficult it was to fit everything in. A particular highlight of one visit to Oxford was going to see the one-ninth scale replica in stone of the village of Bourton on the Water. The children loved being giants looking into the churches and houses. We also saw a train collection in a dedicated store. But these family interludes had to be eked out of our busy, busy lives.

The Britain of the late 1970s was divided by the policies of Conservative politician Margaret Thatcher, who had become Prime Minister in 1979. She was described as the "Iron Lady," and was anti-union. The economic recession in the UK culminated in 1978-79 with a series of strikes by both private and public sector unions in which higher wages were demanded. Labour Prime Minister James Callaghan was in the unenviable position of opposing the traditional base of support of his party, the trade unions, and imposing salary caps. The strikes swayed public opinion towards Thatcher and she was elected with a strong mandate to bring the unions under control, privatize state-owned industries and bring in supports for industry. Many young people left the country at that time including our friends Julian and Eluned Schweitzer; he joined the World Bank and was based in Washington and she pursued further studies in her nursing specialty.

In summer 1979, we flew to Edmonton for a holiday and my parents insisted that we leave the boys with them and go off for a holiday on our own. We had never done this and leapt at the opportunity. We took a bus to Banff where we picked up a rental car. We booked dinner at the Banff Springs Hotel but had several hours to kill so we drove to Lake Louise. The view of the lake surrounded by peaks convinced us that we wanted to have dinner there instead. We went inside and, when Hugh spoke to the young waitress, she was charmed by his British accent and we got a table in the large window overlooking the lake. Hugh called to cancel the booking at the Banff Springs and we sat down to a leisurely meal. I believe we had fillet mignon and Hugh drank much red wine. I am not a great drinker so was always the designated driver. As the sun set, Hugh observed, "Why don't we come to live in Canada." Believing that he had been seduced by the beauty of the mountains, I said that I didn't mind considering this but warned him not to say anything to my family.

Hugh was anxious to visit the US so we headed south through Waterton Park and into Glacier National Park in Montana. The Going to the Sun Road was terrifying with its winding, hairpin turns but also exhilarating. The relatively peaceful roads through rural Montana were a relief and we eventually ended up at Lake Pend Oreille in northern Idaho. Arriving around 7 pm at Sandpoint, we went into a nice motel on the edge of the lake to book a room. The only room left was the honeymoon suite and we booked one night. It had a large fieldstone fireplace and you could walk through patio doors onto the grass, and then onto the beach with its fine sand. We slept very well and, after a big fried breakfast, we went sightseeing and fell in love with the small town with its historic houses surrounded by white picket fences. We returned to the motel for lunch and decided to stay for another three or four days. We knew that we wanted to be back for Hugh's birthday on August 16. We spent time on the beach (Hugh was a strong swimmer while I was not and sat in a comfortable chair and read) and also explored the neighbouring beauty spots (Sandpoint is surrounded by the Selkirk, Cabinet and Bitterroot mountain ranges).

We had several serious conversations about moving to Canada. I warned Hugh that he had been dazzled by the romance of Banff and Lake Louise, and that living day-in-day-out in Edmonton would be different, particularly in winter when it got very cold. I also mentioned that the Edmonton Symphony would not be of a standard that he was used to and he observed, for the first time, that he might consider returning to the law.

We arrived in Edmonton the afternoon of Hugh's birthday (a Thursday) and the boys were in good spirits and happy to see us. They had spent time with their cousins and had been spoiled by my parents. That evening, family members and friends began to gather. We thought we were going to celebrate the birthday quietly but, in fact, my parents had planned a surprise party! Hugh was in high good spirits and, when he stood up to thank everyone for making him so welcome, he said, "We are looking forward to living in Canada when the orchestral season finishes in 1980." The packed living room erupted in cheers and rejoicing, and my heart sank.

As soon as we returned to London, Hugh gave his notice to the Orchestra. Hugh's mother, while saddened by our decision to leave, observed that it was only fair that my parents get to enjoy their grandchildren. That final year had a sense of things coming to an end but also the excitement of new beginnings. While other musicians had taken their families on run-outs and abroad on tours with them, Hugh had not. He said that he didn't want to be distracted by having his family there. This changed in this last year with the Orchestra and I enjoyed this enormously.

One outing took us to The Maltings at Snape for a concert conducted by the new *wunderkind* of British orchestral music – Simon Rattle – who in 1980 was appointed conductor of the City of Birmingham Symphony Orchestra. He was 25. The circular concert hall and other buildings were developed by composer Benjamin Britten and his partner, singer Peter Pears, and overlooked a marsh. They were inaugurated in 1967. The original malting building converted to a concert hall had burned down in 1969 and was rebuilt in 1970. Three Barbara Hepworth statues, part of the "Family of Man" series, were placed strategically on the grassed area around the hall, and the marsh grasses swayed like ocean waves with the wind.

It was one of the most beautiful and peaceful sites that I had ever visited. But I was conscious that I had to keep my six-and-a-half-year-old and four-year-old sons quiet and away from the water and any other dangers. We began by sitting in on the rehearsal and, out of the corner of my eye, I saw Alex moving towards the low stage platform. Rattle, without halting the rehearsal, beckoned Alex onstage and he was followed by William. Thankfully, they sat quietly and seemed fascinated by the music. When the Orchestra took a break, I went to get them and took them outside.

For lunch, we drove to Maldon, a town on the Essex coast famous for the battle which took place there with the Vikings. A raid was beaten off in 924 but the Vikings returned in 991 and were soundly defeated by the locals. The Old English poem "The Battle of Maldon" commemorated this important event and I was thrilled to see the historic structures and walk along the beach with Hugh and the boys. I remembered studying the poem in Frank Bessai's class at the University of Alberta along with other Anglo Saxon works.

Another highlight of 1980 was being able to go to Barcelona with Hugh and the boys when the Philharmonia performed at the Palau de la Musica Catalana. We stayed in a beautiful hotel in the city centre not far from the concert hall and the Sagrada Familia Cathedral, a key work of the architectural style known as Catalan Modernism. The hotel provided babysitters so that I was able to attend the concerts in the amazing "Palace of Catalan Music," which was inaugurated in 1908. Its style resembles art nouveau and it is a feast for the eyes with mosaic columns and incredible stained glass. The main concert hall has a stained-glass ceiling in the form of an inverted bell that depicts a sunburst against a blue sky. Colourful female muses are represented in partial relief on the back of the stage. At the end of the performance, members of the audience threw roses on the stage and I wondered whether any would strike the conductor or musicians. Fortunately, the stems were covered in aluminum foil.

When Hugh was not in rehearsals during the day, we wandered around the city seeing the amazing art nouveau structures (not only buildings but also metro stations and street furniture), in particular, those created by architect Antoni Gaudi. The Sagrada Familia Cathedral was not completed at his death and continued as a work in progress. Our favourite Gaudi work was the Parco Guell on Carmel Hill in Barcelona, built in the period 1900 to 1914. It is a public park at the centre of a neighbourhood of stunning houses and public buildings. The organic shapes of the two buildings at the entrance to the park resemble a kind of fairy tale world but the centre-piece is the enormous staircase. Gaudi designed the elaborate salamander (popularly considered to be a dragon) that was covered with multi-coloured mosaics. The boys loved it as well as the long bench in the shape of a sea serpent on the main terrace.

The performance in the evening was not until 9 pm and restaurants were closed until about 8 pm so we had to give the boys snacks to keep them functioning until we could go out to eat. The restaurants were memorable and our favourites were a rotisserie chicken place in which the stacked grills were placed in an enormous window that was open to the street, and a seafood restaurant in the harbor area. We ordered deep fried squid rings, which the boys loved mistakenly thinking that they were onion rings. We also ate a huge bowl of shrimp fried in garlic and olive oil. We ordered a tomato salad expecting sliced tomatoes with some olive oil, garlic, oregano and sea salt (the Italian style) and were surprised to get crusty bread dipped in the tomato juices with no tomatoes in sight.

Besides these memorable activities, we also had to do mundane things like selling our house and disposing of the contents. Anything with sentimental or monetary value, we planned to take with us and Hugh arranged for these items to be shipped in containers. The rest we gave to friends or sold. Our friends, Elizabeth and Stuart, who were professors at the London School of Economics, had just had twin boys and were the beneficiaries of a bunch of stuff including clothing and the backyard climbing frame. Our beloved child sitter, Sybil, went on to look after their boys and older daughter Amy. By the first week of August when the boys and I flew out from Heathrow, everything was settled. Hugh would remain in the house until the Philharmonia Orchestra left on its North American tour, I believe, in October 1980.

My Father drove us to the Edmonton International Airport to meet Hugh in mid-November and it was still "golden October" weather. The reunion with Hugh was joyous. We arrived at my parents' home in North Glenora and the extended Italian family began to gather for the "welcome to Edmonton" party. The next chapter of our lives was about to begin.

Photo 1: Adriana in front of a Pierre-Elliott Trudeau election poster in a store window in London, Ontario, May 1968. Photo courtesy of Doris Grant.

Photo 2: Estera and Raffaele Albi on wedding day, 1937. Photo courtesy of the Albi family.

Photo 3: Estera Albi and children: Adriana (left), Giuseppe (left) and Rosa (right) on their family lands near Grimaldi, Italy, ca. 1950. Photo courtesy of the Albi family.

Photo 4: Adriana Albi on the family lands near Grimaldi, Italy, 1949. Photo courtesy of the Albi family.

Photo 5: Adriana, Giuseppe, Raffaele and Rosa Albi on the steps of their home in North Glenora, Edmonton, 1960. Photo courtesy of the Albi family.

Photo 6: Rosa, Estera and Adriana Albi in their home, 1961. Photo courtesy of the Albi family.

Photo 7: Giuseppe and Adriana Albi with cousin Pasquale Falcone on her high school graduation night in September 1962. Pasquale was Adriana's escort at the graduation dance. Photo courtesy of the Albi family.

Photo 8: Adriana and friend Silvano Vecchio in cap and gown in front of the Northern Alberta Jubilee Auditorium for their graduation from the University of Alberta in 1965. Photo courtesy of the Albi family.

Photo 9: Adriana's formal photo taken by the Corona Studios, 1965, in Edmonton.

Photo 10: Photograph of the small rosary given to Adriana Davies by Leonard Cohen the evening of November 29, 1966. Photo courtesy of Adriana Davies.

Photo 11: Eli Mandel and Leonard Cohen pictured at a reading of Cohen's work at the University of Alberta in November 1966. Photo courtesy of the U of A yearbook, The Evergreen and Gold, 1967.

Photo 12: Adriana posed in front of the Thai Pavilion at Expo '67 in Montreal in September, 1968. Photo courtesy of Adriana Davies.

Photo 13: Adriana in Trafalgar Square, London, June 1968 feeding the pigeons; the photo was taken by a street photographer. Photo courtesy of Adriana Davies.

Photo 14: Adriana with her paternal grandmother, Alessandra Albi, in the garden of the Albo family home in Grimaldi, Italy, in July/August, 1968. Photo courtesy of the Albi family.

Photo 15: Adriana Albi and boyfriend Hugh Davies holding pet monkeys at the market in South Kensington, London, summer 1970. Photo courtesy of Adriana Davies.

Photo 16: Adriana and sons Alex and William at the beach in Aberystwyth, Wales, Christmas 1980 before the family's move to Canada. Photo courtesy of Adriana Davies.

Photo 17: Adriana and sons William and Alex near the Columbia Ice Fields, Banff National Park, ca. 1984. Photo courtesy of Adriana Davies.

Photo 18: Giuseppe, Adriana and Rosa with their parents on their fifty-fifth wedding anniversary in May 1992 at La Boheme restaurant in Edmonton. Photo courtesy of the Albi family.

Photo 19: Adriana and Hugh Davies in their home on the occasion of Adriana's fiftieth birthday in September 1993. Photo courtesy of Adriana Davies.

Photo 20: Adriana meeting Pope John Paul II at a papal audience in Rome during the Second Rome Conference on Immigration, 1988. She was a delegate from Alberta appointed by Italian Vice Consul Giovanni Bincoletto. Foto Felici, Roma.

Photo 21: Adriana, Executive Director, and Morris Flewwelling, Chair, of the Heritage Community Foundation, at an event at Fort Normandeau in Red Deer, 2004. Photo courtesy of Hazel Flewwelling.

Photo 22: Adriana with Carlo Amodio, President, National Congress of Italian Canadians, Edmonton District, and Alberta Consul of Italy Arnaldo Minuti at the 2005 opening of the "Alberta's Italian History" exhibit, which she curated. The exhibit was hosted by the Ital-Canadian Seniors' Centre in Edmonton and was a centenary project for the Province of Alberta with funding support from the Consulate. Photo courtesy of Adriana Davies.

Photo 23: Adriana at a live poetry performance in a local bookstore in Edmonton, June 2005. Photo courtesy of Adriana Davies.

Photo 24: The Strong Brew Trio at a 2005 reading at Leva Café in Edmonton (left to right): Janet Kozub, master of ceremonies; Adriana; Dawn Carter; unknown woman; and Delvina Greig. Photo courtesy of Adriana Davies.

Photo 25: Adriana, Brian Webb and Tania Alvarado performance of "Love Story," which was based on her poem "The Dark Elegies." This was part of the Brian Webb Dance Company 2007 season in Edmonton. Photo courtesy of Sherry Dawn Knettle.

Photo 26: The Trio avec Brio: Pierrette Requier, Alison Grant-Préville, and Adriana. Photo courtesy of Adriana Davies.

Photo 27: Adriana Davies on a rock formation near the Red Deer River in central Alberta, 2008. This was a favourite spot and features in one of the poems in her unpublished anthology titled "Alberta Pastorale." Photo courtesy of Hazel Flewwelling.

Photo 28: Adriana standing in front of the introductory exhibit panel for the travelling exhibit titled "The Rise and Fall of Emilio Picariello," Fernie Museum, Fernie, BC, 2015. Photo courtesy of Ron Ulrich, the former director and co-curator, with Adriana of the exhibit.

Photo 29: Adriana at the Edmonton launch of *The Rise and Fall of Emilio Picari-ello* at Audrey's Books, 2016. Photo courtesy of Marcia Bercov.

Photo 30: Adriana at the launch of *The Frontier of Patriotism: Alberta and the First World War* that she co-edited with Jeff Keshen, former Dean of Arts, Mount Royal University, 2016, The Military Museums, Calgary. Photo courtesy of the University of Calgary Press.

Photo 31: Governor General David Johnston inducted Adriana into the Order of Canada at a ceremony in Rideau Hall, Ottawa, November 2010. Photo courtesy of John W. MacDonald.

Photo 32: Italian Consul General Fabrizio Inserra presents the Cavaliere d'Italia honour to Adriana in Vancouver in 2015. Photo courtesy of Stephen Fuerderer.

CHAPTER 8

Giving Back

I ARRIVED IN EDMONTON via Air Canada the first week of August 1980 with my sons Alex and William; the former was nearly seven and the latter was four years old. I was met by my parents and taken to the family home in North Glenora where we were soon joined by my sister, brother-in-law and their four children, and my brother Giuseppe. We were joined by members of the Cavaliere and Colistro families. This was the nucleus of my Edmonton family. It was going back to the security of my childhood and all of the people that I was close to. My husband Hugh's English family was swapped with my Italian family.

The boys and I settled into my parents' comfortable, fully-furnished basement that had a living room with a television, kitchen, two bedrooms and a bathroom. This is where my sister Rosa had begun married life in early 1962. She generously passed on clothes and toys including bicycles so the boys were occupied and every day we went to Coronation Park about a block away, and they played in the sandpit and used the climbing frame, slides and swings. They had no problem settling in because of the family ties. The weather was wonderful and I rejoiced in it. Seeing the beautiful prairie sky made me realize how overcast and rainy London had been. This had not been helped by my working five days a week in the basement library of the National Portrait Gallery. The Victorian building had very thick walls and narrow windows at ceiling level so we always worked in artificial light. It seemed as well that I could breathe more deeply because the air was not dense with the lead fumes of too many automobiles, diesel buses and all of the smells of a very large city.

I was in the bosom of my family and living in the country that I had come to consider my home. The only problem was that I didn't have a job and, when Hugh arrived in mid-November at the end of the Philharmonia Orchestra's North American tour, he too would be unemployed. In the spring, Giuseppe had let me know that Mel Hurtig, a local publisher, had announced that he was developing a Canadian encyclopedia and was hiring editors. Giuseppe mentioned that Hurtig Publishers, the small publishing house established in 1972, appeared to be a going concern with a range of Canadian titles. I wrote to Mel, whom I had met when I attended the University of Alberta, to enquire about editorial positions. I frequented his bookstores not only the original one on Jasper Avenue and 103 Street that had opened in 1956 but also the one close to campus that had opened in the early 1960s. Mel had responded promptly and very kindly indicating that he was currently in the process of hiring but, if there were any jobs that were unfilled, he would give me an interview when I arrived in Edmonton.

I called his office and he asked me to give the Managing Director Frank McGuire a call. An interview was quickly set up in the office that he shared with Editor-in-Chief James Marsh, which was in Athabasca Hall on the University of Alberta campus. It was one of the basement bedrooms in this former hall of residence that had been converted to Faculty and administrative offices. I believe that the interview went well and I talked at length about my work on the Collins (Random House) *Encyclopedia of Antiques* and other research and writing that I had done. They seemed to be pleased with my answers and I left keeping my fingers crossed that there would be a positive outcome.

Several days later, Frank called and said, "I have good news and bad news. Which do you want first?" I indicated that I wanted the good news first and he told me that they had been very impressed with me and my credentials, and noted that I was the only person whom they had interviewed with encyclopedia experience. He said they wanted me but, sadly, they could not offer me the Arts Editor position because they had already hired Diana Selsor Palting. Would I accept Sciences Editor, the only senior position that was left? I immediately said, yes, and explained that I had always been fascinated by the sciences and had done well in the Botany and Genetics courses that I had taken for my BA degree. Frank told me that I would start work at the beginning of September after Labour Day, and that he looked forward to having me on the team. He also noted that he liked my sparkling eyes.

Frank was a Scot and I think was impressed by the fact that I had worked in publishing in London and that I also had a doctorate. He had started work at the bottom of the print career ladder as a compositor for printing and publishing company Laidlaw and MacKenzie in Glasgow. In 1953, he immigrated to Canada and worked as a typesetter for the Jewish newspaper in Toronto. He next worked for the Salvation Army and McMaster University in printing and communications. In 1975, he moved his family to Edmonton to become the Queen's Printer of Alberta in charge of all provincial publications and, at that time, there were many. I think that his hiring as Managing Director probably re-assured the province of some oversight for the ambitious project that had been awarded $4 million in funding by Premier Peter Lougheed. Frank told me that his main duty was to secure funding for the project and manage the business activities.

I was on a high and the happy news was shared with my family and Hugh via telephone. We were relieved: at least one of us would have a job and we could begin to establish ourselves in Edmonton. I had always felt a sense of gratitude to Canada for providing me with an excellent education and even grants and bursaries while at the University of Alberta. The culmination was the Canada Council grant that I received for a term of three years that enabled me to get my doctorate at the University of London. Now, it was payback time. I felt that being a Senior Editor of the new Canadian encyclopedia would enable me to use all of my knowledge and skills to serve the people of Canada.

From the outset, the common message that was shared by Mel, Frank and Jim was of the new encyclopedia as a national enterprise that would present Canada in all of its complexities, from past to present, as seen through the eyes of Canadian historians, academics and other experts. The message reminded me of the feeling of pride that I had experienced at Expo '67 in Montreal.

The proposed three-volume work would be accurate, authoritative and current. This could not be said for its predecessor – the ten-volume *Encyclopedia Canadiana* published on January 1, 1958 by The Canadian Company Limited, a subsidiary of The Grolier Society of Canada Limited. This company in turn was a subsidiary of Grolier, an American company that had first published an encyclopedia, *The Book of Knowledge*, in 1910 and the *Encyclopedia Americana* in 1945. While *Canadiana* had been revised in 1974, it did not reflect the Canada that emerged from centennial celebrations in 1967 and which inspired a wave of nationalism across the country and, in particular, on university campuses.

This had occurred in the period 1968 to 1980 when I lived in England and, through my work on the Canadian encyclopedia, I was to discover the new scholarship, much of it emerging from newly-created university Canadian-studies departments. I remembered professors Henry Kreisel, Eli Mandel and Robin Matthews, who had championed Canadian writers, and the movement for a kind of affirmative action hiring of Canadians for academic positions in Canadian universities during my studies at the U of A. I felt thrilled to be able to take on the "mantle of patriotism" that seemed to come with the job.

In those first months, Jim oriented us by talking about the eminent Canadian scholars who were advising him and we also read contextual material relating to Canadian Studies as an emerging discipline. An important source book was T.H.B. Symons' *To Know Ourselves: The report of the commission on Canadian studies*, published in 1975. While the course of the creation of the encyclopedia would not always run smoothly, I believed in the importance of it as a tool for national identity to the end, and even more so today.

I did not know any of the editorial team and accepted their competence based on the short bios that were produced for all of us to share with the Government of Alberta, Hurtig's principal funder, and the media. Diana Selsor Palting was the Arts editor and had a background in the arts including being an excellent photographer; Jim Ogilvy, the Humanities Editor had a doctorate in history from the U of T; and Sandra Monteith, the Social Sciences Editor, had a graduate degree in sociology.

Editor-in-Chief James Harley Marsh, I discovered, was a Virgo like myself (we both had September birthdays) and therefore totally wedded to authority and accuracy. He had excellent publishing credentials including working for Holt, Rinehart and Winston and had served as editor of the Carleton Library Series, which focused on Canadian history and social sciences. From 1970 to 1980, he was responsible for editing 60 books and co-authoring the textbook *New*

Beginnings. This was an amazing achievement since Jim was only 38 (my own age). He seemed to know everyone of note who was writing significant Canadian content whether historians, or writers of fiction and non-fiction. From the beginning, I was aware that there were some who felt that an academic should have held the position of editor-in-chief and that the encyclopedia should have been done through a university, but this was not a course that Mel chose and, in the end, it worked. In any case, Ogilvy, Monteith and I had doctorates.

Mel believed strongly that the creation of a new national encyclopedia would be a fitting gift to the rest of Canada for Alberta's seventy-fifth anniversary in 1980. The grant would be used to defray costs but was also meant to subsidize the gifting of volumes to Canadian schools and libraries, and diplomatic posts abroad. One got to experience the Premier's commitment first-hand at the twin launches for the project held in the Alberta Legislature in Edmonton and McDougall House (known as "the Leg South") in Calgary in early September. I believe that we may have been flown down to Calgary in a government aircraft as a part of the Premier's entourage and treated with respect wherever we went. It was also understood that we could not possibly fail.

The editorial team settled into an office in the basement of Athabasca Hall on the beautiful U of A campus that I knew and loved. In all seasons, to refresh my mind, I went on walks during my lunch break. The small office had four desks equipped with electric typewriters and telephones and four bookcases. We spent the first few months in the U of A libraries so space didn't matter but we soon made a case to Frank and Jim that we needed separate offices so that we could work in peace and quiet. From the outset, it was clear that Mel wanted to spend the least amount of money on the creation of the encyclopedia and that Frank, who was frugal by nature, was his tool to accomplish this. Eventually, they gave way and the editors moved to Ring House 4 near the Faculty Club and, then, as staff expanded, into an old two-storey house at 11043 – 90 Avenue in North Garneau. (We eventually expanded into the house next door as well.) The support staff comprising two secretaries, who were in their fifties, and a project co-ordinator, who took on general administrative work, was located downstairs; the editorial staff was upstairs in the old bedrooms. Jim Marsh shared his office with his administrative assistant, a young woman who was a recent university graduate. Next to the front door, screwed into the white-painted siding was a sign stating "New Canadian Encyclopedia

Publishing." The Alumni magazine *New Trail*, in a winter 1982 article, quoted *Edmonton Journal* writer James Adams' observation that the proposed Canadian encyclopedia was "the literary-reference equivalent of the CPR." Pierre Berton had published his two iconic works on the railway as a nation-building tool in 1970-71. While *The National Dream: The Great Railway, 1871-1881* and *The Last Spike: The Great Railway, 1881-1885*, were popular, academic historians looked down their noses at them.

The research in the university libraries was exciting – this is something that I loved and was good at, and I was also familiar with the encyclopedia format, albeit encyclopedias of antiques. I intuitively understood that subject areas had to be developed from over-arching thematic articles to very specific, single-subject pieces. Marsh had charged us with reading all of the *Canadiana* articles in our fields and had also given us copies of this reference work's article list that he had created. Our research was to result in fully-fleshed article lists for our fields that were current, and reflected the best of Canadian scholarship. I became friends with the U of A's Government Documents Librarian, Sally Manwaring (who also happened to be my parents' neighbor), and Science Librarian David Jones. Between them, they found every book I needed either in their own holdings or through inter-library loans.

I was responsible for "pure" science topics as well as disciplines, and also researched, commissioned and edited articles on Canadian industries including the energy sector. I am proud of the entry on "mega projects," a buzzword of the day that included the James Bay hydro-electric project and oil sands developments in Fort McMurray. I ensured that the environment also received extensive treatment and the entries on environmental and social impact assessments were firsts. Frequently, the only information available was in government reports and industry publications; therefore, developing and maintaining close relationships with both federal and provincial departments was necessary because they held essential information including tables, charts and maps that existed nowhere else.

The University academic and support staff were totally committed to the partnership with Hurtig and he could not possibly have afforded the services that they provided. It's important to remember that this small prairie publisher had the backing of a very large and complex university with a range of experts in all areas of encyclopedia content. Dr. Harry E. Gunning, OC, Killam Professor of

Chemistry and former president of the University of Alberta, served as the chair of the National Advisory Board and Marsh had to keep him and other senior academics content about project development. The board lent the project a level of legitimacy and helped counter arguments that an encyclopedia could not possibly be developed in the western backwater of Edmonton, away from the academic and publishing heart of English Canada in Toronto. Western alienation was alive and well in the early 1980s!

While the editorial team dealt well with the complexities of their work and the occasional lunches for politicians and influentials that Mel hosted at the Mayfair Golf and Country Club in the River Valley when we were paraded out and were expected to perform like trick ponies, all was not well in paradise. It became clear that Frank wanted to micro-manage and this was creating problems for Marsh. A second issue was that the Social Sciences Editor faulted Jim's lack of academic credentials and attempted to undermine his authority, whenever possible, and was a divisive force among the editors. The final issue emerged when Marsh's young editorial assistant, who was a strong feminist, informed the three female senior editors in confidence that Jim Ogilvy was being paid more than the rest of us.

Things came to a head. First, Mel appointed a kind of scrutineer to determine Jim's management skills and the Senior Editors were consulted. Three of us spoke very strongly in support of Jim, as did key members of the advisory council, and, as a result, Mel affirmed his control over content creation and process and, basically, told Frank to back off. The salary issue was addressed and female editor salaries were topped up. The young assistant lost her job and was replaced by a mature and competent woman, Micaela Gates. Finally, an outrageous act of insubordination on the part of the Social Sciences Editor in which she created a rival article list for her field, which she circulated to her consultants and contributors, resulted in her firing. Peace descended though this remained a troubled field and a second and third editor would eventually be hired. Patricia Finlay finally completed the field. Rosemary Shipton would eventually take over the Arts from Diana and Mary McDougall Maude would take on biographies as it became clear that the Senior Editors would not have time to edit these entries though we commissioned them.

The first major achievement of the editorial staff was the creation of complex article lists for every field. These were "tree and branch" type listings from overarching articles down to thematic pieces and single entries, for example, in one of my areas, of a plant or animal species. I also created lists of scientific disciplines including medicine and dentistry; geological eras; and also huge lists of geographic and geological features. Finally, I created a list of biographies of experts in my fields that included "superstars" such as Canadian geophysicist John Tuzo Wilson, the world expert on plate tectonics; Nobel laureate Gerhard Herzberg, astronomer and astrophysicist; and the team of U of T researchers Frederick Banting, Charles Best, James Collip and John Macleod responsible for developing insulin. Banting and Best received the Nobel Prize in 1923.

Marsh was extremely supportive though we did have wrangles about how many words should be assigned to entries. I remember once arguing with him (sometimes "tongue in cheek") that Canadian invertebrates were as iconic as beavers, maple trees and Canada geese. When I told him about the Burgess Shales, which was designated a UNESCO World Heritage Site in 1980, he was convinced. These are fossil beds located in the Rocky Mountains near Field, BC, that show the imprints of 508 million-year-old soft-shelled animals that lacked backbones (i.e., they were invertebrates).

With my background in fine and decorative arts, I made a case for entries and was given, I believe, 12,000 words for "material culture" and 5,000 words for crafts. Once Jim approved the lists (to my knowledge these were not shown to Mel for approval; in any case, he was only interested in political articles and Jim dealt with those). The partnership with the U of A not only enabled access to all library collections but also academic staff. Over a period of several months, the Senior Editors met with deans, department chairs and specialists at the U of A and reviewed the lists with them and obtained feedback. In addition, I asked whom I should approach to be "consultants," i.e., senior people in the field who could review articles and be part of a very broad "community of experts" that gave its blessings to the content.

I found that all were helpful in identifying senior experts whether in academe or government agencies and institutions. I didn't experience even one example of professional jealousy, which was certainly an issue in other disciplines. In the end, I had over 60 consultants across the country including both Anglophones and Francophones. Both with respect to consultants and authors, we were cognizant of the need to show regional balance within an over-arching "national" perspective.

To some extent, we also tried to address the issue of gender balance though this was not always possible, particularly, in the sciences in which many disciplines such as engineering were male dominated. I did my best to identify both established and emerging female academics. One of these was Rose Sheinin, an up-and-coming academic superstar who had received a PhD in Biochemistry in 1956 from the University of Toronto and, in 1975, became Chair of the Department of Microbiology and Parasitology. She was an excellent research scientist and teacher as well as a feminist. Jim appointed her to the Advisory Council. Michelle Veeman was an agricultural economist at the U of A and contributed the article on "Agriculture and Food." I also discovered Claire Tremblay, who worked in a Québec university and was an artist specializing in natural history subjects. She provided a range of artwork for the encyclopedia.

With respect to possible consultants and authors, the elephant in the room was French Canada: the late 1950s through the 1970s had seen the emergence of Separatism in Québec and the so-called "Quiet Revolution." In addition, the Commission on Bilingualism and Biculturalism (1963-69) resulted in the passing of the Official Languages Act in September 1969. The editorial team was committed to ensuring the creation of Francophone content by Francophone experts. From the outset, we knew that there would be a French edition. This was not only an important selling point, it was absolutely necessary to represent the reality of Canada. Premier Lougheed understood and supported this. Marsh would also be charged with representation of Indigenous People, since Alberta had seen the emergence of leaders in this area in the 1960s who were "activists" with respect to Treaty and other rights.

My ability to function in French was a great asset. It resulted in some coups; for example, Louis-Edmond Hamelin had created the Centre for Northern Studies at Laval University that specialized in studies of the North and Indigenous Peoples. He developed the concept of "Nordicité," which emphasized the importance of the North for the twenty-first century not only in terms of resources but also for population growth and development. I was able to introduce the term "Nordicity" as a part of the vocabulary to describe Canada's unique position in the world through the article that Hamelin wrote for me. Pierre Dansereau was an internationally trained scientist who had worked in botanical gardens and had become one of the founders of the new field of ecology. From 1956 to 1961, he worked as the director of the Botanical Institute at the University of Montreal and taught in the Faculty of Science at the University. He was instrumental in setting up the Research Centre for Sciences and the Environment at the University of Québec in Montreal and was the director from 1972 to 1976. He created the concept of "ecosystems" that came to dominate thinking about the inter-relationship between human beings, the built environment and the natural world. Being able to speak to them in French greatly facilitated our exchange of ideas and helped me to better understand the articles that they contributed.

Having solidified the article lists, in January 1981, the Senior Editors were allowed to travel across the country to meet their consultants and to be exposed to the holdings of the universities, government departments, agencies and museums that they headed or were connected with. I became friends with some of my consultants and was in touch with them at every step of the process from commissioning articles to review of edited articles.

This was an amazing experience and gave me a sense of the breadth of Canada and its diverse geology, geography, flora and fauna. I was proud of the fact that I went from the Bamfield Marine Sciences Centre, a University of Victoria research and teaching facility on the outer west coast of Vancouver Island, to C-CORE in St. John's, Newfoundland. The latter was at the time connected to the U of A and focused on ice engineering including iceberg management, and remote sensing. In their offices, I found original photographs taken by photographer Herbert George Ponting during Scott's disastrous exploration of the Antarctic. The photographs of ice sheets, icebergs, ships and boats as well as men and dogs are brilliant, and have a three-dimensional quality about them. I recognized them because I had studied the portraiture of all of the Scott team for the *Dictionary of British Portraiture* that I had researched at the National Portrait Gallery in London, and had visited the Scott Polar Research Institute in Cambridge and seen the originals.

I spent about a week in Ottawa meeting with government departments associated with my field, and identified resource materials including maps and technical drawings that would be useful for the encyclopedia. I had been booked into one of the cheaper rooms in the Chateau Laurier and loved being in Ottawa. One day, outside the hotel, I saw Joe Clark and introduced myself and mentioned that I was Science Editor of the Canadian encyclopedia; he was very positive about the encyclopedia and generally very gracious. I reminded him that I had first met him in the offices of the student newspaper *The Gateway* at the U of A around 1963 when he was an editorial writer.

After returning from my travels, I began the complex work of matching entries to authors and then commissioning the articles. Letters of invitation were sent out (the four editors shared a couple of secretaries though we did some of our own correspondence as well) and these were followed up by telephone conversations. I worked hard to establish a relationship with my authors, who contributed over 1,200 articles, and this paid off. Only one author asked for his name to be removed from an entry when edited copy was sent back for approval. This was not because of the way I had edited the work; rather, it was because he submitted, I believe, 800 words for a species entry that should have been 150 words. He felt that the condensed entry while accurate no longer reflected his style. The other editors had some major issues with some contributors.

When I spoke to consultants and contributors, they would frequently refer to my "editorial team." In fact, for the first year I worked alone. We were allowed to hire editorial assistants for the final three years of the project. I was lucky in finding Gilda Sanders, who was as obsessed as I was about the work and also as precise about fact checking. I had the largest field of any of the editors as well as number of consultants and contributors. In the final year, we were allowed to hire a part-time research assistant and, again, I was lucky in finding Evelyn Phillips who was an excellent fact checker. In the end, Jim decided to get someone else to commission and edit geographical features (e.g., rivers, lakes and streams) because I was swamped. I am proud to say that I met all of my deadlines.

As the workload exploded, Jim did a brilliant job of bringing on freelance editors and other resource people not only to fact check but also undertake photo research and the range of other activities required to ensure that illustrative material was not only accurate but also of the highest quality. He set the bar high for technical standards and the volumes are not only highly readable but also attractive. Additional funding had to be sought and Nova, which styled itself as "an Alberta corporation," provided the funding for the cartography, artwork and illustrations.

While the editors were focused on content creation, we also provided input on maps and illustrations to be created, and also identified photographs and other archival resources though, ultimately, a dedicated person was hired to ensure that all of the artwork would be developed. Jim was forced to hire freelance editors, and also a range of research assistants, who worked directly with him to ensure that all deadlines were met. Not only did he have oversight of the entire encyclopedia, he also took on a range of subject areas, in particular, any that were politically sensitive.

Jim also had the major task of production and dealt directly with the head of university Printing Services as well as designers, cartographers and anyone involved with the artwork. Again, the U of A was invaluable. A *New Trail* 1982 article proudly noted:

> Another novelty associated with the encyclopedia is the fact that, utilizing the resources of the University of Alberta, it will be the first Canadian encyclopedia to use advanced computer technology. Links with the University's computing system are making possible on-line data entry, storage and retrieval, and – using the Bedford publishing system of the campus Printing Services – computer typesetting, formatting, pagination and indexing.
>
> All of this from a sleepy North Garneau house.

This makes the production side sound seamless but, in the end, it was not. For example, there was some flooding in the printing services building, which impacted on the Bedford system causing delays. Jim had many headaches to bear and I cannot think of a more worthy recipient of the Order of Canada, an award that was made to him and Mel in 1987.

At the end of August 1984, Mel informed the Senior Editors that our work was complete and that we would not be involved in the final phases. This was devastating news not only because we would not see the encyclopedia to publication but also because we would be jobless. In a cost-saving move, Mel chose to hire several of our assistants to finish editing work. While I admired Mel for his vision and commitment, he was a difficult employer not only because of his penny pinching but also his massive ego. At a party or event, you never had his full attention because he was looking over your shoulder for a more important person that he should be speaking to. Even though my work ended officially, I continued to do some part-time work until Christmas to ensure that my field was as complete and accurate as possible.

Another impact of being cut loose was that, rather than being a central part of the encyclopedia launch, the Senior Editors felt more like guests. I feel strongly that we were denied our moment of glory. It was the "Mel and Jim" show and that is understandable. None of us had speaking roles at the Edmonton launch at the Citadel Theatre. In fact, even Jim became part of the backdrop to Mel's heroic achievement as the man whose encyclopedia united Canada from sea-to-sea. In the entry titled "The Canadian Encyclopedia: The Biggest Publishing Project in Canadian History" in the online version, the anonymous author writes:

> It was a dramatic moment in the intellectual history of Canada. On the cool evening of 6 September 1985, a crowd of over 1,000 people gathered in Edmonton's Citadel Theatre for the eagerly anticipated launch of *The Canadian Encyclopedia*. On stage, a large replica of the three-volume set opened up and revealed a podium. When Edmonton publisher Mel Hurtig climbed into the mock-up and prepared to speak, the packed house roared its approval.

The Hurtig "hype" machine was in full swing.

The first edition of *The Canadian Encyclopedia* came in on time and on budget, and was published in a three-volume format. It was priced at $125 a boxed set, cheap in comparison to other similar works, and sold out very quickly (154,000 copies in six months). To get it down to the three million words required to allow for maps, illustrations, photographs and other visuals, many articles had to be cut, most from my fields. This was done after I was no longer working for Hurtig. This final task was taken on by Jim and the small team that he was allowed to keep.

Mel described it as "the biggest publishing project in Canadian history" and it certainly was. The small team of professionals that he hired had pulled it off with great passion and commitment. More than 3,000 experts from across the country (and some Canadians who worked abroad) contributed more than 9,000 articles. The volumes are rich in visuals including about 1,600 illustrations and 540 maps. The print run was increased to 463,000 to meet demand. In 1988, a second, four-volume edition was published with an additional 500,000 words. I was delighted because many of the articles that I had edited and had been cut were able to be re-instated. While Hurtig had been on a winning streak, this would end and the threat of bankruptcy would force him, in 1991, to sell the copyright for the *Encyclopedia* to McClelland & Stewart. In 1999, with funding support from Canadian Heritage, the *Encyclopedia* became the property of the Historica Foundation, created by Charles Bronfman and chaired by Avie Bennett. A digital version was created in a CD-ROM format and, eventually, an online version. Jim Marsh remained the Editor-in-Chief until 2013. Professional staff continues to update articles and commission new ones for the online edition.

The reviews were overwhelmingly positive. I recently found a review by Richard A. Jarrell that focused on my articles. I will quote it in its entirety because it gives a sense of the architecture of my content, which he appreciated:

Thanks to the efforts of the science editor, Adriana Davies, and the biography editor, Mary Maude, our subjects are well represented. Lengthy articles on the history of science, of technology and of medicine are joined by shorter pieces on various institutions such as the NRC [National Research Council], provincial research councils, medical education, technical education and related topics. More contemporary are articles on science and society, research and development, science policy, the Science Council, mechanical engineering, medical research. These overview articles are supplemented by many short biographical notices and entries on individual inventions such as Silver Dart, telegraph, telephone and the snowmobile to name a few. The encyclopaedia is probably the single most useful compendium of biographies of Canadian scientists, engineers and physicians anywhere as it includes those still alive and active along with the long dead and forgotten. To give an idea of the coverage, just turning the pages from the beginning of M to the end of MA alone, we find notices on chemists Otto Maas, Charles McDowell, R.H.F. Manske, and Léo Marion, on botanists John Macoun and Marie-Victorin, on physicists J.G. MacGregor and J.C. McLennan, on engineers A.G.L. McNaughton, J.A.D. McCurdy and C.J. Mackenzie, on physiologists and physicians A.B. Macallum, E.W. McHenry, J.J.R. Macleod, J.P. McMurrich and Sir Andrew MacPhail, on ornithologist Thomas McIlwraith, on astronomer Andrew McKellar, meteorologist Patrick McTaggart-Cowan, oceanographer C.R. Mann, marine biologist K.H. Mann, explorer

Sir Robert McClure, agriculturist A. Mackay and manufacturers Daniel and Hart Massey.[2]

Sterling praise indeed. As I researched my various scientific disciplines, I was at pains to discover what was leading edge. I found that a new discipline around the history of science and technology was developing in Canada, particularly at the University of Toronto. In 1967, the Institute for the History and Philosophy of Science and Technology was established offering masters' and doctoral programs. Jarrell, an American, earned one of the first doctorates in this new discipline and became a lecturer at York University in 1971.

One of my coups was to get David Suzuki to write the entry on "Science and Society." When I telephoned him to extend the invitation, I mentioned his time at the U of A in the Genetics Department and his experiments with fruit flies. He was impressed. He had emerged as a science popularizer beginning in 1970 with the weekly children's radio program *Suzuki on Science* and, then, *Science Magazine*, for an adult audience. From 1975 to 1979, he created and hosted *Quirks & Quarks*, and, in 1979 had entered the world of television with the CBC series, *The Nature of Things*. While he was extremely busy, he agreed to write the article assisted by his producer. The article on "Science" was written by Jarrell and "Technology" was written by W.G. Richardson, also from the U of T Institute.

It would be an understatement to say that I was consumed by my work to the detriment of my small family. I could only do this because Hugh stepped up to the plate and looked after the children. He developed a bond with the mothers who accompanied their children on school field trips. He also took them to school and picked them up after school from my parents' home, which was half a block from Coronation School. Initially, he was determined to give up music and approached the Faculty of Law at the U of A to see about qualifying to practice. He was told that he would have to successfully complete undergraduate courses in Constitutional and Property Law, and sit the Alberta Bar exams. Hugh loved learning and chose instead to do

---

2 Richard A. Jarrell, "A Clutch of Reference Works," in *Scientia Canadensis*, The Journal of the History of science, Technology and Medicine, vol 9, No 2(29), December 1985.

a Masters' degree in Canadian refugee law and treatment of refugees. He became friends with L.C. Green, a professor in the Faculty. Leslie taught courses on International Law and Armed Conflict and Human Rights, and was an international expert on refugees. Hugh loved working on the thesis and got great satisfaction from getting his Masters' degree. He even passed the Alberta Bar exams but, when it came to actually practicing law, he rejected it as he had in London. It was too boring and mundane.

Hugh had begun doing work as an "extra" for the Edmonton Symphony Orchestra and, in 1983 he auditioned and was hired, and assigned to the First Violin section. He also began to play with the Alberta Baroque Ensemble, established by Paul Schieman in 1980 and, when Norman Nelson retired to the West Coast, Hugh succeeded him as concertmaster. He loved the Baroque repertoire and excelled at it. He also did recital work with colleagues in the orchestra and appeared happy with both his professional and personal life. It was as if we had switched roles: in London, he was the principal breadwinner and I took on the lion's share of child care; in Canada, I was the principal breadwinner and he looked after the boys and pursued his musical and other interests.

Hugh, unlike me, had the gift of finding activities that he loved and making time in his busy schedule to pursue them. Thus, he balanced his musical activities with weekly meetings with friends Enrico Musacchio (my former Italian professor at the U of A) and Richard Bosley, a philosophy professor. Together they met to discuss philosophers (they read some of their works in the original Greek) and other persons of interest. Hugh also started to study the Burmese language through private lessons with a recent arrival, Win Aungkyaw. He was determined to visit the grave of his Uncle Dawson Corbett, who had been a prisoner-of-war on the Burma Railroad and who had died as a result of appalling treatment at the hands of the Japanese. Hugh overcame all sorts of political obstacles to achieve this.

When my work on the *Encyclopedia* came to an end in late August 1984, I began to look for work. Located on the U of A campus, I had access to a range of employment listings. I saw an advertisement for a course developer and editor for the Local Government Studies and Public Administration Programs at the university. The former was headed by Bert Einsiedel, a Philippine-born and American-trained academic, and the latter by Edd LeSage, an American-trained student of government. I was interviewed and they were impressed with my range of knowledge and experience as well as my work on *The Canadian Encyclopedia*, and hired me.

The basis of the programs that Bert and Edd headed was really government as "democracy in action." I believed this strongly and I enjoyed my work for them. The courses, both credit and non-credit, were offered through the Faculty of Extension. The students were adult learners in full-time employment working for various levels of government, or for organizations whose primary functions involved service delivery to governments. Bert was in charge of the diploma offerings for municipal civil servants and Edd for provincial civil servants. Very close relationships had to be maintained with provincial government departments such as Municipal Affairs, and associations such as the Urban and Rural Municipalities associations. Support staff created the course offerings and ensured delivery; however, the instructors were either Bert or Edd, professors in other U of A departments, or senior practitioners who worked in government or were consultants to government. Courses and workshops took place in Edmonton or Red Deer with an annual conference at the Banff Centre.

The co-directors were very ambitious for their programs and wanted to improve the quality of print materials, and that is why I was hired. Edd at the time was completing his doctorate and I helped him with editing his thesis. I believe that I did my best for them and they were happy with my work. This was the closest to a 9 to 5 job that I have ever had. The only divergence from this routine was the travel to Red Deer or Banff for course offerings. One of the great achievements, not only for me but also for the programs, was the publication of *Alberta's Local Governments and their Politics*, which I saw through the press. It was written by political scientist Jack Masson, and was published in 1985 by Pica Pica Press, a subsidiary of the University of Alberta Press. In his book, Masson presents a history of local government and its functioning in Alberta from about the 1880s, both in times of scarcity and plenty. It describes the complex and changing relationships between municipal governments and the province and, sometimes with the federal government. The book explored the at times conflicted relationship between the province and municipalities, which had the least power to generate revenues of all levels of government but were the biggest providers of services to citizens. It became the textbook for various courses offered to local government officers who included treasurers, city managers and a range of other officials. A second, more comprehensive edition would be published in 1994, co-authored by Masson and LeSage.

While I was content with the job, when the opportunity came up to apply for the position of Executive Director of the Alberta Museums Association at the end of 1986, I jumped at it. I had established some relationships with curators in Canadian museums while researching the material culture section of *The Canadian Encyclopedia* and I knew that was a field that I wanted to return to. I knew that this would be another way of "giving back" to Canada.

CHAPTER 9

Preserving the Past

I DIDN'T KNOW HOW MUCH I had missed London and museums until I convinced Editor-in-Chief Jim Marsh of *The Canadian Encyclopedia* to allow me to create articles on antiques. He agreed and gave me 12,000 words for what became the "material culture" section. I read whatever books I could find on the field and appointed Donald Webster, Curator of Canadiana at the Royal Ontario Museum, as my consultant. In 1979, he had published a book titled *English-Canadian Furniture of the Georgian Period* and was an expert on eighteenth and nineteenth century decorative arts. The Canadiana Collection was exhibited separately from the main Royal Ontario Museum building with its more international scope in collecting and, for me, was symbolic of Canadian history and culture as a kind of "parenthesis" or "adjunct" to the culture of the so-called "founding" nations, Britain and France.

When Donald and I met in spring 1981 and he showed me around the exhibits, we found that we had much in common. With his assistance, I commissioned articles from the eminent curators of the time ensuring regional coverage as well as helping to address the "English Canada/French Canada" duality. Among my Francophone contributors were Jean Palardy and Jean Trudel. Palardy had trained as an artist but had become involved in restoration work and, in 1963, published *Les Meubles Anciens du Canada Français*. He did the research for the federal government for the restoration of the Fortress of Louisbourg and also advised the National Museum of Man (now the Canadian Museum of History), the McCord Museum and the

Château Ramezay. Trudel published *Silver in New France* in 1974 when he worked at the National Gallery of Canada. His expertise included "trade silver" – silver produced for trade with Indigenous People during the Fur Trade Era. As I commissioned and edited the various entries, I also acquired knowledge of Canadian museums.

This was to prove useful at the end of 1986 when I applied for the position of Executive Director of the Alberta Museums Association. To prepare for the interview, I did some research and discovered that the Association had been established in 1971 as a registered society in Alberta, and also had federal charitable status. Its mandate was to serve the province's museums, many of which had come into existence as a result of Canada's Centenary. At the interview, I became re-acquainted with Morris Flewwelling, Director of the Red Deer and District Museum, who was past president. I had met him in 1981when the Queen Mother exhibit from the National Portrait Gallery travelled to his museum and he invited me to give a curatorial talk. I had been involved in the development of this exhibit while working for the Gallery from 1977-80. Because of this, and the fact that I had researched one-third of *The Collins/Random House Encyclopedia of Antiques*, some members of the interview committee were concerned that I was only knowledgeable about "elite" culture, and knew nothing about rural Alberta. I was then able to "dazzle" them with my knowledge of municipalities around the province including their history, knowledge acquired through my work for the Local Government Studies Program at the University of Alberta.

I was offered the job just before Christmas and was told that I would begin work on January 2, 1987. I had an hour meeting with the outgoing ED, Wilma Wood, to serve as an orientation. We met at the offices in the Commonwealth Building on 106 Street and 99 Avenue, and she pointed to a pile of file folders on her coffee table and said, "You are going to have to do something about that. They are overdue grants." The volunteer-run organization had lobbied the Government of Alberta for funding to hire some professional staff so that advisory and grant programs could be established to assist the increasing number of local history museums (at the time, there were about 200). They were successful and, in 1985, were provided an annual grant of $400,000 through the Alberta Historical Resources Foundation. This enabled them to set up an office and hire Wilma, a well-established museologist. Wilma told me that she was "good at startups" and then lost interest. After two years with the Association, she wanted to move on. The staff consisted of an administrative assistant/secretary, grants and education co-ordinators and a part-time book-keeper. Most of the provincial funding went to museum members through a quarterly grants program largely focused on care of collections and exhibitions.

The grants cycle determined the work flow of the organization. Every quarter, with staff support, I provided advisory services to members (both institutional and individual) wanting to apply for grants; reviewed grant submissions to ensure that they were complete; convened a jury comprising members in good standing; couriered jury packages and ensured that jury day went well and that decisions were made; prepared for a Board meeting including developing the agenda with the President and ensuring that board packages were prepared (they ratified the grants); mailed out grant letters and cheques; and, finally, ensured that grant reports were submitted with proof of expenditures. This was important because an organization in arrears could not apply for new grants and, if there were too many in arrears, this could impact on our provincial funding. Thus, one of my big tasks was to deal with the reporting backlog that Wilma had identified but, while time-consuming, this gave me the opportunity to get to know our museum members first hand. I used the information on the grants awarded and the work accomplished by local museums to create a year-end report to the Government of Alberta. The final major activity of the organization was an annual conference held in October. Museum site visits, committee meetings and liaison with a range of peer organizations had to be fitted in to the busy schedule.

My first president, Evelyn Hansen from Peace Country, educated me about the Association since she had been one of the founders. She told me that the conference was scheduled in October to accommodate members who were not available to attend until after harvest. This was her situation as a farm wife. She was a tiny, determined woman who not only helped to run the local museum but also authored community history books and was a shrewd observer of human nature, in particular, of politicians. She had written about the railways and waterways of Peace Country and, in 1968, edited an anthology titled *Brick's Hill Berwyn and Beyond: A History of Berwyn and District* for the Berwyn Centennial Committee. Evelyn was a member of the Peace River Women's Institute, which was instrumental in setting up the Peace River Museum and Archives as a centenary project in 1967.

Evelyn taught me about the operation of a volunteer-run museum. She was one of the large number of able, rural women who were determined to preserve their family and community histories through the setting up of historical societies and, then, museums. They were the brigade of women in "blue rinses and running shoes" (so described by Duncan Cameron, Director of the Glenbow Museum) that were the backbone of the museum field in Alberta.

My calendar was packed because, on top of these administrative activities, I was the museum advisor and also provided support to a number of committees chaired by board members. (This varied from six to ten.) To ensure fairness, not all committees came in to Edmonton for meetings. This meant that I had to travel to various parts of the province, flying when possible (for example, Calgary, Lethbridge, Medicine Hat, Peace River, Grande Prairie), but frequently driving by myself to areas that I had never visited before. Red Deer was a popular meeting site because of its proximity to a range of museums and the fact that it was half way between Edmonton and Calgary. Morris and members of his staff became very close friends and the Museum was a welcoming place not only for the local community but also members of the museum community. Morris became a mentor to me and also many other museum people. He also served on Canadian museums association committees and eventually became President at a time when many interesting initiatives were taking place.

I brought to the job a passion for the past and telling the stories not only of eminent people but also of the nameless and voiceless ordinary people who were, by and large, those who had settled Alberta. I think that these qualities served me well, and I made many personal and professional friendships in the museum community throughout the province. I welcomed the opportunity to go on site visits to remote communities and to be toured around the facility and, then, sat down to talk about work that needed to be done, and to provide advice on how to prepare a grant proposal. They were the same people who were active in the church and ran the seniors' centres and agricultural fairs. I respected these volunteers and they, in turn, came to like and respect me. I could not have worked for the Alberta Museums Association for 13 years without this mutual respect and trust.

My experience with museums in London enabled me to relate to the province's senior museums – the Provincial Museum of Alberta; the Historic Sites Service of the Heritage Branch, Alberta Culture; the

Glenbow; and the University of Alberta Museums and Collections. The AMA had a special relationship with the PMA because, in 1969, shortly after it opened, it established the Museum Advisory Program that ultimately led to the creation of the Association. Ian Paterson was the first advisor going around the province to visit small museums providing information on care of artifacts and archival records. In 1987, Eric Waterton served as the Museums Advisor, initially working for the PMA and later based at St. Stephen's College on the U of A campus within the Historic Sites Service. For 10 years, the PMA also created exhibits (through the Travelling Exhibits Program) and toured them around the province in large trailers providing rural communities access to its collections. The larger museums had the majority of trained staff in the province and many were happy to sit on AMA committees and juries. As provincially-run or funded facilities (the Glenbow got a core operating grant from the province), they were not eligible for grant funding from the Association though staff members of Glenbow could apply for training grants. The staff of provincially-run facilities could not.

My tenure as Executive Director began with a huge controversy. In early January, 1987, I had a telephone call from someone indicating that they were calling on behalf of the Lubicon Cree and wanted to know what "ICOM Resolution 11" was. He refused to give me his name, and indicated that he believed that the Glenbow was contravening the resolution. I said that I would get back to him. I telephoned the Canadian Museums Association and was provided with the wording of the Resolution as follows:

> Resolution No. 11: Participation of Ethnic Groups in Museum Activities Whereas there are increasing concerns on the part of ethnic groups regarding the ways in which they and their cultures are portrayed in museum exhibitions and programmes, The 15th General Assembly of ICOM, meeting in Buenos Aires, Argentina, on 4 November 1986, Recommends that: 1. Museums which are engaged in activities relating to living ethnic groups, should, whenever possible, consult with the appropriate members of those groups, and 2. Such museums should avoid using ethnic materials in any way which might be detrimental to the group that produced them; their usage should be in keeping with the spirit of the ICOM Code of Professional Ethics, with particular reference to paragraphs 2.8 and 6.7.

I discovered that the issue of the relationship between Indigenous People and museums had been brought to ICOM for discussion because of the Lubicon protest.

I next telephoned Julia Harrison, the Curator of Ethnology at Glenbow, and told her about the call and asked her what had been done with respect to Indigenous consultation. She informed me that Glenbow had an advisory committee of national experts and an Indigenous advisory group from the beginning of exhibit planning. I also spoke to Duncan Cameron, who had been Director since 1977 (he was a former director of the Brooklyn Museum), and he told me that the intention of the exhibit was to educate the world about Canada's Indigenous Peoples, and that the exhibit would benefit them as well as museums. I called the Lubicon enquirer back and gave him the wording of the Resolution, and repeated what Julia had told me.

I then set out to educate myself about the subject as quickly as possible. I discovered that the Calgary Olympic Committee's aim was "to bring the world to Calgary." It was thought that a strong cultural component would add to the appeal and that's why a partnership with Glenbow was brokered in 1983. The Glenbow had strong Indigenous collections including material gathered by founder Eric Harvie, who had made a fortune through petroleum discoveries and who had wanted to give back to the community. He did this through the founding of Glenbow and also through various foundations that doled out money to significant public projects such as the setting up of Heritage Park in Calgary and the building of the Confederation Arts Centre in Charlottetown, PEI. Harvie was also a friend of Norman Luxton, a collector of Indigenous artifacts, who advised him on collecting. Since this was a strong suit in the Glenbow collections, it made sense to Cameron and Harrison to create an exhibit on First Peoples. They also had first-hand knowledge of the fascination that foreign visitors had for all Indigenous materials. Julia had an ambitious plan to borrow from Canadian and foreign collections; in fact, the majority of the over 650 artifacts displayed in the exhibit were from institutions outside the country indicative of Canada's colonial past.

While the Glenbow was focused on developing an excellent exhibit and obtaining the range of governmental and non-governmental funding required to bring the exhibit to fruition, a historical grievance was simmering that would challenge the Museum's good intentions. The Lubicon Lake Cree from Northern Alberta, who had been left out of Treaty 8 negotiations, had filed a claim with the federal government as early as 1933, for their own reserve but nothing had been done to resolve this matter. Pressures on their traditional way of life resulting from the number of oil companies drilling on the contested territory had accelerated their need for a settlement. Under a new, young Chief, Bernard Ominayak, the cause received renewed impetus and he sought the help of professionals.

American human rights activist Fred Lennarson became his chief advisor in 1979. His consulting company, Mirmir Corporation, had already done work for the Indian Association of Alberta (under Harold Cardinal). Ominayak and Lennarson aimed to get a $1 billion settlement from the federal government and, to do this, organized an aggressive letter writing and media campaign. By 1983, they were mailing information about the land claim dispute to over 600 organizations and individuals around the world, and had been successful in obtaining the support of the World Council of Churches and the European Parliament. They also undertook a number of lecture tours. Knowing that they would need the support of Indigenous organizations, they had extensive meetings and, among the first to come on board were the Assembly of First Nations, the Indian Association of Alberta, the Métis Association of Alberta and the Grand Council of Québec Cree.

When the Glenbow announced that Shell Canada would be its exclusive exhibit sponsor (it pledged $1.1 million), this was a gift to the protestors. The hated oil company that was drilling on contested lands was supporting a museum that appeared to be exploiting Indigenous culture and traditions. Lennarson went so far as to claim that the museum was in league with the Government of Alberta, and with the oil companies. He pointed out that of the 15-member Glenbow Board, nine were appointed by the Government and that, in 1986, two appointees were oil company presidents and another, a director of an oil company. Lennarson's intention was not only to impact negatively Glenbow's fundraising for the exhibit, but also to have lending institutions abroad refuse loans. He set out to organize an international boycott of the Glenbow exhibit and the Winter Olympics. The Lubicon boycott received support from some European museums and that is why ICOM Resolution 11 was drafted.

The initial exhibit title was "Forget Not My World" because Harrison viewed the proposed exhibit as a companion to the very successful exhibit that she had curated titled "The Metis: The Forgotten People."

This harkened back to a book edited by Harry W. Daniels titled *The Forgotten People: Metis and Non-Status Indian Land Claims*, published in 1979 by the Native Council of Canada. Daniels, a politician and Métis activist, had brought forward a benchmark case, "Daniels v. Canada," that succeeded in guaranteeing that Métis and Non-Status Indians would be considered "Indian" under section 91 (24) of the *Constitution Act, 1867* with all of the attending rights and privileges.

As the Lubicon Boycott campaign ramped up, the exhibit title was changed to "The Spirit Sings: Artistic Traditions of Canada's First Peoples" since the original title seemed to give credence to Lubicon claims that Native People were endangered. When the exhibit opened, Chief Ominayak observed: "We look at the people involved with Glenbow, the people sponsoring The Spirit Sings, as our enemies. They are destroying us at a community level."

The question to me about ICOM Resolution 11 would mark a shift in focus of the Lubicon Boycott with respect to the Glenbow exhibit. While the Glenbow had consulted Indigenous People, in compliance with the Resolution, the exhibit included ceremonial and sacred items such as a "False Face" mask (Fake Face is the preferred term today). The mask in question had been exhibited in museums before but ICOM Resolution 11 empowered Indigenous communities to express their feelings about how museums displayed their materials. The issue would divide museum curators as well as anthropologists (some in Alberta were helping the Lubicon with their protest) and this caused Julia Harrison much personal and professional pain. For example, Joan Ryan, a well-known Calgary anthropologist who had been assisting with the exhibit, resigned in support of the Lubicon. Harrison authored an essay titled "'The spirit sings' and the future of anthropology" in which she describes the curatorial process, and work with advisory groups. In the article she notes that she came to realize that this was not enough and that future dealings between museum and First Nations had to be more egalitarian.

"The Spirit Sings" opened on January 14, 1988 and Siksika Elder Jim Many Bears gave the opening prayer and was shown around the exhibition. Over 130,000 visitors saw the exhibit, the Glenbow's largest visitation for any exhibit at that point in its history. The boycott, rather than keeping people away, stimulated public interest and raised Glenbow's profile. According to staff, only 12 institutions declined to lend objects though Lennarson claimed the number was higher.

Among the most prominent were the Museum of the American Indian in New York, the Peabody Museum, the National Museum of Denmark, the Ethnographic Museum of Norway and the Musée d'Histoire in Switzerland. The final total of objects was 665 and most had never been seen in Canada. There was some fallout for the museum: Julia chose to leave Glenbow to pursue doctoral studies on repatriation and Duncan resigned November 1, 1988. He was succeeded by Bob Janes, who was the Executive Director of the Science Centre of the Northwest Territories and prior to that the founding Director of the Prince of Wales Heritage Centre. He was an anthropologist by training.

While the Winter Olympics was a sporting and cultural success that gave Calgary international profile, the controversy that questioned the role of museums with respect to Indigenous Peoples continued. In 1988, the Canadian Museums Association and the Assembly of First Nations created a working group to examine these issues. Consultations were held across the country and I participated in one hosted by the Glenbow, and also in a national session in Ottawa. In 1992, the report titled *Turning the Page: Forging New Partnerships between Museums and First Nations* was published. It recommended increased participation of Aboriginal People in the interpretation of their culture and history, better access for them to museum collections, and repatriation of sacred objects and human remains from museum collections to appropriate Aboriginal institutions or individuals. The report is prefaced by introductory letters dated January 1992 from CMA President Morris Flewwelling, and National Chief of the Assembly of First Nations Ovide Mercredi.

Because of my early experience attending St. Andrew's School adjacent to the Charles Camsell Hospital in Edmonton, and encounter with racism (my dark southern Italian colouring suggested that I was Native and, in the playground, I was taunted with the word "half-breed"), I became an advocate for Indigenous People. With the support of the Board of the Alberta Museums Association, we created three symposia held in 1988, 1989 and 1990 to address the relationship between museums and First Peoples, repatriation of ceremonial and sacred objects, and "Re-inventing the Museum in Native Terms." For this last, I invited representatives from the Ak-Chin Eco-Museum in Arizona. The community, which was established in 1912 as a reservation, was plagued by poverty and scarcity of resources until it declared itself an "ecomuseum," and focused on preservation of its language and culture to promote economic development. In effect, the whole reserve became a "living history" museum with the twin focus of cultural tourism and agricultural renewal. In 1984, as a result of a settlement with the federal government, the Ak-Chin community obtained water rights to the Colorado River, and was able to implement irrigation schemes. Later, they added a casino. This would become a model for a number of First Nations including some in Alberta.

As a result of information gathered through our symposia and meetings with representatives from various Indigenous communities (both within and outside of Alberta), I was delighted to provide advice to a number of Indigenous museum projects. I could not have done this work without the help of some prominent individuals, who were chiefs, elders and ceremonialists, and who championed Indigenous history. The most important were Russell Wright and wife Julia; Leo Pretty Young Man Senior and wife Alma; and Reg Crowshoe and wife Rose. They participated willingly in the Alberta Museums Association Indigenous symposia, and in other planning and advisory work.

Russell struggled to maintain a museum in the old Residential School at Blackfoot Crossing on the Bow River East of Calgary. In the 1970s, he had helped to develop a Blackfoot studies program for the Old Sun College on the reserve. He was troubled by the high rate of student suicide on the reserve, and firmly believed that it was only through the renewal of the Blackfoot culture and language that this trend could be halted. I did my best in advising him as to how to go about fundraising for a new museum, which had been his dream since the 1977 centenary celebrations of the signing of Treaty 7 (Prince Charles attended the ceremonies). With Leo Pretty Young Man Senior and wife Alma as well as other Elders and their wives, he envisioned an appropriate building that would house cultural artifacts and function as an education centre. The Blackfoot Crossing Historical Park is a legacy to their vision. In 1989, six square kilometres of land were set aside but funding would not become available until 2003 to initiate construction. Neither Russell nor Leo lived to see the museum, which was completed in 2007. The iconic teepee-like structure was designed by architect Ron Goodfellow.

Leo was the former Chief of the Siksika First Nation (from 1971-81 and, again, 1983-87) and was instrumental in taking over the museum founded by Norman Luxton in Banff. Luxton, a successful businessman, owned the King Edward Hotel and the *Crag and Canyon* newspaper, and had amassed an important collection of Indigenous artifacts and needed a place to display them. His interest in Indigenous people was inspired by his wife Georgina, who was a member of the prominent McDougall family that included missionaries and early settlers. She helped her Father, David McDougall, run the Morley Trading Post near the Stoney Reserve. Luxton advised Eric Harvie on collecting and, as a result, his museum was entrusted to Glenbow after his death. In the 1990s, Glenbow decided to remove major parts of the collection (the most important items and those requiring environmental controls). The fort structure with its wooden palisades was left with some bare-bone exhibits. The Buffalo Nations group, headed by Leo, took over and I was delighted to attend planning meetings in Banff and assist them to obtain grants to develop new exhibits, care for collections and undertake necessary restoration work to the building. The Buffalo Nations Luxton Museum is a popular attraction in Banff.

Another of my Indigenous mentors was Reg Crowshoe, a former chief of the Piikani Blackfoot First Nation, who had worked as an RCMP officer. He assisted the Historic Sites Service on various projects and generously shared his traditional knowledge with students at the universities of Lethbridge and Calgary. He founded the Old Man River Cultural Society and followed in the footsteps of his father, Joe Crowshoe Senior. Joe was an Elder and Bundle Keeper and ran Sun Dances; he renewed the Brave Dog and Chickadee Societies. Father and son collaborated with Historic Sites and were instrumental in the building of Head-Smashed-In Buffalo Jump Interpretive Centre near Fort Macleod, which showcases and interprets Blackfoot culture. It opened in 1987 and is run by Alberta Culture. It is a Canadian national historic site and UNESCO World Heritage Site.

Gerald Conaty, Julia Harrison's successor at Glenbow, was an invaluable resource and took me on a number of field trips to Treaty Seven areas to meet with Elders and ceremonialists. Beginning in 1990, he helped the Glenbow to develop and implement repatriation policies with respect to sacred objects. The initial work was done by Hugh Dempsey, long-time Glenbow curator and sometime Acting Director, who had extensive relationships in the Indigenous community going back to his involvement with the Indian Association of Alberta. He married Pauline Gladstone, the daughter of James Gladstone, the first status Indian appointed to the Canadian Senate. In mid-1990, Dempsey with Board approval loaned a medicine bundle to Dan Weasel Moccasin for a ceremony thereby setting a precedent. The bundle was returned.

While Indian Agents in the US regularly collected human remains for academic studies, many of which resided in the Smithsonian Institution in Washington, this was uncommon in Canada though there were some in collections. Gerry studied what the US had done through the Native American Graves Protection and Repatriation Act (1990) with respect to the funding it provided for inventorying human remains and sacred objects, and worked closely with Treaty 7 peoples to ensure appropriate repatriation. He was supported by then Glenbow Director Bob Janes. This policy was not initially adopted by the Provincial Museum of Alberta. The culmination of relationship-building work was the new permanent exhibit titled "Nitsitapiisinni: Our Way of Life," which opened on November 3, 2001. Gerry co-curated it with colleague Beth Carter and stated at the time: "Glenbow has redefined the fundamental nature of our working relationship with First Nations. This project, therefore, acknowledges the claim to special rights and a position of privilege voiced by First Nations." In the exhibit, artifacts are not displayed as art or cultural objects; rather, through text they are placed in a context of meaning for the Blackfoot and demonstrate that they are part of a living culture. Gerry was inducted as a member of the Kainai Honorary Chieftainship and died too young in 2013.

While Indigenous activities monopolized my time in my first months with the Alberta Museums Association, two "powerhouse" committees established just prior to my arrival – Standards and Education – also required attention. The former was charged with investigating how the quality of museum practice in all areas of operations might be enhanced; and the latter with creating educational resources to build capacity of volunteers and staff alike. Diana Anderson of the Red Deer and District Museum chaired Standards and Marlene Smith, of the McKay Avenue School Museum in Edmonton, chaired Education. In fall 1986, the Education Committee had initiated a pilot diploma program in partnership with Grant MacEwan College in Edmonton and Medicine Hat College. The instructors, who included Anne Ewen and Catherine Cole, had developed curriculum around core areas of museum practice. We went on to develop a series of workshops that were offered around the province. At the time, there was no other museum society in Canada that did this in such a rigorous way. Ron Ulrich was one of the original student interns at Fort Whoop-Up in Lethbridge and would eventually become the Executive Director of the Galt Museum in that city.

Some of the early members of the Standards Committee were Anne Ewen, Craig D'Arcy and Marijke Kerkhoven. All were committed practitioners and I was charged with investigating what standards existed in the museum community. The Canadian Museums Association had no initiatives in this area. I contacted the British Museums Association and the American Association of Museums to see what they had in place. I found that the BMA was in the process of developing standards and the AAM had some guidelines with respect to practice that were used to determine grant funding. Drawing on what I was able to discover, and working with the Standards Committee, I took on responsibility for codifying the core areas of museum function. I ensured that the range of museum disciplines was represented on the Committee so that they could advise staff. In the next three years, the *Standard Practices Handbook for Museums* was developed and was ready for use by our membership in 1990. I hired Dianne Smith as Standards Co-ordinator, and she researched and wrote the manual, which I edited. Shari Saunders succeeded Dianne and worked for the Association from 1993-97. By this point, we were working on a second edition (published 2001). Because of the close relationship between the educational needs of museum staff and volunteers and standards, a combined Professional Development and Standards Committee was created.

While core areas of function – administration, collections management (including conservation), exhibits and programming – were easily determinable, I struggled with an over-arching piece that would serve to underpin museum practice. On becoming Executive Director, I had espoused the ICOM definition of museums "as institutions in service to society and its development." For me, museums were public trust institutions not only because of their service mandate but also because they were "non-profit" and frequently received government funding for which they were accountable. My research in the American and British literature revealed that museums were being called to serve various communities, particularly ethnocultural communities. Multiculturalism as a concept based not only on human rights but also ethnic diversity had come to prominence in Canada, the US and Australia. In fact, Alberta had been a leader in this area and German-born Horst Schmid had been appointed Minister of Culture and Multiculturalism for the Government of Alberta in 1971.

In 1986, I became President of the National Congress of Italian Canadians, Edmonton District, and lived and breathed multiculturalism. Thus, for me, it was an easy jump from "museums and communities" to "museums and society" which became the first section of the *Standard Practices Handbook*. In the Introduction, I wrote:

> Museums are integral parts of the societies in which they exist. Museums reflect the cultures they represent, and serve as foundations for collective memory, continuity and social development. This section looks at the various ways in which museums interact with communities and addresses the social responsibilities each museum bears. At a general level, this section deals with the following questions:
> - How do museums shape society, and how does society shape museums?
> - What societal values do museums reflect?
> - Who is the museum for?

In these words, I challenged the notion that collections care and management were ends in themselves, which was a commonly-held view in the first generation of museum development in Alberta. The Alberta Museums Association was the first in Canada to develop museum standards and I was delighted to see that *SPECTRUM The UK Museum Documentation Standard Handbook* cited the AMA Handbook.

I also struggled with the obvious inequality evident in the province's museums ranging from small, totally volunteer-run facilities to large professionally staffed ones. I conceptualized three tiers of museums based on size – small, medium and large – and the *Handbook* presented standards that were achievable for each category in the various areas of core museum function. We also encouraged museums to update their policies to correspond with the standards of practice and to use achieving these standards as justification for specific grant applications. Our course offerings increased and most were delivered as one or two-day workshops in different Alberta communities for ease of access. They were well attended and Certificates were created to acknowledge accomplishment and mastery. The Association also continued to do several other museum studies pilots with Grant MacEwan and also assisted the University of Alberta in one successful pilot undertaken by Museums and Collections Services under Janine Andrews.

While I remained with the Association (I left in November 1999), the standards were voluntary; however, they had an immediate impact with respect to provincial funding. When I became Executive Director, our provincial funding was $400,000 per year, about a year later it was increased to $500,000 and a year later to $750,000. When the *Standards Handbook* was published, the Government of Alberta decided to give the Association control of the operational funding that it provided to specific museums. Our funding increased to $1.2 million and we were charged with ensuring that grants were tied to standards.

The Board supported the range of professional development activities that I chose to enable me to accomplish my job and I, therefore, undertook a number of study tours including to the UK, France and the US, as well as attendance at the CMA and AAM conferences. I viewed these as learning opportunities that resulted in my acquiring the "intellectual capital" that would benefit the association not only in the development of museum standards, but also our education programs and publications (our magazine, *Alberta Museums Review*, and newsletter, *InForm*). Our magazine was ably edited for many years by Catherine Cole and I encouraged our membership to contribute articles not only on the activities of their museums but also with respect to how they were addressing issues relating to museum practice. It became a valuable resource.

On occasion, experts that I encountered would be invited to be keynotes at our conferences and, as a result, conference attendance was high. Sessions were also streamed to ensure that the needs of small, medium and large museums were met. Stephen Weil, Deputy Director of the Hirshhorn Museum and Sculpture Garden, Smithsonian Institution in Washington, DC, had written *Rethinking the Museum* (1990), which focused on serving communities. His example of the "toothpick" museum that did everything perfectly but was irrelevant was a show stopper. After his very successful keynote at the conference in Red Deer, I invited him to do a workshop and this work was cited in a subsequent book, *Making Museums Matter* (2002). Another popular keynote was Rex Ellis, who had done his PhD on slavery at Colonial Williamsburg, and developed the first public program focused on interpreting the slave underpinning of American federal society. I also brought to Alberta, David Anderson, head of programs at the Victoria and Albert Museum in London, who had written *A Common Wealth: Museums and Learning in the United*

Kingdom (1997). The book included some case studies involving work with ethnocultural communities.

Finally, I read Jane Jacobs' seminal work, *The Death and Life of Great American Cities*, which inspired a generation of urban renewal projects that were sensitive to community needs. I researched projects in Philadelphia, Baltimore and Seattle and in Toronto and Montreal and this became a conference theme. This fit with the Alberta Main Street Program, a partnership of the Alberta Historical Resources Foundation, Alberta Culture and the Heritage Canada Foundation, which was established in 1987. Robert Graham, an urban planner, was the first director and did advisory work to interested groups leading to selection as a "main street" community with funding support for building façade restorations and historic streetscaping. Cardston, Claresholm, Crowsnest Pass, Drumheller, Lacombe and Medicine Hat were the first beneficiaries of this program. The Alberta Museums Association helped museums to become part of these "community building" projects supporting them through material in their archives and also a vision as to the importance of "place" and the built environment in the identity of communities.

Through David Goa, Curator of Folk and Religious Life at the PMA, I became acquainted with the "cultural memory and living tradition" work of Per-Uno Agren and his wife Britta Lundgren. They were Swedish museologists who described their country's museum model, which involved inter-locking mandates for museums to avoid overlap and to ensure best use of resources. This was implemented by the state in the early twentieth century and tiers – from national museum to community museums – defined their collecting and interpreting mandates. Agren and Lundgren also undertook oral history research that enabled them to preserve and interpret the life of communities and their traditions. Through Goa, while they were on a visit to Canada, we invited them to do a workshop, hosted by the Red Deer Museum. A direct result of their visit was development of the Regional Museums Grant Program, which offered $30,000 to a group of museums wanting to work together.

Regional collaboration in Peace Country had started as early as 1989 when, in order to host the Association's conference, a consortium of about 30 Northern Alberta museums decided to do it jointly since none individually had the capacity. I supported this initiative and went up to Grande Prairie for the committee meetings. As a result, the Spirit of the Peace (SOTP) museum network was established in December. A highlight of the 1990 conference was a bus tour that visited all of the facilities The group met quarterly and I attended at least a couple of meetings every year since it was relatively easy to do grants advisory in this way. That year, SOTP received a special grant to develop collective tourism infrastructure including a marketing campaign. Signage and brochures were produced and media ads taken out. When the Regional Museums Grant became available, the group applied for funding for the following projects: "Peace Region: Advancing Museum Standards" (1994-95) (this work was done by consultant Roberta Hursey); "Researching the Region: 'A Sense of the Peace'" (1995-97); "Promotion of the Peace: 'Discover the Spirit of the Peace'," a 16-minute video (1996-97), done by Aquila Productions from Edmonton; "Exhibit for the Peace Country and Beyond: 'Treaty #8 Display and Promotion Project'" (1998-2000); and "Education: 'Taking Peace History to the Schools'" (2001).

The second regional group to jump on board involved over 40 central Alberta museums. The project visionaries were Morris Flewwelling from the Red Deer and District Museum, and David Goa from the Provincial Museum. The objective was to undertake cultural memory and living tradition research inspired by Per-Uno Agren and Britta Lundgren. The Central Alberta Regional Museums Network (CARMN) was founded. It was a consortium of mostly volunteer-run museums who wanted to offer exhibits, information and programs to help the public learn about the development of these communities and the region. The Red Deer Museum, funded by the city, had professional staff and served as the project lead. David Ridley was hired as the full-time researcher. The first project that was accomplished was titled "Who We Are: The Women of Aspenland," which began in 1995 and initially involved 11 museums in documenting the lives of local women and creating exhibits showcasing their lives. The second was an anthology titled *Aspenland 1998: Local knowledge and a Sense of Place*.

My service on the federal Canada-France Cultural Accord Committee brought some direct benefits to Alberta. The agreement was signed in 1965 and was intended to promote knowledge of "each other's civilizations" and professional exchanges in the museum field, joint exhibits and other activities that would be mutually beneficial. My appointment to the committee was based on my ability to speak French; this enabled me to participate in committee activities including annual grant adjudications. I enjoyed this work very much and was able to attend a Study Tour organized by the Société des Musées Québécois, in 1997. During a two-week period in early March about 40 museum professionals, most from Quebec, visited a range of museums and historic sites in France. I facilitated the participation of Bruce McGillivray, Assistant Director of the PMA, who was also bilingual. When David Goa set out to develop an ambitious project that he titled "Anno Domini: Jesus through the Centuries" for the year 2,000, he wanted to borrow from French collections. In 1998, I was able to obtain funding through the Accord for him, Bruce and I to do a study tour of religious and state collections. Our trip was very successful and a number of institutions lent rare artifacts and artworks. Ultimately, David would not only develop a hugely popular exhibit, but also a print publication and a virtual exhibit.

I also enjoyed good relationships with the professional staff at St. Stephen's College and there were some collaborations; for example, under Director Frits Pannekoek, a partnership was brokered with the State of Montana to encourage cross-border tourism. Together we developed the *Alberta-Montana Discovery Guide: Museums, Parks and Historic Sites* (1997), a print publication. Provincial Museums Advisor Eric Waterton and I, on occasion, went on joint advisory visits. I remember one that started well but ultimately failed. We were called to provide advice to the Fort Saskatchewan Museum when it was negotiating with the City to take over the old jail and turn it into a museum and interpretive centre. We were given a tour of the empty structure by some former prison staff members and were delighted at the prospect of this entity becoming a historic site. In the end, the City chose to tear it down intending to allow pricy housing to be built there but this was not to come to pass since it was a historic site with remnants of the old Northwest Mounted Police Fort *in situ*. What a waste!

The period 1987 to 1999 was an exciting time to be in the museum community in Alberta; however, signs of shifting government priorities and a brief economic downturn, beginning in 1997, focused attention on museum funding. Amendments to the Criminal Code of Canada in 1967 had authorized lotteries and sweepstakes and gave provinces the authority to license lotteries and casinos. In 1979, the Province of Alberta took complete control of lotteries and the disbursement of the funds received by government from gaming and casinos. Initially, lotteries funding was dedicated to fairs and festivals, sports and recreation organizations, arts and heritage, and social causes. In the next 10 years, clawbacks would occur and, eventually, the bulk of Lotteries Revenues, which continued to grow with the introduction of slot machines, went directly into general revenues.

Seeing the decline in funding for museums, the AMA Board focused its attention on how best to raise the profile of museums and enhance fundraising activities. I had become a member of the Alberta Association of Fundraising Executives, and attended their annual conference and training sessions. In addition, in 1997, I had been appointed to the Government of Alberta's Charitable Advisory Committee that provided the government with advice on the sector and changes to the *Societies' Act*. The Committee developed a Charities Roundtable 2000, which I co-chaired with Sherrold Moore, and was responsible for helping to shape recommendations that would help build capacity in the sector. In 1999, I was also selected to be a sectoral representative for the federal government's review of the non-profit and charitable sector. I became the co-chair of the Research Steering Committee, which was responsible for the first-ever national survey. All of these activities were ways of becoming informed about fundraising.

Morris Flewwelling became the Chair of the AMA committee charged with looking at fund development and the members were all past presidents including Tom Willock and Lori Van Rooijen. They were skilled in lobbying and Past-President Evelyn Hansen provided me with some insight when she described Morris' lobbying style as follows: "He used reason and charm with politicians and senior civil servants and soon had them eating out of his hands like tame deer." As a result of their work, it became clear that the AMA could not take on the onerous responsibility of fundraising on top of the work that it was already doing and that a separate entity should be created. This recommendation went to the AGM in 1998 and was ratified by the membership.

In the next year, the structure of such an entity was worked out and in July 1999, the Heritage Community Foundation was created with the mandate to raise money and awareness for the association and museums. Laird Hunter, an expert on charities law, helped to draft the objects and the foundation was established as a charitable trust with a governing board of Trustees. The membership was introduced to the concept of the Foundation at presentations in Edmonton and Calgary. At the fall 1999 conference, while the majority of the membership ratified the Foundation, there was some opposition. The planning committee initially thought that the two entities could be run out of the Association's offices but the opposition, which included the current President Leslie Latta-Guthrie of University of Alberta Museums and Collections Services, felt that the Foundation should set up its own offices and run its own affairs. I became the founding Executive Director of the Foundation and David Dusome was hired to succeed me as ED. Morris and the other founding members of the Foundation were disappointed and hurt by the opposition (as was I) but, as Morris observed at the time, "If life gives you lemons, make lemonade."

I contacted our landlords at Maclab Enterprises and negotiated a five-year lease for space at the Commonwealth Building where the AMA had its first office. Mark de la Bruyère, CEO, agreed to give us the space rent free and we were only to pay the common area charges. This was a sweetheart deal. The Foundation was given $250,000 for operations by the AMA and this was done because senior civil servants at the Heritage Branch had said that the "rainy day fund" that the Board had built could prejudice the Association's annual grant.

I took with me a project that I had designed and which was to determine the future work of the Foundation. As a result of my work as an Advisory Committee member to the federal government's Canadian Heritage Information Network (CHIN), I had obtained a grant to give the province's museums a web presence. While focused on computers as collections management and word processing tools, CHIN was also looking at the possibility of websites becoming vehicles for the delivery of museum content to the general public. The pilot project, "Museums and the Web," was to be a testing ground to enable museums to use the World Wide Web for educational and awareness-raising purposes.

While staff at the Alberta Museums Association had grown over the years (when I left it was in the range of 12 to 15 people plus consultants for special projects), the Foundation's staff numbered three. Maureen Bedford and David Ridley made the move with me: Maureen became Fund Development/General Manager and David took on a range of programming activities. We had a wing and a prayer and couldn't afford to fail. We needed a bookkeeper and, with some federal funding, were able to hire Win Aungkyaw, who had recently arrived from Burma and was a lawyer in his homeland. On November 1, 1999, we launched the Foundation at a reception in our offices. All of the furniture had been purchased for a pittance in second-hand office furniture stores and paintings throughout the office were lent by my brother Giuseppe. I began to develop a specialist heritage library through thrift store finds that I paid for myself.

One of the first Board activities was to undertake a strategic planning session and we met at Lougheed House in Calgary. With the help of a consultant, it was decided that the Foundation's mission would be to "link people and heritage" and our over-arching goal was for "heritage to be valued by everyone." In order to do this, we needed "to bring heritage to the mainstream." Maureen, who was an experienced fundraiser, confirmed the truth of this – without public profile, the Heritage Community Foundation, let alone our museum members, would be unable to succeed in fundraising.

The CHIN project had given us a perfect marketing product to develop. Project funding enabled me to hire four interns: two with history majors and two with web development expertise. They attended training sessions organized by CHIN and the first website that we developed was a pilot that resulted in development of metadata for tagging of key words on the website. This enabled search engines to get the maximum amount of hits for the site. To do this, we reviewed curricula from across the country in a range of subjects including history, social studies and the sciences, and developed lists of key words for tags.

The Board and staff shared very ambitious goals for the new media that was ramping up to bring knowledge into every home. These included statements such as: "promote Alberta to the world; create opportunities for rural communities to create content for the World Wide Web; supplement curriculum materials at all levels of education; generate revenue to sustain this asset and future content development; and increase investment opportunities and access funds from individual donors and the community in general." We completed the Albertaheritage.net website and the Home page stated:

Welcome to Albertaheritage.net Alberta's first Heritage and Cultural Tourism Website.

Within the pages of this site you will find information about museums, archives, historic sites as well as heritage organizations and foundations that help to preserve and interpret our heritage.

Discover Alberta by visiting our Places to Go and exploring our Guide to Attractions. Whether you are looking to plan a walking or driving tour or would like more information on a variety of cultural resources, Albertaheritage.net is your source for heritage resources. Enjoy your journey of discovery and come back often to find out what's new.

Alberta's Past and Present begins here.

All of the content that I had developed for Alberta museums for the *Alberta-Montana Discovery Guide* was uploaded to the site giving Alberta museums a huge web presence unequalled across the country. For future development, we were in the Catch-22 situation of not being able to raise funds without a product to showcase, and needing funds to create product. What we had going was the strong bond between our past presidents and museums throughout the province as well as my close working relationship with the same museums.

At the end of the first year of operations, we had limited funds and Maureen offered to resign so that we could survive. Win took on her administrative duties. Throughout the existence of the Heritage Community Foundation, it would be feast or famine. While the Province of Alberta acknowledged the value of what we were doing and we received project funding (mostly through the Community Initiatives Program), we never succeeded in receiving core funding for operations though we did try. In the first few years, we survived on federal grants and internships whether through Young Canada Works in Heritage or through the Department of Science and Technology. We received at one point a letter signed by Prime Minister Jean Chretien complimenting us on providing a training ground for students wanting to work in web development.

The successful completion of our first website showed us a way forward. I pitched to the Board that the prime focus of the Foundation should become the development of web content drawing on museum and archival collections and, furthermore, we should create the "Alberta Online Encyclopedia." They wholeheartedly endorsed this and www.albertasource.ca was born. Luck and, I guess, timing was on our side. In March 2001, CHIN launched the Virtual Museum of Canada, which had a grants program, and I knew which project to bring forward. The Spirit of the Peace Museum Network had developed a travelling exhibit titled "The Making of Treaty 8 in Canada's Northwest." It was rich in artifacts, documents and records. I approached Fran Moore and asked whether they would partner with us and the answer was an unequivocal, "Yes!" It was all systems go. I developed the grant application, which was jointly submitted, and we obtained funding to hire some project staff and a firm of web developers. In the end, content and images for the bilingual website were contributed not only by the Museums of the Peace but also the Glenbow, Provincial Museum of Alberta, Treaty 8 First Nations and the *Lobstick* Journal. I remember going up North to test the site with Elders and seeing the excitement on their faces when they began to identify relatives in the archival photos. The website was launched in 2002 and CHIN was thrilled with it.

For the remaining websites that we developed, we moved all technical development in-house because we found that we could better control quality as well as guaranteeing that websites were completed on time. This was crucial because, in some instances, the majority of funding was received on project completion. Of our first four interns, two stayed on with us for a number of years and became permanent staff. Dulcie Meatheringham, a young Métis woman from Northern Alberta, became our first webmaster and Kim Palmer headed research. Over the 10-year life of the Foundation, we had over 450 interns, most for three-month internships.

The next VMC project that we pitched was a no-brainer. It was "Women of Aspenland." The Central Alberta Museums Network was totally onside and delighted to have us digitize collections. The content was rich because each museum that had undertaken research projects and exhibits on women in their community contributed that content as well as images. We also had the essays in the Aspenland book, which were also posted on the website. We were again successful and created a rich multimedia online resource showcasing prairie women and local knowledge. With David Ridley's help, we designed a Youth Program that involved the development of what we described as "edukits," online teacher and student resources.

In a 10-year period, we developed 84 multimedia websites and all involved partnerships. CKUA became an extremely valuable partner. With funding support from the Heritage Branch, they had developed the "Heritage Trails" series of mini history documentaries on a range of Alberta topics. As a result of the partnership, we digitized these and used them in whichever website they enhanced. In addition, we created the "CKUA Sound Archives" digitizing over 900 hours of arts broadcasting and also providing a history of the station, one of

Canada's oldest independent radio stations. Various government ministries including Alberta Environment and Indigenous Affairs allowed us access to content that they developed. Michael Payne, Provincial Historian, based at Alberta Community Development (another iteration of Alberta Culture), gave us access to various publications for our sites.

In 2004, we designed a project to celebrate Alberta's centenary: expansion of the websites in order to cover Alberta's social, natural, cultural, scientific and technological heritage. Albertasource.ca, the *Alberta Online Encyclopedia*, received a $1 million Centennial Legacy grant. On September 29, 2005, the Foundation launched the *Encyclopedia* – the Province's intellectual legacy project – at the Edmonton Space and Science Centre to a supportive crowd including children from neighbourhood schools.

In the grant report, we noted the following achievements: the number of websites grew to 71 comprising over 12,000 html pages with over 40,000 images, over 3,000 audio files and over 300 video files; a total of 1.5 million unique visitors each spent an average of 24 minutes on the site; 70 percent of the traffic represented visitors from schools, colleges, universities and libraries throughout Alberta; and the remainder represented visitors seeking information about Alberta from institutions located nationally and internationally. The Foundation also responded to over 10,000 emails annually. On the strength of these sites, Alberta at the time and still today has more authoritative web content than any other province in the country.

In 2005, the most popular websites were: *Alberta Naturally* showcasing Alberta's natural regions; *Alberta's Natural Resources* showcasing the pillars of the provincial economy; *Nature's Laws* and Treaty 6, 7 and 8 websites providing the largest amount of authoritative online content on Aboriginal history, culture and achievements on the World Wide Web; *CKUA Sound Archives* showcasing nearly 75 years of public broadcasting; *The City of Edmonton Archives Online Catalogue* making accessible over 10,000 images of the City's rich history as the provincial capital; and *Doors Open Alberta* inviting visitors to celebrate Alberta's landscapes, communities and architectural heritage.

The creation of the *Encyclopedia* was a technical challenge in that it required a common database that integrated the individual websites. Not only text but also, images, audio and video were made fully searchable. Many individual websites also had searchable databases of articles, images, audio and video embedded in them. In addition, we created a key word index based on key fields. Next to the Virtual Museum of Canada, the Encyclopedia was the largest purpose-built, authoritative repository of Canadian digital cultural content. While the VMC sites were created by different institutions, ours were created in-house.

Public recognition included the Edmonton Historical Board 2003 Recognition Award; Museums Alberta 2003 Museums and Society Award; the Alberta Chamber of Commerce Award for Business Excellence in Youth Employment (short-listed); the ZOOM Communications Award for Excellence in Marketing for the "It's Our Alberta Heritage" campaign that we developed (awarded to the Foundation in 2004 and 2005); and the Public Legal Education Network of Alberta (PLENA) Pyramid Award for Public Legal Education. I received the following recognition: Global Woman of Vision Award, YWCA Women of Distinction (Arts & Culture) Award and the Alberta Centennial Medal (all in 2005). In 2010, I was invested in the Order of Canada for my contributions to heritage.

There are certain groupings of websites that the Trustees and I take particular pride in; among them are the over 30 websites that are either wholly or partly devoted to Indigenous content. These include sites on individual treaties as well as *Alberta's Métis Heritage, People of the Boreal Forest* and *Elders' Voices*. The last included content from the "Ten Grandmothers Project" undertaken by Linda Many Guns of the Nii Touii Knowledge and Learning Centre; the *Centenarians*, a nine-minute video production celebrating Indigenous women resulting from a partnership between Aboriginal Affairs and Northern Development, the Institute for the Advancement of Aboriginal Women and EnCana Energy. We also undertook some oral histories of Métis veterans. The Provincial Museum of Alberta and Glenbow Museum provided access to resources for a number of Indigenous websites.

Foundation Trustee Catherine Twinn played a pivotal role in the development of the *Nature's Laws* website, which deals with the legal codes and traditional governance of Alberta's First Nations in the areas covered by Treaties 6, 7 and 8. The material examined was evidence found in oral histories, as well as case law, and the scholarly literature relating to Indigenous Peoples. Project resource people included Cree scholar and practitioner of traditional wisdom, Chief Wayne Roan, Mountain Cree at Hobbema; Earle Waugh, Professor Emeritus, Religious Studies, University of Alberta, who wrote *Dissonant Worlds:*

R. Vandersteene OMI Among the Cree; and Catherine, who served as the legal consultant. The project involved consultations with Elders in Alberta and Saskatchewan as well as ceremonialists and other resource people. New oral history work was undertaken.

Thirteen Edukits draw on the content of the various websites and provide teacher and student resources directly related to the K-12 curriculum. They are: *Alex Decoteau, Origin and Settlement, First Nations Contributions, Culture and Meaning, Language and Culture, Spirituality and Creation, Health and Wellness, Leadership, Physical Education, Sports and Recreation, Math: Elementary, Science* and *Carving Faces: People of the Boreal Forest.*

Another grouping of websites deals with ethnocultural communities. *The Albertans: Who Do They Think They Are*, the first developed, provides profiles of over 70 groups and draws on education resources developed by Alberta Culture and Multiculturalism in the 1970s and 1980s. Thirteen deal with Alberta's Francophone community and were developed in partnership with the Campus Saint-Jean, University of Alberta. Two deans, Frank McMahon and Marc Arnal, were particularly supportive of the projects and historian France Levasseur-Ouimet contributed content. Aside from contributing content, Franco-Albertan historian Juliette Champagne also undertook translation with Yves Le Guevel. Other sites include: *Celebrating Alberta's Italian Community, Alberta's Black Pioneer Heritage* and *Alberta's Estonian Heritage*. These involved partnerships with the National Congress of Italian Canadians, Edmonton District; the Black Pioneer Descendants' Society (Western Canada); and the Estonian Society of Alberta. In addition, a series of Multiculturalism Edukits were created.

The Heritage Community Foundation not only took on a range of digitization work with and for Alberta museums and archives, it also inspired a number of projects. For example, the Glenbow began digitizing its photographic archive under the able leadership of Doug Cass, and the resource became a significant revenue generator for them. The Foundation digitized over 10,000 images and created the City of Edmonton Archives' first online catalogue as a VMC project. The wealth of local history books, developed with funding provided by Alberta Culture and its successors over the years, were digitized under Frits Pannekoek's leadership at the University of Calgary. The digitization of the Peel's Prairie Collection at the University of Alberta came out of collaboration with the Heritage Community Foundation.

I helped Library staff including Ernie Ingles and Merrill Distad to develop the application as well as writing letters of support to their principal funder, Canadian Heritage. I was also involved in framing an inter-provincial collaboration: in 2004, the Galt Museum in Lethbridge received funding from Canadian Heritage through the Cultural Capital of Canada program. The project involved a consortium of museums stretching from Fernie in BC to Drumheller in Alberta, who collected and interpreted coal mining history. The Heritage Community Foundation digitized a range of materials contributed by the partners and created the website *When Coal Was King*.

While the Heritage Community Foundation had demonstrated that, "if you build it, they will come," at least on the World Wide Web, we were still going from project to project and needed to build sustainability. We found that few corporate donors wanted to invest in the *Alberta Online Encyclopedia* though we did receive funding support for specific websites, for example, from the Real Estate Association of Alberta, the Law Society of Alberta and the TELUS Foundation. The generally-held belief was that government should fund such projects. By 2008, government grant programs at the federal level were becoming more competitive and we went from a high of 75 percent success rate to about 25 percent.

After a strategic planning session, the Trustees concluded that the *Encyclopedia* should be gifted to a university that would have the technical expertise and also graduate students, who could maintain the websites and create new ones. Negotiations with the U of A were led by Dean Marc Arnal. Laird Hunter, the Foundation's legal counsel, worked with the Foundation and the University staff to create "the deed of gift" that ultimately totalled about 100 pages. Clearances had to be obtained from partners and some contributors of content. This was all done and the University Libraries, the entity that would oversee the *Encyclopedia*, was given responsibility for the project.

As part of the negotiations, we provided a budget for a core staff to maintain the websites, which was in the neighbourhood of $250,000 to $300,000. Everything was signed off and, on June 30, 2009, the offices were closed and numerous boxes with hard files and books were delivered to the University of Alberta Archives. In addition, a hard drive with the entire Encyclopedia was delivered to Library Services. Management at the University decided not to honour the terms of the gifting agreement because of an economic downturn.

Rather than using the database that we provided to them to post online, Library staff used Archive-It software and this management system rendered the subject index inoperable and also rendered many of the internal databases with articles, documents, photographs, videos and other content inaccessible. This was not the outcome that the Trustees and I had planned. Having said this, the *Encyclopedia* is still accessible online and continues to be used. The Virtual Museum of Canada and Collections Canada still provide linkages to the websites that they funded. Alberta still has more heritage digital content than any other province.

With respect to the museums that we served, we put many of them on the Information Highway and they became part of the "knowledge economy." The Alberta Museums Association was able to focus on the creation of the Museum Excellence Program, the first museum accreditation program in Canada. I believe that the Heritage Community Foundation fulfilled its obligations to the Association and the Province's museums. This could not have happened without the planning and commitment of our Trustees: Morris Flewwelling, Chair; Satya Brata Das, Vice-Chair; Bruce Alger and Kristina Milke (Treasurers); Dianne Darlington and Mark Ferguson (Secretaries); Jerry Gunn; Doug Leonard; and Catherine Twinn.

CHAPTER 10

Poet

LIKE EVERY LYRIC POET, it was pain and intense emotions that started me writing verse. In late middle age, I found myself in a metaphorical dark wood. I described it at the time as a "muddle." After 16 years in Canada, my husband Hugh, who desperately missed his homeland, decided to take a sabbatical in London, playing with his old orchestra, the Philharmonia, from mid-May 1996 to early September 1997. I became the proverbial "cat lady" living alone with my aged cat, Charlie. With Hugh away, I realized that I had allowed my work for the Alberta Museums Association to consume me and had become a workaholic. Hugh had taken on the load of driving our sons not only to school but also to various activities including sports events. I still did most of the shopping, food preparation, household chores and hosting of family events, which being a member of a close-knit Italian family required. We invited friends over for dinners and parties, and I went to Edmonton Symphony Orchestra and Alberta Baroque Ensemble concerts; Hugh was a first violinist with the Symphony and concertmaster of the ABE.

I was always juggling various activities and never had time to rest. The AMA quarterly Board meetings were particularly stressful. While most Board members were supportive, there were some who had a more authoritarian style and tried to micro-manage. I prided myself on having made accommodations to the board style of each of my presidents and handling the pressure but it took a toll on me and, I guess, by extension, on my family. If I was feeling strung out, I was not always the patient mother and wife that I should have been.

When I reflect on it, while doing things together, emotionally, Hugh and I had been living separate lives. Each summer he returned to London and stayed with his Mother and did freelance work with the Philharmonia. He stayed as long as possible, from the third week of May to early September when the orchestral season began in Edmonton. I remember writing a postcard to him in June 1996 when he had started his sabbatical. I was in Vancouver for the Canadian Museums Association conference and, in a strange city, I am always more reflective. I wrote, "I don't know whether our marriage is going to survive this sabbatical."

This was prophetic. A year later, I became infatuated with a younger man who was unavailable. As a born Catholic, I believed that marriage was a sacrament so, in a sense, I was hedging my bets. I needed change but was not prepared to abandon all of my values and beliefs to achieve it. I had fallen away from the practice of religion during my early years in London when I found that the Catholic Church there was still very traditional and different from St. Joseph's College at the University of Alberta where I went to Mass. The latter was a progressive church and introduced changes as they were made as a result of the Second Vatican Council.

I had returned to regular worship in 1984 after Pope John Paul II visited Edmonton. He arrived on September 16, my sister's birthday, and then said an outdoor Mass on September 17, my birthday. As an intuitive person (my husband Hugh referred to this as the Italian "witch" part of my personality), I should have realized that something significant was to happen that day. My brother Giuseppe obtained three tickets from his friend, City Councillor Lance White, and invited Rosa and I to go with him. More than 125,000 people gathered in a farmer's field in Sturgeon County and heard the Pope say Mass. He was raised high on a huge stage so he could be seen by everyone. The weather was blustery and the sky was overcast but there was a sense of holiness about the event; perhaps, it was the buzz of being in such a large crowd worshipping together. I had the sensation that Christ wanted me back in the fold and reached out.

To return to my mid-life crisis, in view of my beliefs, walking away from a 25-year marriage was not on the cards for me. In September 1997, shortly after Hugh returned from the UK, I was in Montreal for meetings and I had dinner with Sister Patricia Simpson. I had met her in June 1986 while visiting the city before going to Ottawa for the CMA conference. A quiet, contemplative member of the Montreal-based Congrégation de Notre-Dame, she inspired confidences. She had taught at the school run by the Order as well as being the biographer of the founder, St. Marguerite Bourgeoys. She was also involved in the restoration of the Order's Chapel, Notre-Dame-de-Bon-Secours, the first version of which was built on the site overlooking the St. Lawrence River in 1655. It is known by many as Leonard Cohen's "Our Lady of the Harbour" in the poem/song "Suzanne."

During a quiet dinner in Old Montreal not far from the Chapel, I told her of my quandary. She was silent for a very long time and, then, said, "You must listen for God in the silences." I caught my breath and immediately responded, "There is no silence in my life." She said, "You must make room for silence" and, by implication, God.

I began to read spiritual and self-help books, and also started a journal confiding to it stuff that I felt I couldn't discuss with anyone. The journal became a dialogue between my two selves: the one who was dutiful and obedient and a good Catholic, and the other, the one that wanted change. I read Kathleen Norris' *Dakota: A Spiritual Geography* and *The Cloister Walk*; Jonathan Star, *Two Suns Rising: A Collection of Sacred Writings*; Philip Novak, *The World's Wisdom: Sacred Texts of the World's Religions*; Thomas P. McDonnell, *A Thomas Merton Reader*; Leo Tolstoy, *A Calendar of Wisdom: Daily Thoughts to Nourish the Soul*; and many others. I found the writings of the mystic Dame Julian of Norwich particularly inspiring and the dictum, "All shall be well, all manner of things shall be well," became my mantra.

On September 29, 1997, I had written the following quotation in the journal from Thomas Moore's book *Soul Mates: Honoring the Mysteries of Love and Relationship*: "All intimate relationships require some degree of magic, because magic, not reason and will, accomplishes what the soul needs." I reflected on my life and concluded that there was little of that kind of magic in it. I wrote that I felt that I had "dwindled into a wife & mother." I continued, "How can I grow myself and be everything I have been to all those I love?" I further reflected that I was two-thirds of the way through my life and, as a menopausal woman, I was no longer "fruitful" without heroics so I could not re-invent myself through marriage and childbirth, as many middle-aged men did.

All my doubts, hopes and fears are expressed in the pages of the journal, which eventually stretched to multiple notebooks. I didn't give up on my marriage and my strong Catholic upbringing stopped me from having a conventional affair so I lived in a state of turmoil. I think that poetry saved me because it provided me with a vehicle into which to channel my strong emotions. Twenty-three years later, re-reading these pages, I can still feel the pain that I was experiencing and I marvel how I was able to live through it and heal.

In my journal, I refer to a quotation from Alfred, Lord Tennyson: "A use in measured language lies." He had written the epic poem, *In Memoriam*, over a number of years while mourning the death of his friend Arthur Henry Hallam, who died of a cerebral hemorrhage in 1833 at the age of 22. The sum of Tennyson's doubts and fears about life including the difficulties of being a poet without a fixed income are contained in the various verses. It was published in 1850 when Tennyson was 41 and was very well received. Queen Victoria appointed him Poet Laureate giving him the income and the standing in the community that he craved. She later told him that she loved the poem and that it helped her to come to terms with the untimely death of her husband, Prince Albert, on December 14, 1861.

On March 18, 1998, in Montreal where I was attending a meeting, I wrote the first poem in the journal. It is titled "Longings":

To possess without possessing –
Humankind's way of understanding Godhead.
But how can I, who know only this place, this time, comprehend
                                                                [eternity?
Eternal forms, timelessness, paradisial bliss –
When I only know the fever in the blood.
To be in time and out of time,
Flesh and bone but also incorporeal.
To feel and not be trapped in the web of feelings that is human love.
Balancing the glory and the darkness requires juggling abilities
that I do not possess;
A fineness and clarity of vision that I can only aspire to.

And here am I, mole-like,
Moving in underground passages
Toward the light.

The glory is there at the end of the tunnel
But my eyes are unaccustomed to light
After years of blind burrowing.
Is my mole body going to be shed for something else?
Am I going to be changed utterly?
Something is stirring in me,
Growing in me,
But, Oh God, what?

While I had written a few poems in the past, after I wrote this one, the journal became a mix of prose and verse. All of my life became the subject matter of my poems and, eventually, the poetry eclipsed the prose.

I re-read the poems of my friend Jon Whyte and one, in particular, resonated with me. It was a circular poem, which is engraved on his gravestone in the Banff Cemetery. The following words can be made out in the circle of letters: "earth," "hearth," "heart" and "the art." These would be the subjects that I explored in my poetry. I dedicated the cycle of poems that I titled "A Personal Cosmology" to Jon. These were written in 1999 and there are 10 poems in each section. The "Earth" section begins with the poem "Powers":

How can I encompass all that Earth is –
In words?
Like trying to cram the myriad grains of sand into an hourglass,
The ebb and flow of tides into power-generating turbines,
The Earth's inner fires into furnaces,
And the turbulent winds into mere drivers for electric machines.
Subservience to our will, a litany of uses;
These do not explain the mystery at the heart of Nature,
The raw power and energy defying imaginings.
Is it any wonder that past civilizations invented deities
To represent these primal forces,
Making them powerful and capricious.
Satellite images allow us, now,
To observe the birth of hurricanes:
Winds mass into a whirling vortex,
The eye of the storm the stillpoint,
In that uncontrolled fury,

Soon to be unleashed on vulnerable human habitations.
No matter how many roads we tarmac,
Powerlines erected to straddle continents,
Streams, brooks and mighty rivers channeled,
Meadows and hills saddled with houses,
And space, that last frontier, become a might communications
                                                    [medium
It will never be just man's world.

I drew on all of the knowledge that I had acquired as Science Editor of
The Canadian Encyclopedia and close observation of nature throughout
my life. I think that I was searching for the deity behind the creation
and also affirming the limitation of the power of human beings over
the universe.

The "Heart" section begins with a poem titled "Heartline," where
I move from the contemplation of the cosmos to the microcosm of
the self:

I contemplate the crisscrossing lines on my hand,
Wondering what they mean –
Are they a map of my personal destiny,
Or aspects of genetic identity like my fingerprints?
How have I strayed,
If at all, from my predestined path,
The heart saying, "go hither";
The head, holding me back.
What opportunities missed,
Hinted at by a simple convergence or divergence of lines,
Or is it only fools who circumscribe their freedom,
By following star signs and auguries.
But that is my head speaking,
And my silent heart nods dumbly,
Like a timid, younger sister,
Thankful to be led.

I did not write a separate section on "Hearth" but the final section, "The
Art," hints at family and roots as part of my craft. It begins with the
following poem:

Ever since I can remember,
Stories have been part of my life.
My Father's fairy tales,
Told to restless children.
Family stories of emigration –
Adjustments to a new land and customs,
The difficulties of acquiring a new language,
And the overcoming of barriers,
Whether in the work place, school or playground.
Before I felt the compulsion to write –
To use language to order and assign meaning –
I found I too had to spin tales,
Like elaborate cobwebs glinting in the sun,
The creations of my innermost being.
Doing this not only provides perspective,
On the unruly and sometimes chaotic elements of life,
But also makes me a part of the human narrative,
The utterances of all literature since the first Word.

I considered myself a full-fledged poet by this time (I had written several hundred) but had no way of sharing what I was writing with others. This was to change.

In 1999, I discovered a small café and antique shop called Grounds for Coffee; it was behind the Winspear Centre for Music on the corner of 97 Street and 102 Avenue in Edmonton. Gitta and Robert Lederer owned it. He was an industrial art instructor at the University of Alberta (originally from Australia) and Gitta was a Jewish-Albertan, who loved antiques. She ran the café and shop. I had started collecting "old stuff" as I travelled around the province on Alberta Museums Association business, and this was a way of relaxing on Saturdays and days off. I started to frequent the café and had conversations with Gitta and Robert. The place was a fascinating mix of modern and old. Robert had made the tables and had applied an acrylic colour wash finish making them look like marble in all sorts of crazy colours. At the back were the antiques, largely, western Canadian in origin. It was a good place to hang out after I did some grocery shopping at the Italian Centre Shop in Little Italy on Saturday.

One day, I saw a notice that advertised poetry readings and live music. One of the organizers was poet Mark Kozub. The readings, described as "Grounds for Jammin," were held once a month on Saturday afternoon. I got my courage up and decided to try to read. It turned out to be an exciting experience which I enjoyed enormously. I didn't suffer from "platform nerves" probably because I am gregarious and outgoing but also because I had taken a drama course in grade 10 at St. Joseph's High School taught by John Rivet, a famous local actor and teacher. I had also acted in two year plays. This experience built confidence and has stood me in good stead both in lecturing and public speaking.

I next learned of another organization, the Stroll of Poets Society, which was started in 1991 and among whose founders were distinguished poets Alice Major, Bert Almon, Olga Costopoulos, Doug Elves, Ruth Donovan, Rhona McAdam, Diane Zinyk, Glen Kirkland, Ken Wilson and Ivan Sundal. In October, they had "Stroll Day" with readings in various venues in Old Strathcona. I joined and, I believe, my first Stroll reading was in the basement of Bjarne's Books, which was a lovely blend of old and new books as well as antiques. It was another of my Saturday haunts when I left museum work behind and did things that pleased me and fed my soul.

The Grounds for Jammin' performances would be the prelude to the creation of another live poetry reading series, in part the result of a rift between the Stroll "traditionalists" (so-called "arm chair poets") and those who espoused "live" poetry. At the time, Mark Kozub was president of the Stroll, Thomas Trofimuk, volunteer co-ordinator and Gordon McRae, treasurer. They and their young supporters wanted to see more dynamic readings. It's no coincidence that Mark styled himself "the Alberta Beatnik" harkening back to the coffee culture and performances of the Beat Generation poets in the US. Allen Ginsberg and Gregory Corso come to mind. They were associated with improvisational jazz as the music of the people, and rejected classical and pop music as too mainstream. Ginsberg's epic poem "Howl" inspired an obscenity trial in 1957, though the judge later deemed it was not obscene.

In spring 2000, Mark and Thomas began the Poetry Tuesdays' reading series with sessions taking place evenings at the Backroom Vodka Bar on Whyte Avenue. These events were raunchier and wilder than Stroll readings and gave birth to performance poetry married with music in Edmonton. The "fathers" of the Raving Poets were

Mark Kozub, Thomas Trofimuk, Randy Edwards and Gordon McRae. The "open mic" series allowed poets who wanted to perform to simply enter their names on a signup sheet until all slots were filled. Just before the poet was to read, they would indicate the "mood" or "tone" and an improvised performance ensued. The Raving Poets Band comprised Mark on bass, Thomas on keyboards, Randy on guitar and synthesizer, and Gordon on drums and percussion. Thomas and Mark served as the first MCs but, later, this role was taken on by Mark Gravel, who was not only a fine poet but also great at engaging with poets and audience alike. He made readers feel like rock stars.

Evenings were given quirky titles such as, "Peace Talks," "The Beat Goes On," "Pig Poetry" (Phil Jagger was the jester of the group and on this evening donned a pig's snout), "Fall of Love," "Mumbo Jumbo, A Word Circus," "Kill Phil," and other witty and evocative wordmarks. Some poets wrote new poems using the evening's theme. Some performances were recorded and CDs made available for purchase; a few were videotaped. (Mark served as the sound guy and general techy.) Readings went on for about eight years and moved from the Vodka Bar to Yiannis Taverna, a popular Greek restaurant on Whyte Avenue. The Raving Poets Band eventually drifted away from these readings, which took place in the basement Kasbar Lounge. The core performers burned out and different groups formed and found new reading venues and opportunities.

Tuesday evening became the highlight of my week: I shed my business suit and donned my "reading" attire: in summer, a T-shirt and a short black leather jacket and jeans; and, in winter, a polo neck black sweater and long, black leather coat that had belonged to my brother-in-law Robin Davies, who had died in 1990. I remember how excited I was as I chose the poem that I would read (mostly the ones about heartbreak initially). A teetotaler, I normally drank only the odd glass of wine on social occasions, but my new persona needed a different drink. Thus, over the years that I performed, I allowed myself a glass of good Scotch whiskey; later, at the suggestion of the Irish bartender, I added Irish whiskey to my selection.

I kept my work and personal life separate and my life as a poet, which was my "secret" life, helped me to overcome the end of my marriage in 2000 when Hugh returned to London to live permanently. I got to know an amazing number of poets and musicians including not only Mark, Thomas, Randy and Gordon but also Laurie MacFayden,

Michael Appleby, Adam Snider, Mandie Lopatka, Mary Pinkoski, Patrick Pilarski, Louis Munan, Paul McLaughlin, Kathy Fisher, Janice Kozub, Delvina Greig, Dawn Carter, Jocko Benoit, Anton Capri, John Chalmers, Corey Hamilton, Margaret Haugen, Cathy Hodgson, Phil Jagger, Wendy Joy, Gary Lee, Rusti Lehay, John Leppard, Kerry Mulholland, Anna Marie Sewell, Nicole Pakan, Jadon Rempel, Mario Flecha, Shima Aisha Robinson, Kelly Shepherd, Mingus Tourette, Deborah Vos, Amy Willans, Francis Willey and Rosemary Wilson.

It was a dynamic group of varied ages, genders, ethnicities and interests but all were committed to the spoken word. Their subject matter and styles were very wide ranging from introspective, expletive-laced misogynistic rants to tender love songs; from political diatribes to nature poems. There were no forbidden subjects or censorship of any kind. Eventually, slam and hip-hop and other more contemporary forms became part of the mix. I didn't feel outraged by any of the content (many of my friends and work associates would have been) though sometimes the poems were painfully bad and I couldn't wait for the normal five-minute time limit to be reached.

In 2009 an organizing committee led by Gordon began to meet at Pub 1905 on Jasper Avenue to plan a 10-year anniversary bash for the Raving Poets. As part of the RP10 commemorative event, Gordon wanted to create a scrapbook and asked for feedback on the question, "What the Raving Poets has meant to me?" On February 4, 2010, I answered as follows:

> The Raving Poets at the Backroom Vodka Bar was the place where I discovered my poetic voice. It was a supportive atmosphere where no-one judged anyone else. Many of us spoke of the uncertainties in our lives and processed pain and somehow healed. Anything was allowed as we used poetic utterances of all kinds to understand ourselves. It was a way of sharing our mutual love of the written and spoken word. For me it was a place where strangers became friends. But it wasn't just a substitute for the psychiatrist's couch – it was also a fun place where old and young mixed! I changed and grew through the readings at the Backroom and completed a cycle in my life as well as half a dozen cycles of poetry. Clearly, I wouldn't have written what I've done and become who I've become in this phase of my life without that experience. I thank the Founding Fathers

who, beginning with the readings at Grounds for Coffee, conceptualized the Raving Poets and made it happen.

The RP10 event took place on Saturday, April 10, 2010 at the
Riverdale Hall and VIP's in attendance included Mayor Stephen
Mandel. Wendy Joy and Phil Jagger played the Homecoming King
and Queen and were dressed in thrift store finery selected by Rosemary
Wilson and myself. A great time was had by all.

It was inevitable that I was drawn to other like-minded poets and
I was part of two performance groups that emerged from the Raving
Poets. One evening, a distinguished-looking, older gentleman who was
sitting next to me said, "Why don't you, me and Paul McLaughlin do
some readings together?" He observed that we were among the oldest
of the poets. Louis Munan was a retired epidemiologist who was not
only a poet but also a playwright and sculptor. His penthouse apartment in a run-down high-rise building near City Hall in Churchill
Square reflected a life well lived and full of interests in the arts and
culture. He became a good friend. Paul attended Osgoode Hall Law
School and practiced in Ontario before coming to Alberta in 1981
with his family. He worked for many years for the Alberta Law Society
and lived on an acreage with wife, Carol. They bred Papillon dogs,
which I had never seen before and who were astoundingly cute. We
met for coffee at the Bistro Praha, the restaurant established in 1977
by Frantisek Cikanek. It was an old-style eatery that served Czech
specialties and had classical music on the soundtrack. It was a popular
haunt for Edmonton Symphony musicians.

Over incredible food and wine, the three of us created the Bistro
Trio in homage to the restaurant. Our range was incredible including
poems dealing with love, family, nature, history and politics. We met
at our respective homes to rehearse and wonderful, new friendships
formed. Since Louis had given up his car, I drove to Paul's acreage
where we frequently went to rehearse, and we had fascinating conversations. Among our topics were all things Italian since Louis and
I shared this heritage. His grandparents immigrated to New York in
the early part of the twentieth century and he was fond of mentioning
that his parents returned to Italy to live in the 1920s but, because of
the rise of Mussolini, they returned to the US. The family name –
Mugnano – was changed to Munan. Louis began to write poetry as

a young man serving in the American military in the Second World War. For most of his professional life, he was based in Washington, DC, but then moved to the Université du Québec à Trois-Rivières to set up an epidemiology program. When he turned 65, his wife forced him to retire and they moved to Alberta to be close to two of their children who had moved here. Louis and I also discussed our respective divorces – his after over forty years of marriage. We read together for perhaps two years but our friendship lasted until his death in 2014; he was a young 93 at the time.

The three of us planned readings and did a number of educational performances including sessions at Ross Sheppard High School with a classroom of aspiring poets; and at Louise McKinney School (all girls) where we focused on poetry inspired by the landscapes of Alberta. We did a Remembrance Day performance at the long-term care facility where Paul's father was living. In the introduction to the November 11th performance, it was noted that Louis was a veteran of the Second World War serving in the US Army in Europe; Adriana was born in 1943 as the Allies landed in Sicily and made their way North in the liberation of Italy; and, Paul was born in 1946 and belonged to "a blessed generation that didn't have to go to war." We read some renowned war poems among them Isaac Rosenberg's "Break of Day in the Trenches" and Wilfred Owen's "Doomed Youth," as well as some of our own.

Bistro Trio also did several performances of love poetry. We mixed our own poems with some from poetry greats including Shakespeare, Browning and Yeats. The first was at a café on Whyte Avenue and the other at Il Forno restaurant on Valentine's Day, February 14, 2002. The restaurant was full and, in intervals between the five courses comprising the sumptuous meal, we performed. It was truly the "food of love" with main course selections including stuffed salmon, crabmeat, shrimp and scallops; Cornish game hen stuffed with wild rice; or roast lamb and garden fresh herb stuffing. The desert was tiramisu or *zuppa Romana* (Italian trifle). My son Alex was visiting from London and saw the performance at the café and afterwards observed, "Mum, I wish you would stop spilling your guts in poetry and concentrate on writing nature poetry!"

Through Raving Poets' readings, I developed a friendship with two younger women: Delvina Greig and Dawn Carter. We started to meet at a small café in downtown Edmonton near the former Edmonton Telephones' Art Deco building in Churchill Square. We focused on poems of love and loss since that was a strong suit for all of us. We called ourselves "Strong Brew" not only because of our love of coffee but also because of the strong emotions that were expressed in our poetry. Our reading titled "The Lover's Journey: Women on Men," which was held on Friday, November 26, 2004, was mentioned by Malcolm Azania in an article titled "Poetry Out Loud," which appeared in *Alberta Views* (July/August 2005). Dawn was one of the four poets featured (the others were Mark Kozub, Gail Sidonie Sobat and Mingus Tourette) and he wrote of our performance as follows:

> Sister Dawn, regal, beautiful like a 13th century Benin carving in ebony, tonight has a mouthful of other women's words. It's a November jam in the capital city's Liva [Leva] Cappuccino Bar. Through the window, the artificial aurora borealis of Christmas lights on a construction crane sanctifies the event. Strong Brew Trio: Adriana Davies, Delvina Grieg [*sic.*] and Carter—a benefit for the TRI-Shelter Christmas hamper program, MCed by Janice Kozub. The poets are all women, and tonight they'll be reading each other's work. Such surrender of ego would be unthinkable in Toronto, Carter says.

The readings were grouped under three headings and each section included poems by each of us. I read "Beginnings"; Dawn read "Middles"; and Delvina read "Ends." We each brought to our first meetings poems that dealt with falling in love and relationships. We then selected those that fit together into a kind of narrative, and presented a range of feelings.

The bios that we included in the program are downright edgy, though mine less so than those of Delvina and Dawn. They are as follows:

> Adriana A. Davies in her working life is a researcher, writer, cultural executive director and encyclopedist. She writes poetry to better understand herself and the human condition. She believes that language is both a medium of communication and vehicle for lies and coverups. No armchair poet, she is a member of the Stroll of Poets and the Raving Poets at the Backroom Vodka Bar.
>
> Delvina Greig is part hermit, part exhibitionist, and all parts passion. Whether she's playing the sex kitten or the eccentric recluse, her mind is always moving, thinking, and feeling. Her one

guilty pleasure is hanging out with other hopeless poets – currently
the Raving Poets and Strong Brew.

Dawn Carter is a shaken-not-stirred mix of north side E-town,
downtown, T dot O, prairie town escapee, funky music junkie,
bred-in-the-bone BBC (British Barbadian Canadian). She's been
published in Other Voices, SEE Magazine, and Contemporary
Verses 2, appears on Raving Poets CDs and shamelessly performs
poetry to speak her mind.

The performance was well-attended and the audience was not turned
off by the strong feelings that we expressed about relations between
the sexes. Sadly, it was not repeated though we all continued to read
at the Backroom Vodka Bar. Mark Kozub was our sound tech.

In 2005, Alice Major was appointed Edmonton's first Poet Laureate. In 2006, in collaboration with The Stroll and other groups,
she inaugurated the Edmonton Poetry Festival, which has gone from
strength to strength. The first festival saw poems being chalked on
the concrete in Sir Winston Churchill Square and readings in various
venues. The Stroll of poets presented the first-ever "Blinks" poetry
event that involved 60 poets reading for 30-seconds each. The fun
and goodwill was palpable. The organizers also began the tradition of
inviting "headliners" from across the country. At the first festival, the
Parliamentary Poet Laureate, Pauline Michel was brought in. I read
and hosted an event not only at this festival but also at a number of
others over the years. I also took part in The Stroll's Haven series at the
Upper Crust Café on Monday evenings. I enjoyed MC'ing and reading.

My life as a performance poet was kicked up a notch as a result of
a chance encounter. At the Edmonton International airport, I believe,
in fall 2004, I saw dancer and choreographer Brian Webb waiting in
the boarding lounge. We were both on the flight to Ottawa. I had
attended some performances of the Brian Webb Dance Company and
went up and introduced myself. We had a nice chat and I learned that
he was going to Ottawa to prepare for a festival at the National Arts
Centre to celebrate Alberta's centenary in 2005 titled "Alberta Scene."
He was also artistic director of the Canada Dance Festival at the NAC.

I was going to take part in meetings of the committee that I
co-chaired that was looking at building capacity in Canada's charitable
sector. We weren't seated near each other but, during the long flight,

we made the opportunity to talk as we walked to stretch our legs. We continued our conversation and I mentioned that I was a performance poet and that I felt some of my poetry was musical, and the subject matter could lend itself to contemporary dance. By chance, we were on the same return flight and, at the Edmonton airport, before we said goodbye, we agreed that I would send him some poems and we would meet to discuss them.

I made selections from a series of nature poems that I called "Alberta Pastorale," and from a long poem that I titled "The Dark Elegies." When Hugh returned to the UK in May, 2000, I felt that I needed to write about the end of our marriage. I remembered that in Elizabethan and Jacobean poetry there was a poetic form, the *epithalamium*, which was a poem or song celebrating a marriage. I thought that I would turn the genre on its head and write about the ending of a marriage. I read various examples and particularly liked one written by Edmund Spenser, which had 24 stanzas, one for each hour of the day: 16 stanzas dealt with the preparation for the wedding including the dressing of the bride and the actual ceremony, and eight stanzas dealt with nighttime and consummation. I decided that, in my poem, sixteen stanzas would deal with loss and grieving, and eight with metaphorical rebirth.

In early 2005, Brian and I met for coffee at Vi's for Pies in the west end, and he told me that he loved the "Dark Elegies" and would like to work on a dance/music/spoken word performance. He was noted for doing innovative performances including one that involved him performing naked. In fact, when I told friends about the collaboration many asked, "Do you have to perform naked?" I laughed nervously and said, "No." Brian felt that the collaboration and the content would be a creative challenge for him and his dance partner, Tania Alvarado. We agreed to meet to discuss the possibilities and to begin the creative process, which was based on improvisation. From the outset, Brian envisioned two performances in different BWDC seasons; therefore, the first titled "A Love Story (A First Draft)," was scheduled for May 4-6, 2006 (Thursday through Saturday) at the Catalyst Theatre; and the second, "a love story," on February 23 and 24, 2007 (Friday and Saturday) at the John L. Haar Theatre, Grant MacEwan College in the west end.

The two-year period that we collaborated on performances was immensely fulfilling but also challenging. I was working more than full-time on the creation of the *Alberta Online Encyclopedia* and it was difficult to carve out time for rehearsals. But, after each rehearsal, I felt emotionally renewed and re-invigorated. Brian and Tania were used to working together and he was her mentor. He was the best-known and most influential dancer and choreographer in Alberta with a national reputation. I was thus very much the odd person out – I was older; not a dancer; not particularly fit though I had been going to a gym to work out for nearly 10 years. The team also included Linda Rubin as dramaturge and David Fraser as the lighting designer.

Salena Kitteringham in a feature article titled "Fresh Start: Brian Webb Unveils New Season of Intimate, Incendiary Dance," (*See* Magazine, Oct. 6 – Oct. 12, 2005) discussed the Company's 2005-06 program. Noting that Brian's impact on dance in Canada had been "staggering," she focused on the uniqueness of his style and quotes Brian describing his dancing as follows:

> … very physical, it uses the floor, there's a lot of fall and recovery, weight is important, and leading from the head is the key. I'm still really interested in what the body can do, and what my body can do at different periods in my life. So the vocabulary is always evolving.

In another article titled "Creating a new vocabulary: Tania Alvarado uses her words, gets back to dance" (*See* Magazine, May 4 – May 10, 2006), Kitteringham quotes the dancer as follows:

> I do not aim to be romantic with the movement. I never have. I've always thought of it as work and attacked it in a very physical way. I would say in my past work, that I have been reckless; it's like I've had my heart hanging out my chest all the time.

It was fascinating to see how the work came together as a result of numerous meetings and rehearsals. Brian and Tania took on the role of the lovers, sometimes caring and sometimes combative, and we agreed that there would be 24 dance movements, one for each of the stanzas. The physicality and athleticism of their performances were amazing. At the beginning, it was agreed that they would not "act out" the stories embedded in the poem. In a sense, the words themselves and the musicality of the language served as a kind of "tone poem" for the production. I was integrated into the dance by movement and had to memorize all of the words so that my reading was spontaneous rather than studied. It was a big task. To limber up, Brian suggested I do yoga with him and we also did some Pilates classes. Brian suggested that we use excerpts of music from Wagner's *Tristan and Isolde* throughout the performance.

The performance in 2006 at the Catalyst was definitely lower tech than the one in 2007 at the John L. Haar Theatre. The stage properties at the former were very rudimentary; whereas the latter was a fully-equipped theatre with all the bells and whistles. Brian decided that we should integrate video projected on a back screen, and Tim Folkmann filmed and developed this so that the second performance really lived up to its name of being multimedia. Brian suggested that I buy a "sexy" nightdress for the video. I went out and bought an expensive cream silk, long nightie with spaghetti straps – this was more in keeping with my age, I felt, than some black lace number. The images were of dramatic sunsets and turbulent skies and I lounged on a sheet in the aftermath of what I imagined was good sex.

David Fraser's lighting for the production was brilliant and set the mood for the various movements. Dramaturge Linda Rubin kept an eye on the overall performance as it was created, and ensured that the different elements fit together to form a pleasing whole. Besides the recitation and movement, I also had some other stage business, which was enhanced in the second production on the professional stage. Brian had been able to purchase (or get donated) big rolls of craft paper and also large sheets of coloured paper. At the beginning of the performance, Brian and Tania unroll the sheets so that they overlap each other across the stage; this served as a kind of prelude to the dance. Several stacks of the large sheets were also positioned on the stage. During several stanzas I not only recite the lyrics but also write them on the white newsprint still connected to the roll. It is as if the word was given flesh through the physical act of writing. At a point of conflict between Brian and Tania later in the sequence, I pick up a dozen or so of the sheets and fling them, being careful not to hit either of them as they moved around me. At the finale, some dance students mill around at a social gathering as the poet re-integrates into life. The program summed up the intent of the production as follows:

Tania Alvarado/Brian Webb and Adriana Davies explore the politics of desire, obsession and love (found and lost). Through this maze they locate the integrity of the self as a complete being. All of this to the glorious music of Wagner's Tristan and Isolde, played live by a palm court orchestra. And, in a wonderful environment created by David Fraser.

The media coverage for both productions was excellent and the audiences loved the performances. Sherry Dawn Knettle in the review titled "Love Story Puts Poetry to Motion" in *Vue Weekly* (May 4, 2006) wrote:

> Local poet Adriana Davies has been making big moves towards expanding her artistic range of activity in preparation for her upcoming performance A Love Story (a first draft) with dancers Brian Webb and Tania Alvarado, which involved both dance and poetry. "The movement is enriching and amazingly creative," she says of the improvisational rehearsals the three have been immersed in. And she's discovering the universality of languages as she sees her text translated into dance.

She quotes Brian as follows: "We're trying to give strength to both the dance and poetry. So we're not illustrating each other, but rather empowering one another's work. Each artist is taking a challenge to go where we've never gone before."

Pamela Anthony in an article titled "Multimedia show explores mysteries of love" (*The Edmonton Journal* February 19, 2007) writes:

> Ah, the sweet – and bittersweet – mysteries of love.
> Artists have tried to convey the joy, heartache and transformative power of love since the beginning of time.
>   Now six Edmonton artists want to chart the intricate pathways of love with a multimedia performance called, simply enough, a love story.
>   Dancers Brian Webb and Tania Alvarado play the lovers, representing a very specific love based on Adriana Davies's poetry, an elegy to passion and love lost.
>   They also present the universal condition of love between two people, searching out the nuances of how love affects the lover.

On the Friday night of the second production in 2007, there was an opportunity for the audience to speak to the performers. Again and again, people noted how the poetry resonated with their own experiences and wanted to purchase a book. This led to my self-publishing a slim book of poetry titled *Changing My Skin: The Dark Elegies and Other Poems*.

While others used falling in love as a means of re-inventing themselves, I think that writing poetry and performance played that role for me and, just as at the end of the "Dark Elegies" the poet moves from darkness to light, this happened to me as well.

I believe that not only in the "Dark Elegies" but also in all of my poetry, I draw on both my own experiences and feelings, and the works of poets from all ages and cultures. As a student of literature, I have felt part of a great tradition. That is why I have been drawn to works that explore myths and rituals such as Sir James Frazer's *The Golden Bough* and Joseph Campbell's *The Hero with a Thousand Faces*. For me, each moment in our own lives is mirrored in myth and ritual.

In 2012, as part of Alberta Culture Days, a call was put out for poets to create a performance around the theme "Visions of Alberta." It had to be collaborative so I thought of Franco-Albertan poet Pierrette Requier, whose work I admired. Her bilingual grandparents had left the Isle of Jersey in 1914 and settled in Peace Country. The pioneering experience of her family fascinated her (the struggle to break the land and eke out a living) as did the dynamics of male/female relationships and the influence of the Roman Catholic priests on their parishioners. These were the subjects explored in her poetry and I felt that we were poetry "soulmates" in many ways. She was a specialist in elementary education (bilingual) and also had a Masters' degree in Philosophy, and was a member of the Stroll and had been doing poetry workshops and mentoring.

I telephoned and asked Pierrette whether she would like to work on a performance. She immediately said, yes, and told me that she had met a young musician/poet, Alison Grant-Préville, and would like to include her. Alison is a multidisciplinary musician, who plays a range of instruments including flutes, piano and harmonium as well as being a fine singer. She was also a student of world music and ethnomusicology. I readily accepted and we agreed to select poetry to bring to a first meeting, which took place in Pierrette's attic studio above her garage. This was the beginning of many meetings that were both creative and joyful. We became the Trio avec Brio and our performances were a blend of spoken word, music and song. Our proposal was accepted and we performed at Government House in September 2012 under the dome in the Cabinet meeting room at the top of the historic house.

I had been inspired by Alberta landscapes since the mid-1980s when I wrote poetry for a brief period. Beginning in late 1998, when I began to write poetry seriously, nature poetry was one of my favourite genres. In 2001-02, I had written a series of poems titled "Reflections on Nature and Life." Sometimes a memory would trigger a poem and, in this instance, it was a line from Shakespeare's Sonnet 73, "bare, ruined choirs where late the sweet birds sang." This came into my head as I was sitting in a taxi in October 2001 going from the Ottawa airport to my hotel for a few days of meetings. I saw a large deciduous tree silhouetted against a dark sky. It was covered in dark leaves but all of a sudden the leaves seemed to explode into the air, and I realized they were crows that had been resting on the branches and, then, as if on a silent signal, they had all flown off together.

There are a total of 21 short poems in the cycle. The largest cycle of nature poems that I wrote is titled "Alberta Pastorale: A Journey in Time and Space." This was written in the same period and drew on memories of Alberta landscapes over my entire adult life. They deal with "unspoilt" nature and nature adversely impacted by human habitation, fire, drought and other natural and unnatural phenomenon. There are 31 poems in all.

Pierrette, Alison and I shared an affinity that went beyond our performances and encompassed both our beliefs and values. Pierrette challenged me to translate my immigration poems into Italian and thanks to my friends, Carlo and Lina Amodio, I was able to translate several for our performance thus making it trilingual. After the successful Alberta Days performance, we went on to a number of others including taking part in the ArtSpirit Festival, May 23 – June 1, 2013 at Holy Trinity Anglican Church in Old Strathcona. These focused on women's experiences. Pierrette went on to become the City of Edmonton's sixth poet laureate in 2015 (she had served as MacEwan's Writer in Residence in 2012) and also turned a number of her poems dealing with her family's history into a play, *Les Blues des Oubliées* (Blues of the Forgotten), performed by Francophone theatre company l'Unithéâtre, at the Cité Francophone. It was produced by Brian Dooley in 2015.

Alison has also gone on to other performances including, in 2015, a solo performance at the Skirts Afire Festival and, another with members of New Music Edmonton, at the Edmonton Fringe Festival. This was *Sticks and Stones* by Christian Wolff.

The last entry in my journal was May 28, 2009. This marked the ending of my life in poetry though I continued to perform. The last paragraph states:

> So, I go back to that plane trip in September, 1997, when I read the article about Jane Jacobs who did not find her cause and begin to write about it until her fifties and was productive for the next thirty years. I wrote then about changing my skin thinking that it might be a process accomplished in a year or so. In fact, it's been happening for the past ten years and, I suppose it will continue until I die and my adventure on Earth is finished.

The next part of my adventure would be in prose.

CHAPTER 11

Author

IT WAS AT ST. JOSEPH'S HIGH SCHOOL in Edmonton that I first wrote prose accounts of any length. My Social Studies teacher, Maria Biamonte, the daughter of a pioneer Italian family who arrived in Edmonton around 1905, required that we write a university-style term paper on any subject that we liked. The school library was a treasure trove of unexpected works donated by parents and alumni, and I had discovered Leo Tolstoy and read *War and Peace* and *Anna Karenina*. I was fascinated by Russia and its Revolution so I chose to write about that.

I don't have a copy of that paper but remember that I consulted various historical texts to write it. It was the longest prose piece that I had ever written and producing it nurtured development of research skills. My next influence was literature: at an open house at the University of Alberta, held by the Department of English in 1962 when I was finishing grade 12, one of the professors talked about D.H. Lawrence's *Lady Chatterley's Lover*. He told us that the book had been privately printed in 1928 in Italy and 1929 in France with some crucial cuts. An unexpurgated edition was published in 1960 by Penguin Books in the UK and they were charged with obscenity. While they were acquitted, it was still a "hot" issue at least at universities. As students from a Catholic school I think we were surprised that we were being introduced to a "banned" book but I was secretly intrigued by the shocking nature of the relationship between the lady and the gamekeeper, and thought that I would like to write novels someday.

In the short term, I decided that I wanted to be a journalist. Since there wasn't a journalism program at the U of A, I chose English as a major and French as a minor for my BA degree. Miss Biamonte's assignment stood me in good stead and I wrote many term papers and did well in most of them. My favourite profs were very good writers so I had excellent models. I remember my first year English prof, Rowland McMaster saying, "There is no such thing as writing. There is only re-writing!" I also wrote for the campus newspaper, *The Gateway*, and later for *The Edmonton Journal* during the summer of 1964.

It was a period in academe when writing well was not only something to aspire to but also essential. In addition, professors took seriously their task of helping to teach young minds to think critically. Classroom discussion focused on being able to argue various points of view intelligently. I also read voraciously not only works that I studied but also a range of other literature. This was a habit I had acquired in elementary school when I used to take my sister's and brother's library cards so I could borrow more books. I read so much that at one point my parents worried that I would damage my vision. The prose writing skills and also the fascination with life and learning have been important throughout my career, as I undertook university lecturing work, research for fine and decorative arts publications, writing and editing for encyclopedias, work as a cultural administrator and, finally, as a historian.

Until my retirement on June 30, 2009 most of my writing was focused on work. I didn't choose the subjects: they were chosen for me. This also applied to the 84 multi-media websites that I developed for the *Alberta Online Encyclopedia* (www.albertasource.ca) in the period October 1999 to the end of June 2009. Topic selection was not only based on what was appropriate for an Alberta encyclopedia but also the partnerships required in order to create the various websites, and the grants that could be obtained. I researched and wrote the prospectus for each website and always chose some key essays to write. Writing was the carrot in my all-too-busy life. This was particularly true for the *Celebrating Alberta's Italian Community* website for which I wrote all of the thematic essays.

But this was not the same as choosing my own topic from the get go and being entirely focused on the project. Whenever possible, I created opportunities to do freelance work that allowed me to explore subject areas that I was passionate about. David Goa, Curator of Folk and Religious Life at the Provincial Museum of Alberta, in the planning of his incredible exhibit, *Anno Domini: Jesus through the Centuries*, gave me the opportunity to explore religious art. As a freelance contractor, I wrote three discussion papers for him and also arranged loans from British and some Canadian collections.

My fascination with religious art goes back a very long way. I remember my wonder when I visited galleries and churches in the United Kingdom and Europe when I went to London to do doctoral studies in June 1968. The six weeks that I spent travelling on a Eurail pass allowed me to walk around some of the major cities of Western Europe, and discover their cultural treasures. I have a highly developed visual memory and can still recreate in my mind's eye some of the wonders that I encountered.

In the early 1970s, when my PhD supervisor Leonée Ormond and husband Richard were working on a biography of Sir Frederick Leighton, artist and British Royal Academician, they required translations of some letters in Italian from the period that he studied in Rome. Through them, I became aware of the German artist with whom Leighton had studied: Eduard von Steinle, a historical painter. They told me that he had been influenced by a group of young artists who wanted to renew German art by going back to religious painters such as Albrecht Dürer. The original group included Friedrich Overbeck, Franz Pforr, Ludwig Vogel, Johann Konrad Hotlinger, Joseph Wintergerst and Joseph Sutter. They left Vienna in May 1810, and arrived in Rome on June 20 where they found lodgings in the monastery of San Isidoro, an Irish college and monastery. It had been vacated as a result of the French occupation under Napoléon. Not only did they proceed to absorb as much as they possibly could of the art of their favoured Italian religious painters, in particular, Raphael, they established a monastic/artistic commune and chose for themselves the name of the Brotherhood of St. Luke, the patron saint of medieval artists' guilds.

Various accounts exist of how they came to be called the "Nazarenes." One story has it that it was because they were followers of Christ; another notes that it was initially a critic's derogatory reference to the group's affectation of long hair and flowing cloaks (in the manner of Jesus' image in religious works); while another ascribes it to their pietistic behaviour. However, it so aptly described them that they themselves came to accept the name. Having mastered their themes and technique, the majority of the initial group, as well as others who followed them to Rome, returned to Germany where they initiated other Nazarene groups (for example, besides in Vienna and Frankfurt, at Düsseldorf, Munich and Prague). Many became teachers in academies, thus, influencing the next generation of artists. They also undertook many religious and historical works including frescos in public buildings, and inspired renewals of religious art throughout Europe and the UK. The style they developed was also used to illustrate fairy tales of the period; for example, artist Hermann Vogel's illustrations for *Auserwahlte Marchen* (Selected Fairy Tales) by Hans Christian Anderson, which was published in 1881.

In 1999, after research in France facilitated by a Canada-France Cultural Accord Study Tour and a research trip to the UK, I wrote two discussion papers. "Mere Papistical Fantasy: The Religious Art of the Nazarenes and the Pre-Raphaelite Brotherhood," which dealt with the religious art movements in Germany and Britain; and "Four Portraits of Jesus: From Romantic to Historic," which focused on works by William Holman Hunt. The first is the iconic image of Christ titled "The Light of the World" gifted to Keble College in which he stands in a darkened doorway with a lantern. The image of the "man who is God" glows with a spiritual light but the doorway and plants around him are depicted painstakingly. Hunt travelled to the Middle East to see where Jesus had actually lived and produced two works depicting him at different stages in his life. These were decidedly realistic. "The Finding of the Savior in the Temple," shows Jesus as a thirteen-year-old surrounded by the elders and rabbis, his youth contrasting with the age and self-importance of the greybeards. "The Shadow of Death" depicts him as a young carpenter at work in his shop; behind him two timbers form a cross-like shadow portending his death. The final work is a life-sized version of "The Light of the World" that Hunt completed in 1904 and which toured to Canada, South Africa, New Zealand and Australia before being gifted to St. Paul's Cathedral in London.

The final essay that I wrote for David Goa, "François Édouard Meloche: The Last Nazarene," deals with one of the many "painted churches" of Quebec. My interest in Meloche was inspired by a visit to Notre-Dame-de-Bon-Secours in September 1997. The so-called "sailors' church" (many votives in the shape of sailing ships hung from the ceiling) in Montreal's old harbor was undergoing a massive restoration. Sister Patricia Simpson, the biographer of the founder, St. Marguerite Bourgeoys, showed me around. She pointed to the ceiling where canvas was peeling away to reveal grey frescoes under-neath, and told me that these paintings had been done by Meloche and it was thought that they had been destroyed in 1908-10 when the chapel was redecorated.

I later discovered that a contract for the work had specified how many coats of whitewash were to be used to cover them to provide a fresh ground for new works. Sister Patricia observed that, after a new copper roof had been placed on the chapel, the heat had been turned up to dry the ceiling that had experienced water damage over the years. To everyone's surprise, canvas that had been pasted on the ceiling began to peel away revealing Meloche's masterpieces. Whether the artist who was to paint over them used canvas rather than paint to respect the work of his predecessor, or simply because it was easier than applying numerous coats of paint, is not known. Sister Patricia told me that Meloche had been influenced by the Nazarenes and I was inspired to tell her that I would do some research and write a paper that could be used to interpret the chapel. The *Anno Domini* exhibit gave me the opportunity to do so.

I read whatever I could find on Québec religious art, and dis-covered that various religious orders commissioned art works and decorations for churches as was the case in Catholic countries around the world. As a result of my research, I discovered that, in order to unravel the mystery behind some of Montréal's church frescoes, it is important to understand the influence of the illustrated bibles of the nineteenth century. The most important is that of Julius Schnorr von Carolsfeld: *Die Bibel in Bildern* (The Bible in Pictures), published in 1860. The son of a painter, he was trained at the Vienna Academy and arrived in Rome in 1818 when the Nazarenes had already established themselves, and followed in their footsteps.

I found that several of the frescos in the Jesuit chapel, L'Église du Gésu, built in Montreal together with a new Jesuit college, the Collège Sainte-Marie, in 1865, were drawn from the Schnorr von Carolsfeld *Bibel*. These were executed, on a commission from the Jesuits, by Daniel Müller, who was either trained or influenced by the Naza-renes. He was relying on a very recent publication and no doubt had a copy of the bible with him. Meloche studied at the Collège and was exposed to these artworks. His teacher was the established Québec art-ist Napoléon Bourassa, who he assisted in several commissions includ-ing the decoration of Notre-Dame-de-Lourdes. I also discovered that

Meloche's maternal great-grandfather, David Bohle, was a silversmith from Hanau, Germany, who came to North America as part of a regiment of hussars, which fought for the Americans in the war of independence. Bohle was based with troops along the south bank of the St. Lawrence River. His name appears on the list of 317 former German soldiers who chose to remain in Canada after the American Revolution and he is also listed in the Lower Canada Land Petitions at the National Archives in Ottawa. According to the records, he arrived in Canada in 1783; he married a local woman and had three sons who were also silversmiths. One of them, Peter, was Meloche's grandfather and some of the hallmarked domestic and Indian trade silver that he produced survives. Meloche's father worked for his father-in-law and the family also lived in the Bohle residence. It is likely that they had a copy of the Schnorr von Carolsfeld *Bibel* and Meloche was familiar with it.

Meloche undertook a range of commissions, mostly in the Province of Québec, among the most important being the frescoes in Notre-Dame-de-Bon-Secours, which were done in the period 1885-90. When the restoration work on the chapel was completed, I was able to see all of the frescoes on the ceiling and walls, and using a replica edition of the *Bibel* that I had purchased, I was able to make a comparison. I was delighted to discover that Meloche had wanted to focus on the life of the Blessed Virgin Mary and copied the following scenes from the *Bibel*: the Nativity of the Virgin, the Presentation of the Blessed Virgin, the Marriage of Joseph and Mary, the Annunciation, the Visitation, the Nativity of Christ, the Purification of Mary, the Life in Nazareth, and the Crowning of Mary as Queen of Heaven by her son Jesus. The frescoes were executed using the ancient encaustic technique, which involved applying heated beeswax to a surface and then painting on it using coloured pigments. Meloche decorated over 40 churches including Saint-Michel in Vaudreuil, Saint-Philippe in Saint-Philippe-d'Argenteuil and as far away as Vermont, Ontario, PEI, Manitoba and Saskatchewan. A number were churches associated with the Oblates of Mary Immaculate – early in his career he had written to the Superior to ask for work and mentioned his particular devotion to the Blessed Virgin. I imagined Meloche lying on a scaffold for months painting heavenly scenes. He appears to have become an alcoholic and there were no commissions after 1900.

Meloche's paintings at Notre-Dame-de-Bon-Secours are in the *grisaille* style in which various shades of grey are used to create a three-dimensional effect. Paintings in other churches are poly-chrome and are not directly linked to the *Bibel*. My research was encouraged by Cécile Belley, who in 1989 had completed a Master's thesis titled, "François-Édouard Meloche (1855-1914) mural-iste, professeur de décor de l'église Notre-Dame-de-la-Visitation de Champlain." She gave me a copy of her thesis as well as her research files. Since her research was done before the uncovering of the works at Notre-Dame-de-Bonsecours, she had not been able to deal with them and was delighted by my discovery. The *Anno Domini* exhibit included some artworks from Québec.

While I enjoyed writing essays and occasional papers, I was frustrated: I was a would-be author in search of a major subject. In 2008, I would find this at the opening of the exhibit titled "The Group of Seven to Takao Tanabe" at the Whyte Museum of the Canadian Rockies. It was curated by Michale Lang, the Executive Director. As we walked around the exhibit, we stopped in front of a glacier work painted by J.B. (Jack) Taylor. It was startling in its simplicity: a band of aquamarine across the top of the painting was reminiscent of the glacial silt in mountain lakes and the white of the ice, which covered most of the painting, showed dark, particulate matter that had been embedded in the glacier over eons. I observed casually, "I would love to curate an exhibit on Taylor." In September 2010, I signed a contract with the Whyte to curate a retrospective exhibit.

I had first become aware of Taylor as one of the artists featured in the *Alberta's Arts' Heritage* website that I developed for the *Alberta Online Encyclopedia*. At the launch at the Art Gallery of Alberta in 2003, Taylor's son, Chris, had talked to me about his desire to have a book written about his father's work. I suggested that he find a good web designer and develop a website, which he did. The site includes a comprehensive catalogue raisonné of his work put together by Chris.

John Benjamin Taylor was born in Charlottetown, Prince Edward Island, in 1917. He was the son of Reginald Taylor, a jeweller, and Elizabeth Chappel, a housewife who was an amateur artist. She nurtured her son's artistic talents: Jack received lessons from local artist Mabel Gass, who studied at the Art Students League in New York and also in France. Following in her footsteps, Jack studied at the Art Students League and started his own studio in Charlottetown after completion of these studies. With the outbreak of the Second World War, he enlisted in the Air Force and was assigned to the creation of

"recognition rooms," a type of diorama used to train pilots in iden-
tification of enemy aircraft. After the war, he attended the Ontario
College of Art and Design and, when he finished, in 1947, was hired
by H.G. Glyde, the founder of the University of Alberta's Department
of Fine Arts, and became the second professor of art.

Taylor was an accomplished landscape painter and many of his
works are associated with the Rocky Mountains around Banff where
he taught summer courses at the Banff School of Fine Arts. He also
taught art classes for the Faculty of Extension in different parts of
Alberta and these landscapes also feature in his work. The post-war
period and early 1950s were an exciting period in Alberta when the
provincial government supported development of the Department
of Fine Arts at the U of A as not only the supplier of art teachers
for schools but also of visual artists to reflect the Province's cultural
coming of age. Both Glyde and Taylor are represented among the 15
artworks purchased by the Province in celebration of the fiftieth anniversary in 1955. These works are exhibited at Government House in
Edmonton and form the basis of the provincial collections now under
the stewardship of the Alberta Foundation for the Arts.

Part of the work of the exhibit curator is to create a manual that
includes a short biography of the artist; the context for the development of the artist's style; an essay on the primary subject matter of
the works; an assessment of the artist's place in the context of Canadian and international painting and overall achievement; and a list
of paintings to be exhibited and collections from which loans can
be obtained. Both primary and secondary research is required and,
for a modern artist, this includes contacts with family, professional
colleagues and friends. The curatorial manual presents the vision for
the exhibit and also justification for choice of works to exhibit. As I
completed this, I came more and more to admire the originality of
the works and Taylor's sheer talent. I realized that this was a book that
I wanted to write.

I knew that the University of Calgary Press had a Canadian artists' imprint – the Art in Profile Series – and drew on the curatorial
manual to produce a proposal. I sent it to Editor-in-Chief Donna
Livingstone as an email attachment and heard back from her the next
day. The consensus was that they loved it and to go ahead and write
the book. Initially, the book was going to have the same title as the
exhibit: "J.B. Taylor and the Idea of Mountains," but, in the end,

I chose to deal with all of his works, which included other landscapes as well as portraits.

As I learned more about Taylor's life and his artistic techniques, I realized that he had made an enormous breakthrough from representational or "realist" art to abstraction. He also had moved from watercolour and oil paints to acrylics, and was an innovator in the use of the latter. I traced the formation of his style, which was influenced by one of his teachers at the Art Students League of New York, Frank Vincent DuMond, who was an exponent of the American Sublime School of landscape painting. This was the earliest landscape school in the US and the works represented dynamic natural scenes in which effects of light were a feature. For the earliest exponents of the so-called "Sublime" style, such as the German Caspar David Friedrich, the light represented the Divine in nature.

For 12 years, Taylor created luminous mountain paintings but his style was to change as a result of new influences on his work beginning with a sabbatical year in London, England, in 1955-56. There he took some courses at the Slade School and was exposed to the works of contemporary artists such as John Piper. He also visited Italy several times and was captivated by the architecture and produced many sketches and some paintings. I traced Taylor's movement to abstraction, which was inextricably tied to his use of acrylics. This medium allowed him to create a textured ground evoking the surface of pitted rocks, ice sheets and glaciers. He used the same techniques for his later Italian pictures in which aged walls and architectural elements suggest the ravages of time. Taylor's untimely death in 1970 cut short his innovation and further development of his very personal, abstract style. My book, titled *From Realism to Abstraction: The Art of J. B. Taylor*, was published in 2014 and was well received.

Donna Livingstone did me an enormous favour: when I submitted a first draft of the book, she responded that all the facts were there but it was "dry." She observed, "You know more about this man than anyone else. Get inside his head and write about what he thought and felt." She introduced me to the literary movement described as "creative non-fiction." Ultimately, this advice forced me to rethink how I presented Taylor and his work. I believe that, as a result, Taylor comes alive as does his work. Audrey, his wife, had kept exhibit programs, newspaper reviews and a range of other material that helped me to gain insights into his life and work. His sons, Philip and Chris, provided me with reminiscences and observations as well. Discussions with Taylors' peers including Allison Forbes, David Cantine, Norman Yates and Robert Sinclair inspired further insights.

Documents such as grant applications, performance appraisals and tenure reviews revealed the highly-fraught environment at the U of A as the "publish or perish" mentality took hold and was applied to practicing artists. One of my external reviewers noted that this resulted in many artists abandoning academe because they had no desire to write art historical essays. The frustrations and pressures (when Glyde retired, Taylor was asked to step in as acting chair), which added enormous stress, are evident in letters and reports. To the end, he bore the university politics because he believed in the importance of not only the teaching of art in institutions of higher learning but also in artistic creation as a part of the celebration of the human spirit and in service to Canada's identity and culture.

Taylor's work sold well not only in commercial galleries but also to fellow professors at the U of A and few paintings have come onto the art market. He was not an automaton, who painted compelling pictures. The family has a number of failed works that he did not want exhibited or sold. The stunning glacier paintings were preceded by some muddy green or brown paintings that did not work. These failures eventually led him to the glacier and mountain landscapes in which close-ups evoked the whole and also suggested the thousands of years in which they had evolved and changed. Taylor also liked the idea that his paintings could be flipped around and hung upside down and still make a successful artistic statement. His last series of paintings were also in the abstract style, in which angular brush strokes represent prairie landscapes formed by the retreat of glaciers and covered with undulating grasses and stands of poplars and birches.

My next book also began as a museum exhibit. I first encountered Emilio Picariello, a notorious bootlegger, while working on the *Celebrating Alberta's Italian Community* website in 2002-03. He and his so-called accomplice, Florence Lassandro, were executed for the killing of Alberta Provincial Police Constable Stephen Lawson in a bootlegging incident in September 1922. This tragic story intrigued me and, when I was contracted to do some curatorial research for Glenbow's new Western Canadian gallery titled, "Mavericks," I suggested that he be included. The inspiration for the gallery was Aritha van Herk's popular history, *Mavericks: An Incorrigible History of*

Alberta, which was published in 2002. She was part of the exhibit team headed by Glenbow VP Michale Lang, and provided researchers with the following definition: "Maverick: a unique character, an inspired or determined risk taker, forward-looking, creative, eager for change, someone who propels Alberta in a new direction or who alters the social, cultural, or political landscape."

The permanent exhibition opened on March 25, 2007. Picariello was part of the immigration story and represented a type of the hard-working immigrant. The profile that I created was the source of information used in the section of the exhibit devoted to him. Picariello arrived in the US as a young man in 1900 and moved to Toronto where he established a confectionery store. His next move was to Fernie in 1911 where he ran a number of successful businesses with the help of his wife Maria and older children, Steve and Angiolina (Julie). This included a pasta factory and also a collection service for liquor bottles, which he sold back to brewers and distillers. In 1918, he purchased the Alberta Hotel in Blairmore from Frits Sick of the Lethbridge Brewing Company. Picariello ran afoul of the Prohibition law when Alberta like other provinces went "dry" and police were expected to enforce a life style choice that had been rendered illegal. The Crowsnest Pass and southwestern BC had voted against Prohibition so there was little support for it other than among Methodists and other Protestants. While many made lots of money including the Bronfman family, others, like Picariello faced tragic consequences.

Because of my interest in Italian immigration history, I wanted to discover the back story. Was Picariello guilty? Did he receive a fair trial? My research, which involved going through all of his lawyer's files (John McKinley Cameron's wife donated them to the Glenbow Archives), suggested that he had been "framed" as a result of a police "sting" operation. Two of his bootlegging rivals, Mark Rogers and Jack Wilson, assisted the Alberta Provincial Police to set the trap. The section on Picariello in "Mavericks" included a video production that involved a re-enactment of the crime. I was the "talking head" expert, who provided commentary and insights. While I enjoyed doing this work enormously, it did not allow me to explore the story fully and I felt that a larger treatment was required. I convinced Ron Ulrich, Executive Director of the Fernie Museum, to develop a travelling exhibit titled "The Rise and Fall of Emilio Picariello." This time my research was more in-depth and I also was able to consult with Picariello family members including his son Carmine's daughters. I treated my enquiry as a "cold case" and investigated every piece of evidence that I could find including not only the defense case records but also a range of newspaper accounts.

I found two vital pieces of evidence in the case files, which I had missed in 2005. One is the liquor order placed by Mark Rogers to be delivered by Picariello, and the other was a letter dated November 13, 1922, from assistant legal counsel, Sherwood Herchmer, to senior counsel, McKinley Cameron. In it he names Mark Rogers, a Studebaker dealer in Lethbridge and a very successful bootlegger who owned the King's Liquor Co. in BC, as the individual who helped the police set up the sting with its tragic results. He was assisted by John (Jack) Wilson, a recent immigrant from Ballymena, Northern Ireland, who operated a garage in Fernie and, who rumour had it, had been loaned $1,000 by Picariello to start in the liquor trade. Around 4 pm on September 21, 1922, the police were waiting for Picariello, his son Steve and chauffeur, Jack McAlpine, when they returned to the Alberta Hotel. He had, legally, bought liquor in Fernie (BC had overturned Prohibition legislation while it was still in place in Alberta) and, illegally, transported it across the BC/Alberta border.

When Picariello was challenged by APP officer Sergeant James Scott, he signaled to Steve, who was carrying the load, to return to BC. Steve turned his vehicle around and headed back towards the provincial border but, while driving through Coleman, was ordered to stop by Constable Lawson. Steve disregarded the order and Lawson fired a shot at the moving car that struck Steve in the hand. It's important to remember that Lawson only suspected that Steve was transporting liquor and was also aware that he was 16 years old. The use of violence was not warranted; Lawson also followed Steve into BC in a borrowed vehicle until he had to stop because of car trouble. This also violated standard police practice.

After the incident, Constable Lawson ordered Picariello to bring his son to the APP barracks in Coleman, threatening that there would be trouble if he didn't. He then returned to the Coleman APP barracks, which also served as his family's home. Around 7 pm, Picariello went to meet with Lawson accompanied by Florence, who was the wife of his bar manager and friend, Charles Lassandro. What happened next was like a Keystone Cops movie: various Alberta Provincial Police, local police and rival bootleggers were lurking in the dark in Coleman.

Picariello called out to Lawson who came to the car and stood on the running board, and the two argued and struggled. According to Lawson's nine-year-old daughter, Pearlie, who was the only witness, her father "hugged Mr. Pick." Various shots rang out and Lawson was killed. Picariello and Lassandro fled and, after a night-time manhunt in which APP and RCMP officers were brought in from Lethbridge, some by Mark Rogers, Picariello was arrested in Blairmore and Lassandro turned herself in. No notes were taken of their interrogations in violation of all rules of police conduct and Lassandro buckled, and confessed to the murder. This was not the outcome that the APP wanted and they tried to get her to say that Picariello did it. Various reports in the media, some attributed to her mother, indicated that Picariello "forced" her to confess because a woman would not receive the death sentence.

The prosecution case was that Picariello thought that Steve had been killed and went on a rampage to avenge him. If that was the case, why, would he bring a female family friend who helped his wife to look after the children? Wouldn't he have brought her husband Charles Lassandro, or his mechanic Jack McAlpine, or any number of people who assisted him in the bootlegging enterprise?

In fact, Picariello knew that his son had suffered a minor injury. This was confirmed in evidence provided by William Hilton, a BC provincial policeman who Steve spoke to when he stopped in Natal at 6:30 pm to enquire where he could find a doctor to tend to his hand, and where he could find a telephone so that he could call his family. Hilton also confirmed that there was a lot of liquor in Steve's vehicle. According to the family, Picariello went to see Lawson because he was ordered to and to get his help to bring Steve safely back to Blairmore. The peaceful intent would explain why he took Florence with him.

To the end, Picariello claimed that he was innocent and that there had been a shooter in the alley who had actually killed Lawson. The question arises as to whether this was a "friendly fire" casualty? In my opinion, this was certainly the case and the fact that Rogers committed suicide at his home in Lethbridge two years later on September 30, 1924, suggests that a guilty conscience did him in, in the end. Picariello certainly violated the law of the land and deserved to be punished, but the "race card," the expression that McKinley Cameron used at the trial to suggest police bias, certainly stacked the cards against him. The British establishment viewed him as an undesirable alien and his success and perhaps arrogance made him a target.

The Attorney General attended the trial in contravention of sound legal practice. McKinley Cameron, while believing in the innocence of Picariello and Lassandro, who were tried together, knew that he couldn't win the case and his focus was on technicalities such as the fact there were no written records of the questioning of the suspects. He didn't even bring up the fact that the majority of the front windshield lay shattered inside Picariello's car, evidence that there was a shooter or shooters in the alley. As a result of the guilty verdict and execution, Prohibition was finally repealed in Alberta. My book was released by Oolichan Press in 2016 and sold out. I believe that it has led to a questioning of the establishment view represented in bootlegging books and such creative works as the opera *Filumena*, composed by John Estacio with a libretto by John Murrell. This presents Florence as the innocent victim of the much worldlier Picariello. Many believed, among them high-ranking APP officers such as APP Commissioner Willoughby Charles Bryan, that she was, in fact, Picariello's or Steve's mistress. There is no evidence of this.

Besides the case files at Glenbow, there are a series of letters that Picariello wrote to his family from prison. He was literate in English and though there are ungrammatical passages, the letters communicate his instructions and thoughts well. The letters counter the image of the criminal and murderer presented in the media. The family man emerges: an individual worried about the fate of his illiterate wife and his young family of whom Steve is the oldest. In one letter, Picariello apologizes for having forgotten his seventeenth birthday in November because of worry about the trial. He provides instructions to him and Julie on what business dealings to do; who not to trust; and what outstanding bills to pay including those of the lawyers. He knew that the world was a difficult place for them to navigate. In the last letters, the ink is very thick in places as if he was having trouble writing and the words are sometimes difficult to decipher. The appeal had been lost and he was facing death. Mariannina (the diminutive by which his wife was known) would be facing the future alone. She had been having health issues after the birth of their last child and could not visit him in the Fort Saskatchewan Gaol near Edmonton where he was sent after the trial in Calgary. Steve would become the head of the family and, according to his two nieces (brother Carmine's daughters), he was incredibly strict. Steve moved the family to their farm near Spokane and forgot their life in Canada. Carmine's daughters told me that they found out about their Grandfather's story when they were in junior high school in Fernie – their father had gone to work for family friends who ran a wholesale fruit business and who lived in the old Picariello duplex. They were distraught.

Florence Lassandro left no letters or other personal material so she is very much a shadowy figure. Her plight was taken up by journalists, who initially commented on the fact that she was well dressed at the trial and, eventually, focused on her frail figure and fearful countenance. Her cause would be taken up by two individuals: a religious brother, who became her confessor, and a man who wanted to see the abolition of the death penalty. Father Fidelis Chicoine, a Franciscan monk from Quebec who ministered to the Fort Saskatchewan parish, visited her in prison and provided the comfort of religion in weekly visits. He continued to see her until the execution and was a source for Jock Carpenter's book *The Bootlegger's Bride*. She is presented as a "child bride" (she was 16 when she married) in an unhappy, arranged marriage to 24-year-old Charles Sanfidele (Sanfedele). Carpenter, who admitted that the book was a blend of fact and fiction, presented Florence as a victim not only of her husband but also of Picariello. This was true also for John Kidman, Secretary of the Canadian Prisoners Welfare Association based in Montreal. On May 28, 1923, after the executions, Kidman sent a draft of a proposed pamphlet to John McKinley Cameron for review. Titled "Thumbs Up, Thumbs Down," it begins:

> In ancient gladiatorial style the women of Alberta turned thumbs DOWN, with the result that in the 20th century of Christianity and in the New World civilization, a young married woman of 22 years of age, was placed in the hands of a group of public male officials, and dropped from the scaffold on May 2, 1923, at Fort Saskatchewan Alberta, and the manner of death took eleven minutes.

A petition for commuting of the death sentence to life in prison for her had failed and among the opponents was magistrate Emily Murphy who believed in her guilt. Kidman makes a case that Picariello killed Lawson and told Florence to say she did it because he knew women were not sent to the gallows. Cameron rebuts all of Kidman's assumptions and emphasizes that Picariello did not have sufficient knowledge of the law and also that once he dropped her off in Blairmore at the friend's house where she was staying, he never saw her alone again and was, therefore, unable to give her any instructions. Florence's confession came when she was interviewed, alone, by Sergeant Scott at the APP barracks in the Frank Sanatorium. He waited to interview her until the matron left. Scott stated as evidence that when Florence confessed, she laughed and noted that she was glad that she was alive and Lawson was not. This sounds like something that a shell-shocked young person might say.

Any biographer has to believe that they speak for the dead. I have done this not only in the book but also in various talks that I have done associated with the travelling exhibit and book launches in Fernie, Coleman and Edmonton. Picariello family members came to the exhibit and book launches and some shed tears. The largest number turned out at St. Joachim Cemetery in Edmonton where I gave a graveside talk when the travelling exhibit opened at the Fort Saskatchewan Museum in 2019. There was another piece of the story to tell there. Justice Kevin Feehan was sitting on the Queen's Bench in Lethbridge, Alberta, on December 19, 2017 when the Picariello exhibit was at the Galt Museum. A colleague took him there and he was stunned to discover the information in the final panel that stated that Picariello and Lassandro were buried in unmarked graves. Feehan knew this to be untrue because, in 2011, he had seen to the placement of concrete tombstones over their graves. According to the Connelly family, their grandfather, Joseph William Connelly, founder of a local undertaking business, had been present at the hanging on May 2, 1923 and was convinced of their innocence. He gave his son, William James Connelly, a hand-drawn map of the burial site and suggested that he find money to see to the erection of gravestones. William was intrigued by the story and did his own research and was also convinced of their innocence so much so that the following bequest appeared in his will: "The sum of $2,500.00 to provide a suitable marker for the graves of Emilio Picarello [sic.] and Florence Lesander [sic.], who were executed at Fort Saskatchewan, for historical purposes." His wishes were honoured when his will was finally probated in 2010 and, in December 2011, the Connelly family saw to the placement of headstones. They cost much more than the bequest.

On October 19, 2019, a lovely fall day, members of the Picariello and Connelly families, Justice Feehan, representatives of the Fort Saskatchewan Museum and the Edmonton Heritage Council, who jointly sponsored my talk, and members of the public watched as flowers brought by the Picariello family were placed on the graves. It was a blustery fall day but for the entirety of the talk (about an hour), brilliant fall sunshine illuminated the graves and participants. I felt that Emilio and Florence were looking down with pleasure at the proceedings.

My next writing venture occurred when my friend and colleague Peter McKenzie-Brown with whom I worked on the Petroleum History Society Oil Sands Oral History Project connected me with Jeff Keshen, the new Dean of Arts at Mount Royal University in Calgary, in 2013. Jeff, a military and political historian, wanted to commission an anthology exploring Alberta's role in the First World War. I believe Doug Cass, the head of the Glenbow Archives, also recommended me as someone with extensive knowledge of Alberta history. Jeff telephoned me and I agreed to do an essay on the role of women on the home front. Shortly after, Jeff called back and asked whether I would commission and co-edit the book. I immediately agreed since war historians were not, by and large, interested in local, regional or provincial perspectives. My experience with Alberta's museums had led me to an understanding of how important the world wars were at the local level. Most used Remembrance Day on November 11th as an opportunity to celebrate local heroes and display memorabilia. I had seen many such exhibits. In addition, all Alberta local histories included family stories of war-time experience.

It was a pleasure to work with Jeff, who had published a number of books on twentieth century military history, and, from the outset, our perspectives fit together nicely and I don't remember any differences of opinion. Our biggest challenges were to get articles in on time and edit them down to the prescribed word length. I made a case for taking a social historical perspective and Jeff agreed that this would be the right approach. We also wanted multiple authors to give us the best scope and reach. Since it was to be published by the University of Calgary Press, and would undergo peer review, it had to be scholarly; however, we also aimed at a general audience including high school and university students as well as general readers interested in the history of war.

In the end, 40 authors contributed and they ranged from academic military historians to graduate students to local historians. We were also sensitive of the need to deal with a range of subject areas including the perspectives of under-represented or marginalized people such as women, Indigenous People, conscientious objectors, enemy aliens and others. An introduction provided an overview of the First World War experience of Albertans, on the battle front and the home front; in addition, we developed a timeline and a table to provide information about regiments and battalions. The stories and experiences of soldiers on the front are represented through letters and journals. The majority of essays document the home front experience and impacts since this was the history that was unknown.

As Jeff and I edited and re-edited the essays, we discovered that just as armouries and other military-related structures popped up in the landscape, new organizations were set up as established institutions struggled to fill the demands placed on them. It can be said with certainty that the First World War created the foundations of the Alberta that we know today. Every generation re-thinks and sometimes re-invents its history. Significant anniversaries provide an over-riding incentive to do this, and the perspective of 100 years spans several generations of lives as well as the movement away from British Empire. The roots of independence, both in thought and action, can be found in Albertans' responses to the war and what they accomplished. It might be said that the war signaled Alberta's entry into the modern world.

It was an age of belief with the Protestant churches – Presbyterian, Methodist, Unitarian and Anglican – dominating (in 1911, Presbyterianism was the largest denomination in Alberta). This faith enabled communities to accept the horrors of war as fathers, husbands and sons failed to return, or returned maimed in body with disturbed minds as a result of "shell shock," and the horror of the slaughter of their own and enemy soldiers. Referring to the two Kirton brothers killed in the Somme campaign, the *Edmonton Bulletin* maintained that "[A]lthough saddened by the blow which deprived them at one stroke of two sons who were a credit to the rising generation of the city," the parents "took pride ... that they laid down their lives in defence of everything humanity holds dear...."

The Frontier of Patriotism: Alberta and First World War was published in 2016 by the U of C Press. It was a monumental 550 pages and was very well received. It is an attractive book with many period photographs. There were two launches: the first at The Military Museums in Calgary and the second at the Prince of Wales Armouries in Edmonton. In addition, I was invited to the Alberta Legislature on Monday, April 10, 2017 on the day dedicated to the commemoration of the Centennial of the Battle of Vimy Ridge. Alberta's military were recognized as was the team responsible for the book. This was written into Hansard. I was pleased and humbled to be able to work with Jeff and the authors to create such an important work.

My first paper, titled "The Gospel of Sacrifice: Lady Principal Nettie Burkholder and Her Boys on the Front," dealt with the contributions to the war effort of the students at Methodist Theological/ Alberta College South (later St. Stephen's College), one of the first colleges on the University of Alberta campus. In 1912, Nettie became Lady Principal and, when the war began, developed an extensive correspondence with the students from the college serving in the military. She provided news from home as well as moral and spiritual support, and the letters are very moving. The "boys" wrote of their fears, religious doubts, the horrors of the battle front and even pain at receiving "Dear John" letters.

Nettie also organized care packages with "soldier comforts" to be sent to them. The University of Alberta Archives holds 302 letters and cards written by students in response to Nettie's letters, and four of her returned letters (the recipients being listed as missing in action or killed). These are very revealing because they demonstrate what an intelligent human being she was, both caring and compassionate. From the summer of 1914 to the end of the First World War in November 1918, 484 University of Alberta staff and students served in the Canadian armed forces and 82 paid the ultimate price for their commitment. Just under a quarter of the enlistees from the university were from Methodist Theological. In May 1915, Herbert Joseph Ball, one of the Methodist students, became the first student killed in action.

My essay explores Nettie's role as a pioneer woman educator and also the relationships that she established with the young men from the college. Many were studying to take religious orders and were appalled by "man's inhumanity to man" in wartime. Several asked to be moved to the 11th Field Ambulance, a unit containing students from universities in BC, Alberta, Saskatchewan and Manitoba, in order to avoid having to kill. Others believed strongly that they were fighting the war for God and to bring peace to the world. They were among the brightest minds of the age and, many, including Nettie, questioned the proliferation of religious denominations and, when they returned to Canada, played important roles in the creation of the "United Church."

My second essay, titled "Alberta Women in the First World War: A Genius for Organization," dealt with the overwhelming contribution of Alberta women that occurred through a range of volunteer activities. Many of the organizations that were created to further women's causes including the rights of women were patriotic in nature, and there was a seamless shift to war-time volunteer work. The war itself, and the perceived threat to democracy and Anglo-Canadian values, also spurred the desire for suffrage and put additional pressure on the Alberta government to approve it. According to the Women's Press Club of Calgary, in 1913, forty-two women's societies had about 3,000 members. In 1916, the Edmonton Women's Press Club reported sixty-one societies and over 7,000 members. Since the population of the two cities was similar, the growth evidenced in Edmonton is significant, and can be attributed to the onset of the war and opportunities that it created for women's involvement. Edmonton was also the seat of a number of provincial organizations.

Letters, newspaper articles and books of the time reveal the excitement felt by women wanting to participate fully in building the new province. There was a remarkable convergence of strong women, both newcomers and long-term residents, who worked together to further common causes. This is the "sisterhood" revealed in the pages of the Calgary and Edmonton Women's Press Club publications. The leaders, in many cases, are the "literary" women, who take pride in their intellectual powers and communications skills. The press clubs became the vehicle for forging feminist agendas. Among the "sisterhood" were journalists and authors Emily Murphy, Nellie McClung, May L. Armitage Smith, Miriam Green Ellis, Elizabeth Bailey Price and Ethel Heydon. These women were the documentarians of not only the women's societies but also the women's movement in Alberta. The women's clubs were involved in a range of organizations that supported the war effort including the Red Cross, St. John's Ambulance and Imperial Order Daughters of the Empire (IODE). Women were also instrumental in setting up "Soldier's Clubs" to provide support to men on leave and their families. Their number was staggering; for example, Edmonton had over 500 women involved in the IODE.

Julia Ponton, Honorary Secretary of the Edmonton Branch of the Canadian Red Cross, noted that the Canadian Pacific Railway helped to set up the society in November 1914, and it was operational by January 1915 in rooms in the CPR building. The initial work was to purchase material for garments, and Ponton notes that the Great West Garment Co. and Emery Manufacturing Ltd. cut the garments and bandages free of charge. City Red Cross Sewing Circles crafted bandages, bags, slings, operation stockings, etc. Some sewing was also sent out to individual workers. This "cottage industry" extended beyond Edmonton to volunteer auxiliaries in the district and northern towns. Ponton notes the existence of 161 city circles – averaging about 3,000 workers. In the first seven months of 1916, 100 boxes per month were packed with an average of 125 women working per week. The production is outstanding and an enormous saving of revenues for the Government of Canada. Ponton is able to assign a cash value to the production: "From the date of inception to the end of October, 1915, there was sent from Edmonton a total of 976 boxes and 215,440 articles, the approximate value being $63,464.10."

In most of my work in the heritage sector, I dealt with the "dominant" culture in Alberta, that is, people of British ancestry. While it is understandable that ordinary citizens live in the present, it is important that historians and public officials be aware of the past. Some claims are made that it's only in recent times that immigrants have encountered racism. While it is important to acknowledge the truth of some of these claims since many come from visible minorities, it is important not to forget the past and the obstacles placed in front of individuals perceived by the dominant society as "undesirable aliens." Having said this, I think it's important not to vilify the power elites from past generations for not possessing today's values. Hindsight is always 20/20 but doesn't change what happened in the past.

As an immigration historian, and myself having a hyphenated identity, I think that I felt finally that I needed to deal with my own history in a significant way. The impetus occurred when the Edmonton Heritage Council approached me in 2016 to "map" the Italian community for a website that looked at the City's ethnocultural roots, and provided images and contexts for major landmarks associated with a particular community. I agreed to do this, and asked for the opportunity to create essays based on the three principal eras of Italian immigration. The common thread was "There Were No Safety Nets." Post the passage of the Charter of Rights and Freedoms, rights have been guaranteed and, it is important to remember that prior to this, there were few guarantees and racism was systemic. It was not only Indigenous People, Blacks and Chinese who were discriminated against;

at different times, Southern and Eastern Europeans and others were considered unsuitable as potential settlers. This has been forgotten and one sees the paradox of recent Syrian immigrants complaining in the media about their treatment and letters to the editor from descendants of Ukrainian settlers who recount stories of their ancestors' internment in the First World War. Their rights and those of other "enemy aliens" including the Japanese, Germans and Italians in the Second World War were violated as well.

I decided that I needed to write about "Alberta's Italian history" not only to address issues of race and discrimination but also to affirm the capacity of almost all immigrants to assert themselves, and make a home and belong in this country. The research and writing of what became my book, *From Sojourners to Citizens: Alberta's Italian History*, allowed me to tell stories of success and failure that represent the Italian community and, by extension other immigrant communities, within the context of "province building." It is incredibly important to undertake social history research otherwise "official" history will continue only to focus on mainstream political and economic histories.

My personal life-span covers about half of the over 140-year-period that Italians have been in Alberta. I have thus been a participant in some of the changes brought about through multiculturalism and charter legislation. The immigration stories of my grandparents, parents and my own cover the broad span of the Italian presence in North America. I have seen the changes beginning in the 1960s and 1970s, as historians began to study the experiences of ordinary people in the past to illuminate public history that focused on major political figures and events. Social history has been described as the "history of the people" or "history from below." Subfields include demographic, ethnic, labour, gender, family, and urban and rural histories. This is the history that dominated as I came of age and in which I became a practitioner.

I began my work in community history as a volunteer: I was part of the team that developed celebratory activities for the 25th anniversary of Santa Maria Goretti Parish in 1983. Father Augusto Feccia, the pastor at the time, had brought with him from his last parish in Chicago the desire to document local Italian history, and to preserve Italian culture and traditions. He incorporated the Italians Settle in Edmonton Society and asked local high school teacher Frank Sdao and I to head up a project. I helped develop an oral history project; wrote a historical booklet (*Italians Settle in Edmonton*); and

created a photographic exhibit documenting the early history of settlement. These materials were all deposited in the Provincial Archives of
Alberta. Subsequently, working with community leader Sab Roncucci,
I created the Italian community profile for the City of Edmonton as
the City embraced multiculturalism.

In 1996, I was recruited by Sab to become the President of
the National Congress of Italian Canadians, Edmonton District and
for the next six years took part in all community events locally, pro-
vincially, nationally and internationally. This included not only the
core activity of organizing the Italian Pavilion at the annual Heritage
Days event on the August long weekend but also being a delegate for
Alberta, appointed by Vice Consul Giovanni Bincoletto, at the Second
Rome Conference on Immigration. It took place from November 28
to December 3, 1988. The conference theme was "Gli Italiani all'Es-
tero" (Italians Abroad). As a member of the Canadian delegation,
I took part at the joint meeting with the American delegation in New
York (June 1988) and in Toronto (November 1988).

We formulated positions on various conference themes including
culture, language retention, political rights, pensions, etc. Discussions
were heated and were complicated by Italian party political differences
as well as regional differences, which also impacted on the opinions
of American and Canadian delegates. As well, there were among the
representatives more recent immigrants, who had kept their Italian
citizenship, and truly considered themselves "Italians abroad." They
wanted to retain full rights of Italian citizenship while making a living
abroad. The total number of conference attendees was 2,239 (1,189
were delegates, 600 invited guests, 50 observers and 400 journalists).
Travel and accommodation expenses were paid by the Italian government. Countries represented ranged from Algeria to Venezuela. Most
of Italy's parliamentarians attended at least some of the sessions.

I was also part of the redress efforts for Italian-Canadians interned
during the Second World War, which were led by the National Congress under President Annamarie Castrilli, a Toronto lawyer. At the
time, she was a member of the board of governors of the University of Toronto. (She later served as chair.) A brief was prepared and
reviewed by the executives of regional congresses across the country.
The NCIC succeeded in obtaining a verbal apology from Prime Minister Mulroney at a luncheon in the Toronto suburb of Concord, on
November 4, 1990. This event was the highlight of the NCIC biennial

meeting and was attended by 500 members and guests. Some members of the Italian community wanted more than an apology; they wanted compensation. For them, the issue continues to be a sore point. Quiet lobbying continued and, on April 14, 2021, Prime Minister Justin Trudeau announced in the House of Commons that his government would be issuing a formal apology in May, which he did.

For the *Alberta Online Encyclopedia*, I not only created the *Celebrating Alberta's Italian Community*, the first multimedia website (2002) in Canada to deal with an ethnocultural community but also an overarching site titled *Albertans: Who Do They Think They Are*, which includes profiles of about 75 communities. My interest in ethnocultural history resulted in the creation of a series of Francophone websites (all bilingual); and Estonian and Black pioneer heritage sites in partnership with these communities. Indigenous history was a particular focus because of the lack of authoritative material for educational and community engagement purposes. I worked with the Treaty 6, 7 and 8 organizations and the Métis Nation of Alberta to create thematic websites including five Indigenous teacher and student resources described as "edukits."

This experience was brought to bear on my Italian history project, the largest research project that I have ever undertaken, and which involved reading all of the local histories funded by the Government of Alberta (over 500), the academic literature pertaining to immigration of ethnocultural communities and various newspaper accounts. In addition, I listened to about 100 oral histories, some of which I was involved in undertaking. For the book, I created an over-arching narrative that sets the context of immigration of Italians (and other ethnic groups) based on government policy beginning in the late nineteenth century. In addition, I created a specific timeline of Italian immigration to Alberta. I didn't want the book to be a dry recounting of facts so I selected and included stories of individuals (male and female) drawn from oral histories as well as family histories, memoirs and newspapers accounts. I did this to enrich and particularize the settlement experience of Italians.

The chapters are thematic in nature but also deal with the history in a chronological fashion. The majority of immigration from Italy, in the late nineteenth and early part of the twentieth centuries, was to small communities where railways were being built and resources exploited. In chapters titled "Working on the Railways," "When Coal

Was King" and "Breaking the Land," I told the community stories. The earliest immigration was from Northern Italy and this is reflected in the community and oral histories. The Italian labourers and their families embedded in statistics are given names, faces and life stories. Not all of them were happy: mining, in particular, was dangerous work and people were killed or maimed with terrible repercussions for families who lost their breadwinners. I was also able to show that families pulled together to help each other, and women and children helped to till the land and harvest crops.

Others used their trades or just winged it and set up small businesses and prospered. I documented the value that many parents placed on education for their children that enabled movement from the working class to professions, and discovered that only in mining communities did you find five generations of individuals who worked in the mines. Social mobility apparently was inhibited in working class occupations and resource hinterlands.

Restrictions on immigration after the First World War resulted in a very static Italian population in all of Canada: family reunification and farm labour were the only criteria for entrance. Thus, most Italians, whether first- or second-generation, considered themselves Canadians. The shock of being designated enemy aliens as a result of Mussolini's declaring war on the United Kingdom on June 10, 1940 was felt across Canada. While the number of Italians interned in Alberta was low, six in all, this resulted in a feeling of shame for the entire community. Over 600 were interned Canada-wide with the majority from the largest population centres in Ontario and Quebec. While many individuals interned had been part of the setting up of *fascios*, Fascist cells, in Edmonton, Calgary, the Italian agricultural colonies at Venice and Hylo, and in Lethbridge, for most, it would have been inconceivable or impossible to undermine Canada's security and the war effort.

The second major wave of Italian immigration that occurred post-1949, was to cities, primarily Edmonton and Calgary. This was my own era of immigration and I was part of a group of "child" immigrants who received most if not all of their education in Canada. Most of us experienced some type of discrimination whether at school or in the work place but we were also beneficiaries of the new "multicultural policies" leading to the Charter of Rights and Freedoms. From 1968 to 1980 I lived in London, England, first as a doctoral student and, then, as a working wife and mother. Thus, when I returned to Canada in early August 1980 I marvelled at how "ethnic" Alberta had become. Little Italy was a fixture in the inner-city Boyle-McCauley neighbourhoods; Italian restaurants had proliferated; and every year on the August long weekend, a heritage festival took place in Hawrelak Park. It became important for me to document these stories and my work in the heritage field gave me the necessary knowledge and skills as well as access to archival resources.

I spent over five years writing and rewriting *From Sojourners to Citizens: Alberta's Italian Community* and drew on knowledge and projects dating back to the oral history work that I was involved in, in 1983, for the Santa Maria Goretti commemorative project. It was a personal journey of discovery to listen to oral histories of members of the Italian community; mine the content in the community histories of Alberta; consult archival records; and search genealogical records made accessible online by Ancestry.ca and other providers. This allowed me to flesh out the life stories of a number of individuals both unique and representative of a particular occupation or trade.

While the stories of enormous achievement are an important part of Italian community history, there are also those of ordinary people whose lives were marked by tragedy. These still haunt me. The early entrepreneurs including Louis Pozzi, the great builder from the Crowsnest Pass, the Nigro-Anselmo families of Edmonton, the Gallellis of Calgary, the Forzani brothers and others are noteworthy. So also are the five generations of Oliva family members who worked in the mines and the many miners whose names appear in lists of accidents that resulted in death. I will never forget the stories of the young mother, newly come from Italy, who was washing clothes in the Red Deer River on a hot summer's day, drank the water and died a painful death from typhoid because she was too shy to go to the new hospital in Drumheller; or of the children of a miner who were consigned to pauper's graves, also in Drumheller. I hope that my book honours their memories.

When I embarked on the research and re-discovered the treasure trove of documents and copies of oral histories in my own basement, I realized that if I died before writing the book, all of this material might end up at the City dump. It was a pretty compelling reason to undertake the research and writing. As I saw the work moving to publication guided by Michael Mirolla, Editor-in-Chief and Publisher at

Guernica Editions, I was thrilled that these community stories would be available for future generations. I have also organized all of the research files and the boxes containing them are clearly labelled as is their destination, the Provincial Archives of Alberta.

Each of the books that I authored allowed me to explore an area of interest in my life. *From Realism to Abstraction: The Art of J. B. Taylor* was a culmination of my life-long love of fine and decorative arts. *The Rise and Fall of Emilio Picariello* dealt with a small slice of Italian immigration history but also represents my personal commitment to justice and equality. *The Frontier of Patriotism: Alberta and the First World War* deals with the horrors of history and the impact on the lives of ordinary people. Finally, *From Sojourners to Citizens: Alberta's Italian Community* allowed me to celebrate my Italian heritage and Canada as a place where immigrants can not only make a home but also belong.

CHAPTER 12

COVID Reflections

But at my back I always hear
Time's wingèd chariot hurrying near;
And yonder all before us lie
Deserts of vast eternity.
—**Andrew Marvell**, "To His Coy Mistress"

Humankind cannot bear very much reality.
—**T.S. Eliot**, *The Four Quartets*

As a historian, I've read about wars and disasters, and how they impacted on the lives of not only the rich and famous but also ordinary people. These stories reveal that human beings do not control their world. French author Antoine de Saint-Exupéry titled his 1939 memoir *Terre des hommes*, literally, "man's world." The English translation of the title, *Wind, Sand and Stars*, missed his true meaning and intent. As an aviator, flying above deserts and other immense landscapes, he could see how minute human beings were in the totality of the cosmos. His ironic title captured that it was not "man's Earth," but rather, something that was huge and majestic, and beyond the control of human beings.

Expo '67 in Montreal took the words literally and the various pavilions were meant to celebrate the diversity of the world, both human and natural. I was blown-away by the Expo site and the worlds of meaning contained in the pavilions. I remember, in particular, the Thai Pavilion with its gilded relief work. I visited Expo twice: in September 1967 and late May 1968. The first viewing was just before I went to the University of Western Ontario to teach for an academic year; the second, because I was going to board a ship to Liverpool to begin doctoral studies at King's College, University of London. I was a young adult and firmly believed that all was possible. My studies had given me a progressivist view of history, which, by and large, I have kept over the years.

Living in a first-world country with a high standard of living, it's been easy for me to delude myself in the belief that I control my life. Disasters have been at a distance seen through media reports of countries in the developing world in the grips of civil war, disease, famine or natural disasters. Charitable appeals provide opportunities to donate money for humanitarian relief and re-building, and we can then go on with our ordinary lives. In Canada we are blessed and, thankfully, sheltered from those kinds of occurrences.

This all changed in March 2020 when external circumstances impacted on my life and that of many others throughout the world. The COVID-19 virus, whatever its origins, made its way around the world causing illness and, in many cases, death, first among seniors and immuno-compromised individuals. Alberta Premier Jason Kenney, because of the spread of the virus, declared a public health emergency on March 17, 2020.

My daughter-in-law Sabrina gave birth to her second child, Miles, on March 18 at the Royal Alexandra Hospital in Edmonton. On March 29, six years earlier, her Mother Jean and I were at the same hospital with my son William for the birth of their first child, Dawson. At Miles' birth, only his Father could be there, and had to wear protective covering and a mask. The rest of the family waited at home for the happy news, which we received via texts accompanied by photos of the smiling mother and sleeping baby. We couldn't rush over to see the baby as we did with Dawson, either in the hospital or in their home.

I can't help but reflect on then and now, and how diminished my life is as a result of the COVID outbreak. Thankfully, FaceTime visits have allowed me to see Miles and witness his big brother's love and occasional jealousy, the latter manifested by Dawson's "hogging" the screen. While I was accustomed to speaking to my son Alex in the UK and twin grandsons, Oliver and Ciaran, it seemed somehow unnatural to be using the same technology to see William and family in Edmonton just a ten-minute drive away. But these FaceTime calls became a life-line and it's like watching a favourite movie, again and again.

As spring turned to summer, I mostly stayed inside. I ate to live rather than living to eat, and an unexpected benefit occurred: I lost fifteen pounds. I didn't want to take solitary walks though nature beckoned. I bought potted annuals at nurseries and placed them around the front and back yards, and on the back deck. The perennials I planted over the years flourished through a wonderful summer. It was as if nature was making up for the restrictions to my movements by making every window a picture window through which I could look at the glorious flowers and birds that visited the birdbath that I filled daily.

While common crows and magpies came every day, so did a pair of blue jays; they daintily drank from the birdbath before flying off. As well, funny, red-breasted birds came; they were not like the large American robins pictured in bird guides. These were smaller and had dusky bodies and, clearly, were less inflated with self-worth. They were more diffident, Canadian birds. Occasionally, I also heard a woodpecker since the trees planted over 60 years ago by the first owners of my house have some dead branches. The largest tree, an elm, is half dead and the gardening firm I called to get rid of some dead branches last year suggested I cut it down. I couldn't (it was still too alive) and gave them permission only to remove obviously dead branches to prevent them from being blown down in a storm and hurting the neighbour's children playing in the yard next door, or causing property damage. The squirrels use this same tree and others as a "jungle gym" leaping from branch to branch in impressive acrobatic displays. They are a constant source of amusement.

As a life-long reader, it was natural to turn to the comfort of books but I found that I couldn't read any serious literature, only historical romances; I also binge-watched Home and Garden TV programs, and silly romantic movies. It was an escape and I don't apologize that a woman of my age and education had sunk so low. Many years ago, when my older son Alex discovered that I read romances, after a flood in the basement required the wholesale removal of my books, he observed, "Mum, what a pity: a fine mind gone to mush!"

He couldn't understand the mix of academic books, histories, biographies and romances. (He excused the science fiction and fantasy titles because I had introduced him to these genres and he loved them as much as I did.)

My mind had certainly turned to mush as a result of COVID restrictions. It was only in dreams that any intellectual activity occurred. My past and present lives merged in a cinematic way, and I took on the role of the director editing and inter-cutting scenes from my past and present. I re-lived aspects of my marriage and had some pleasant discussions with my ex, Hugh. In one dream, he was advising me on the rebuilding of my house (our former marital home), which had been destroyed by fire. This was paradoxical since, in the last years of my marriage, I had a recurrent dream in which I searched for my "forever" home only to find each old house that I visited was a warren that I couldn't escape. In my dreams, I talked with family members and friends both living and dead, and reflected on matters of faith and conscience.

I also relived a trip to Italy that I took in September 2018 with a group including family members and old friends. The group of 18 seniors toured northern and central Italy for about two weeks. Afterwards, the majority returned to Canada and, with my sister Rosa, cousin Rudy and his wife, Rita and sister, Anna, I spent just over a week in our home province, Calabria. We visited our ancestral home town, Grimaldi; spent time on the beach at Amantea; and visited the museum in Reggio Calabria as well as doing other sightseeing.

In my dream, I got separated from the group while visiting a museum in northern Italy and my cell phone stopped working so I couldn't connect with them. I had forgotten the charger at the hotel. I became more and more desperate and even visited a local police station but, though I spoke Italian, they didn't seem to understand me, and ignored my more and more frantic pleas for help. I was wandering around the streets like a confused old woman when I witnessed a minor car accident and, when a couple of police officers arrived, a man and a women, I was able to tell them what I saw. They were so grateful that they took me to their police station where they recharged my phone. Numerous text messages began to pop up on the screen, the gist of which was "Where are you?" They were sent by my cousin Rudy, who was the tour organizer. I called him immediately and we were able to arrange a meeting place and I woke up as the nightmare ended.

I've had other desperate dreams in which I am similarly helpless running up and down unfamiliar streets trying to find my destination. It was terrifying to feel this way because my whole life had hitherto been marked by my being in control. In fact, both at home and at work, I was a bit of a control freak. I didn't like what I had become during the COVID outbreak: a powerless old woman.

I wasn't reassured when I looked in the mirror. After five months of not seeing a hairdresser, my hair, which is normally dyed auburn, was white and grey, and fly-away. When I looked in the mirror, I was uncomfortable with what I saw – a resemblance to my mother, in the long-term-care facility where she spent the last six years of her life before dying at the age of 94 in 2015. In the last years, she was confined to her bed because of degenerative arthritis. When we visited, my sister, brother or I brushed her hair but to little effect, other than soothing her by our touch. It continued to go every-which-way as a result of lying in bed, day-in and day-out, no matter how it was cut. Sometimes I woke up crying from my dreams as a result of missing not only long-departed, loved ones but also living family members and friends.

I had been alone since my husband returned to England in May 2000 and we were divorced; so living alone wasn't new. But this was different. During the early months of the COVID-19 pandemic, I grieved my freedom and lost life when, at a whim, I could visit my son William and family, my sister Rosa and brother Giuseppe, and my friends. I missed the thrifting excursions, coffees, lunches and occasional dinner parties. These social activities added balance to my working life as a freelance writer and occasional curator of exhibits. This work was mostly solitary as I undertook research in libraries and archives, and spent long hours writing at the computer.

On September 17, I turned 77 and became very conscious of my age: there was no denying that I was a senior and in the "at risk" group. I described this sense of vulnerability that I had not experienced before (other than for a couple of months after my car accident in January 2019 when I was homebound) to a friend as the feeling that I was walking around with a target on my back. She laughed and agreed.

I knew that I wanted to be around for at least another 15 years to see my grandsons grow up; therefore, I didn't mind the restrictions imposed by the various levels of government. I was, and still am, very cautious and venture out only to do essential shopping. I don't need any new clothes or luxury items; I basically have everything I need and question the conspicuous consumption I see daily on TV.

I have tried (and mostly succeeded) in not being jealous of family and friends who have significant others, and do not live alone. My correspondence via email has blossomed, like the letter writing of old, and I spend many hours on the telephone and emailing to sustain my wide network. I sometimes even FaceTime with my sister and brother, and have Zoom calls with distant friends.

Throughout my life, I have followed the news on television at home and on the car radio. This has changed and I now watch the TV news sparingly because I find it so depressing: talking heads constantly on the attack, assigning blame for one thing or another; and only making matters worse. Apparently, there is no "good news" and I can't stomach the onslaught of the disease, and its impact on individuals and the economy.

I have seen its impact on the latter first-hand: my son William was unable to obtain work as a heavy equipment operator. I did job searches for him daily via the job line Indeed and put in applications for him. Any equipment operator job in the greater Edmonton area, based on the stats that I received, had anywhere from 150 to 500 applicants. It was a huge relief when the government approved the Canada Emergency Relief Benefit (CERB) and, when it was about to run out, my prayers were answered, and he miraculously got a job through a friend. This involved working 12 hours a day, seven days a week in a gravel pit. He was delighted to have the job and didn't mind the hard work. When the work ended in late November, he qualified for employment insurance.

Thankfully, my older son Alex's banking job in London was safe and he began to work from home and continued to do so. London moved quickly into the third-tier of severity and everything shut down. My grandsons went to school until just before Christmas when some COVID cases prompted an early shutdown that continued until early March 2021. They had no trouble adjusting to online learning and their parents created efficient study areas in their bedrooms including new desks and comfortable chairs. Alex worked in the kitchen and Catherine in the attic spare bedroom. They all rode the stationary bike that Catherine had rented at the suggestion of her physiotherapist to deal with a running injury. The twins, who are also great hockey players, shot pucks into a net that their father placed at the end of their garden. The yard got heavy use and, at the end of the summer, the shrubs had taken a beating and the grass lawn was dead.

Alone at home, I struggled with a kind of "low-grade" depression – not one that could result in self-harm but, rather, a feeling that I could not deal with any other pressure or discord of any kind. The media attacks on Prime Minister Justin Trudeau and his Liberal government, and other world leaders, as they struggled to deal with the pandemic's challenges to the public health service and the economy, depressed me. I also found that sad happenings even in Rom-Coms that I watched for escape brought me to tears.

I do not feel qualified to talk about occurrences in other countries, but, by and large, I believe that both the federal and provincial leaders were doing their best in the difficult circumstances and didn't find the "blame game" on television productive. Public officials are novices at dealing with these issues and the ones who had dealt with life-threatening situations during the Second World War are all dead.

As a historian, I am amazed that there has been little or no learning from past experiences. I have no patience for "anti-vaxxers" and the extreme followers of President Trump, whether in the US or in central and southern Alberta. I blame Premier Kenney for pandering to them for too long with the result of escalating rates of infection in late fall and winter 2020 requiring a lockdown around Christmas. I am very selective in the ways I keep informed: I focus on the various news apps on my I-Phone and I-Pad: I read only what I feel I can deal with. In the first months, I viewed the COVID stats (local, national and international) several times a day but, since then, I only want to get a sense of the "big" picture: rates of transmission and deaths, and outbreaks in Alberta; London, England; Italy where I still have distant cousins; and the US.

Too much illness and too many deaths threatened my peace of mind and made me feel more and more powerless. Sharing COVID stats, comic videos and other humorous material, and uplifting sayings and songs via email with family and friends seemed to help. Telephone calls made by me or returned served the same function. It was good to receive samples of "British" humour because they have an edge; North Americans would reject them because they are not politically correct.

The only relief in my day came when I watched the Daily TV Mass from the Loretto Abbey Chapel in Toronto. As a museum professional, I liked the fact that the Abbey was an all-girls Catholic secondary school established by the Loretto Sisters in 1846, making it one of the oldest educational institutions in Toronto. I remembered that my mother had watched the TV Mass and first looked for it after an automobile accident on January 26, 1919. My Toyota Highlander was totalled when it was hit broadside and the seatbelt caused massive abdominal bruising. For about six weeks, I was in enormous pain and housebound. I started to watch the Mass but then, when I got better, I returned to going to the "real" thing – Sunday Mass at St. Joseph's Basilica at 8:30 am with Giuseppe and wife Sylvia. Afterwards, we would go for coffee at Remedy on 124 Street and meet with old friends, Marjorie and Jack. It was both a spiritual and social experience.

During the pandemic, the TV Mass has provided me not only with comfort but also a context for seeing the discomfort of the present in a larger, perhaps even eternal, context. I am selective about what I take away from the experience choosing to focus not on the punitive, "Old Testament" God but, rather on Christ, the Redeemer, who preached the "Gospel of Love," and the imperative to treat others as we would like them to treat us. On the news, I see a broken world that needs healing and, as a life-long Catholic, the teachings of Christ seem to me to be the answer. Above all, I personally and society, generally, need hope. My over-arching desire is that COVID will end and that we will be able to continue our lives, perhaps a little wiser. In the meantime, I had to learn acceptance and resignation in the face of things I could not change.

The first phase of my life as a COVID recluse ended in August 2020, and I now reflect on it as a golden month. William and Sabrina agreed that I could have Dawson two days a week and, in addition, they said I could visit Miles the other days. My life changed dramatically. I used to look after Dawson twice a week before he went to kindergarten and I missed his presence in my life. We quickly picked up our old routine. We talked endlessly and we started each morning with milky tea and doughnuts that I bought in the local IGA or Safeway on the way back from picking him up. I sometimes used a "character" teapot with relief figures of an owl and a pussycat at sea. I cooked pasta for him at noon and sometimes even in the evening before taking him home. We also went for long walks in the neighbourhood and along Valleyview Drive overlooking the North Saskatchewan River Valley. Sometimes I drove down Buena Vista Road and parked near the Storyland Valley Zoo and we walked the paths next to the River.

I talked to him about flowers and trees, and also beavers and other wildlife; I drew on the information that I retained from my days as Science Editor of *The Canadian Encyclopedia*. The twins, when they were three, told me that they liked the explanations that I gave them about science. I continued this tradition of "mini-lectures" with Dawson and also warned him about the dangers of the swift river currents and the danger of walking too closely to the eroding river banks. I remember doing this with his Father and Uncle Alex and images from my past as a Mother and my present as a Grandmother seemed to be superimposed one on the other emphasizing my advanced age. In fact, at times as we walked and I would have to tell Dawson to slow down, he responded, "Don't worry, Nonna, I'll look after you when you're really old and I'll cook pasta for you!"

We talked endlessly. He told me stories that he made up on the spur of the moment: he is a child who loves heavy equipment, the police and the fire department so his stories are always about disasters. I kept toys (some that belonged to his father and uncle as well as some I bought for him) in my library upstairs and also in the basement rumpus room. He created elaborate towns including airports and parking lots as well as farms, and then "destroyed" them like a tornado would. We then became doctors and other emergency service workers and tended to the casualties. All the while he was inventing the stories that we were enacting.

The other five days of the week I went to their home for several hours. Initially, I took Dawson and Miles out for a walk together. I pushed Miles in his stroller and Dawson walked, skipped or jumped beside me. After a few days, Dawson said that he preferred to stay home with his Mummy (William, by this time, thankfully had got a job with a local gravel company). Most days, I took the boys out for walks separately and I could feel my body gaining strength with each walk; my skin also took on a healthy glow. This was important because I felt that my body had aged at least 10 years in the past few months. I also felt a peace of mind coming back that I had lost as a result of COVID.

The walks reinforced the bond I had established with Dawson and I began to create a new one with Miles. I continued with Miles the tradition of singing popular folk songs including classics by Gordon Lightfoot ("In the Early Morning Rain," "Pussywillows, Cattails," "The Way I Feel" and "Bitter Green"), and Ian and Sylvia ("Four

'Strong Winds") and other music icons. These songs reflected my passion for Canada and its landscapes that I missed the 12 years that I lived in London, England, where I first sang them to my sons. Baby Miles listened intently and hummed along quietly and, occasionally, shouted some gibberish before falling asleep. Prior to this, he had only seen me masked on their back porch, or through the glass of their living room window. He had seen my bare face only on FaceTime and he knew me, and smiled brightly whenever he saw me. This happy period ended in early September when Dawson returned to school and joyfully was reunited with his friends. He still told me stories when we FaceTimed but it was different: there was no physical presence, even though masked.

I returned to my solitary reflections. I remembered that the University of Alberta had put out a call for COVID stories to post on a blog and I thought about doing this. I began to write a "COVID Memoir" that I titled "In My Head" but only succeeded in writing a few pages. What struck me was the notion of being "cloistered" from life and reflected on this. Having read sixteenth and seventeenth century works about the religious life of women who turned away from the world to become "brides of Christ," I tried to imagine what that was like, and how it differed from the imposed social distancing that I was experiencing. I wrote in the fragment:

> Reliance on self; I don't think I was cut out for this. It is like being cloistered but not as in a cloistered religious order where there are other nuns. But rather like the women who walled themselves up to dedicate themselves completely to God – like Holy Jeanne Le Ber in Montreal.
>
> But it isn't God that motivated this retreat to the cloister but a virus that has spread from an animal vector to humans.
>
> It isn't like all of the Sci Fi/Zombie Apocalypse stuff I've been reading for years with the scenes of violence and dog-eat-dog existence.
>
> It is being solitary and learning to accept that the only contact is virtual – emails, telephone, FaceTime, Zoom, etc. – at least for the first three months.
>
> I imagine myself like Jeanne in her walled-in sanctuary/prayer room living inside her soul – with me it's my head – memories of real life my preoccupation.

It brings to mind Tennyson's Lady of Shalott in her solitary tower looking through the windows at the real world, and weaving a tapestry scene of it. But, as Tennyson writes, the Knight rode by, a colourful, three-dimensional being, and she "grew half sick of shadows." The tapestry split "from side to side" and she died, the last scene being her exit from life lying in a boat floating down the stream.

In the dictionary, a recluse is a person who lives in voluntary seclusion from the public and society. The word is from the Latin *recludere*, which means "shut up" or "sequestered." Historically, the word referred to a hermit's total isolation.

From a number of Google searches, I discovered that, in the Middle Ages in Europe, women were not allowed to live alone. That is why convents were set up.

St. Bernard de Clairvaux wrote that woods and secluded places were dangerous for women because the Evil Tempter could draw close and seduce them to commit an Evil Act. The reference, of course, being to the Garden of Eden and Satan, in the form of a serpent, tempting Eve to eat of the Apple, which brought Knowledge of Good and Evil, and the Fall of Mankind.

But, by the twelfth century, there were women recluses. Margherita Colonna lived in a cave on the Prenestine Hill in Rome before becoming a Poor Clare.

Those early women recluses escaped the will of parents or husbands, maintaining control of their bodies and minds.

I realized that my situation was very different from these early feminists. Isolation can and does lead to negative thoughts that can take over one's mind creating a downward spiral. This is evident with the increase in suicides being reported, and the warnings by public health officials of the looming suicide "pandemic." Contemporary human beings are more social than at any other period in the history of our race and, unless an individual is introspective by nature, the forced isolation is a frightening state to be in.

On the positive side, there seems to have been an enormous growth in the "nesting" instinct as evidenced on life-style programs on television, and the boom in purchases of items and materials to enhance living at home. Many, particularly wealthy and middle class people with secure jobs, have extra money as a result of not being able to go on holidays, and can spend it on home beautification. This gives credence to the saying that one's home is one's castle, in the sense of a fortification against the world and, by extension, disease.

The disadvantaged do not have this option: there is an exponential growth in those suffering from poverty resulting from loss of work. This is particularly true for those with resource-based employment. Environmental concerns about the impact of the oil industry on the health of the planet, supported by government action to limit carbon emissions, together with the decline in use of petroleum products associated with COVID restrictions, has meant the loss of many jobs. Some will never return and new, so-called "green" jobs resulting from reclamation of industrial sites and alternative energy models haven't materialized yet. Any historian can tell you that for economic recovery to occur, massive "make work" schemes like those implemented in the Great Depression of the 1930s, supported by dollars from all levels of government, are required. Hopefully, this will come as vaccines and government restrictions on movement of citizens bring COVID under control, and governments can focus on rebuilding the economy. At least this is my view of the "macro" situation.

In my own, small world, I've been thinking about my family and remembering what it was like to be an immigrant. My father, Raffaele Albi, left Italy in 1949 and didn't see his mother, my Nonna Alessandra, until 1975 when we visited Italy. They connected via a monthly letter and, later, an occasional telephone call arranged ahead of time so that Nonna could go to visit a friend, who was lucky enough to have a telephone.

This lack of "connectedness" is within my living memory. When I went to London, Ontario to teach at the University of Western Ontario in September 1967, I began the habit of writing weekly to my parents left behind in Edmonton. This continued for the twelve years that I lived in London, England. When my son Alex went to London to finish his schooling in 1990 and, then, to Oxford University, letters were replaced by emails and enlivened by telephone calls on special occasions. Summer and Christmas visits made living apart bearable.

What COVID has done is make the distance from family and friends the norm, rather than an exception. This harkens back to the great eras of immigration in the nineteenth and first half of the twentieth centuries. That is why it is so challenging. While immigrants stoically accepted distance from loved ones for years as necessary to elevating the quality of their life, and creating opportunities for advancement for their children, there is none of that payoff for COVID isolation.

Seniors in long-term care facilities are isolated from their families and dementia symptoms are escalating: there is no stimulation to keep them connected to ordinary life. My sister Rosa sees this in her husband Frank, who is now 90. Under COVID restrictions, he has become depressed and sleeps most of the day. During the summer she was able to bring him home on Sundays, and he enjoyed the special meals that she prepared for him that they ate on their covered back porch. Not being able to go home, even for a short while and, then, Rosa not being able to visit him as a result of the shutdown of visits to elder facilities where outbreaks of COVID became the norm, sapped Frank's will to live. While some families could connect via FaceTime, Frank is profoundly deaf and this is difficult. It also relies on the goodwill of staff and they don't always have the time. To raise Frank's spirits, Rosa drove to his facility and parked the car below his window on the second floor of the building. He looked down at her and waved and they talked via the telephone.

Keeping one's spirits up has become the new imperative and conversations via various media, the accepted tool for doing this. On a regular basis, I am overwhelmed by a wave of sympathy for others, reinforced by the sermons that I listened to on the Daily TV Mass. With immediate family and friends this meant "remembrance of things past." Since our current lives were on hold, we only had memories of our former lives to reflect on and share. I told my sister and brother that I was writing a memoir, and this prompted Rosa to sit down and write her own story for her four sons and their families. Because I wanted some photographs for the memoir, I went through the photograph albums that I had inherited when my Mother moved into a long-term care facility in 2010 and we sold the family home. Giuseppe suggested that I scan some of them and share them with him and Rosa, which I did.

In daily emails with my old friend Natasha, who is like a second mother to me, I gained new understandings of exile and isolation. Her father was a White Russian general, who after losing the battle with the Bolshevik armies, ended up with many of his friends and former colleagues in Harbin where Natasha was born. The city was founded in 1898 with the arrival of the Chinese Eastern Railway. Many Russian families settled there and re-created, to the best of their abilities, their former lives. Few learned Chinese (only enough to function) and they re-created their churches and social institutions and organizations. After the end of World War II, Natasha's father was arrested and disappeared into the Gulag leaving his wife and daughter bereft. Natasha connected with some archives and museums in Russia and, as a result, wrote several articles about her past. These intrigued a young Russian academic who is focusing his research and publications on the fate of the White Russian Army. I scanned for her relevant photos from her albums and sent them to him via email. At the age of 97, she still has an amazing memory and was able to identify the "White Army" generals in social gatherings at their family home in Harbin. This has been invaluable to the young academic who, as a result, has a "living" link with the past.

For Natasha, these exchanges with Andrey have brought back memories of the horrors of history as they impinged on her parents as they became exiles from their homeland. This loss became her experience as well. She is intensely Russian though she has never lived in Russia and, when the Chinese Communists came to power and took over her husband's cigar factory in Harbin, they became stateless persons living first in France and re-connecting with wealthy family members, who had fled the Russian Revolution and settled in Paris in 1916. Natasha and her husband were poor and, what is more, couldn't settle in France: no European country was interested in granting landed immigrant status. For a time, they lived in Florence and she mastered Italian and was able to make a living as a translator. An opportunity presented itself for her to undertake doctoral studies in the US and she left, trusting that her husband and son would join her. They never did and she obtained a divorce and subsequently remarried. She was successful in getting American citizenship and, eventually, Canadian citizenship when her husband John got an academic job at the University of Alberta in Edmonton. Reliving these memories with her somehow made the restrictions required by the COVID pandemic pale in comparison.

I was finally shaken out of my state of lethargy when the Edmonton Lifelong Learners Association asked me to teach a course via Zoom beginning in January 2021. In 2001, when the Faculty of Extension, University of Alberta, discontinued adult non-credit courses, some professors and interested individuals decided to create a non-profit society to take on this role. In the past twenty years, they've offered courses in established disciplines such as art (painting, drawing and history of), linguistics, classics, writing, history, music, current affairs, ethics, anthropology and literature; physical activity including yoga; and issues-based courses such as aging. I chose the topic "Alberta in World War One" and drew on the book that I co-edited with Jeff Keshen, former Dean of Arts, Mount Royal University in Calgary.

I had to choose themes for the 15 lectures which began in mid-January 2021. I needed to balance the experiences of soldiers on the Front with stories of women on the Home Front; changes in industry and the life of communities as they struggled to supply the military and the Allies; the impact of the returning wounded and demands on the health system; as well as post-war concerns including the re-integration of the physically and mentally wounded into the work force and society in general. My brain went from "idle" to "super-charged."

As well, I had to learn the technology of delivering Zoom lectures. We were given orientation to the technology by ELLA but I felt I needed more instruction and approached my last webmaster for the Heritage Community Foundation, who had helped to build websites for the *Alberta Online Encyclopedia*. Clifford had remained a friend and was a go-to person for all my computer needs. In addition, I approached a coffee buddy, Travis, who taught law at MacEwan University and had been using Zoom for a year. My biggest challenge was to master the "sharing" of my screen so that I could show power points that I had developed as well as short documentaries; I felt that this enriched the learning. When the course started, I also had the able assistance of Dennis, a life-long learner, who volunteered to deal with signing-in students and other technical matters.

The need to prepare stimulating and interesting lectures energized me and I painstakingly planned each one and wrote extensive notes. In addition, I also brushed up on the four power points that I had prepared for some public lectures that I had done when the book was launched in 2016 including ones for the Canadian Club of Edmonton, and the Edmonton and District Historical Society. I had also helped Allan Kerr, founder of the Canadian Militaria Preservation Society in Edmonton, and Dixon Christie, a young film producer who was fascinated by military history and created the *Battle Scars* television series, in the creation of short videos on the history of the

Loyal Edmonton Regiment. I also shared short excerpts from several talks done by military historian Tim Cook of the Canadian Museum of History and the War Museum in Ottawa.

The 15, one-hour lectures also turned out to be social occasions. I dressed up so that I looked the part of the "professor" sharing knowledge with my students. My study became the classroom. All of the students brought not only a love of learning but also life experience, and stories of their own ancestors and their involvement in the war. We were immersed in all aspects of Alberta history in the first decades of the twentieth century and discussed not only the war on the Front and the Home Front but also its impacts on communities both mainstream and marginalized. I shared with them content from James Dempsey's paper on the participation of Indigenous People from Alberta in the war; the treatment of enemy aliens, many of whom were Ukrainians who, before immigration, had been part of the Austro-Hungarian empire; and conscientious objectors.

I found many similarities between the fractured world of the early 1900s and today. The most startling one was the similarities between the Spanish influenza pandemic of 1918-19 and today's COVID Pandemic. Newspapers in 1918 showed how to make masks and how quarantine was implemented; scientists struggled to find vaccines and these efforts were doomed to fail because the medical science of the time did not know about viruses; the lack of medical personnel – half the doctors in the Province were still in Europe and there were few trained nurses; public health measures were in their infancy; and the few hospitals that existed were filled with wounded soldiers. Thus, individuals and communities were dealing with the aftermath of war as well as fighting a pandemic that killed more than the guns on the battle front.

Teaching this course provided me with a context for viewing the sufferings resulting from COVID. People in their seventies today, like myself, who are now the de facto elders of our society, have not experienced war, and the threat to life and individual freedoms as well as deprivation and hardships. We have been singularly blessed in this. Teaching the ELLA course provided me with a lens through which to view contemporary suffering.

In the end, it was remembering that took me out of my depressed state. I know that I am in a much better place. I can continue to count my blessings: I live in a country with a good medical system; I have a strong network of family members and friends; I love reading and other cerebral pursuits; I can sit at my computer and search out information about anything that interests me; and, once spring comes, I can go for walks in nature and refresh my spirits through seasonal rebirth. I also know that there will be medical breakthroughs that will enable us to see our families and friends again. Let us hope that the suffering experienced during the pandemic will make us all more caring and giving.

ACKNOWLEDGEMENTS

Many people have helped to shape my life including my parents, Estera and Raffaele Albi, and my grandparents and great-grandparents who went before them; my siblings, Rosa and Giuseppe; my ex-husband, Hugh Davies; and my sons, Alexander and William, and their wives, Catherine and Sabrina, and children, Oliver and Ciaran, and Dawson and Miles. I've been blessed with an extended Italian family, English in-laws, and Northern Irish and Chinese extended families through my sons' wives. Many friends and professional colleagues complete my circle. Some of their names can be found throughout *My Theatre of Memory: A Life in Words*.

I would also like to thank the wonderful teachers and professors who helped to shape my mind and encouraged my professional endeavours. I have also benefitted from a number of mentors both formal and informal. While my doctoral studies suggested a career in academe, the cutbacks at universities in the UK and Canada in the early 1970s set me on other career paths: as a lecturer in adult education; researcher, writer and editor; cultural executive director; curator, historian and author; and, lastly, a performance poet. I feel that this suited my temperament much better than a life in academe would have done since I am a life-long learner, a necessary quality when one lives in "interesting" times.

I would also like to thank my publisher and editor, Michael Mirolla, at Guernica Editions and the Editorial Board and staff for making the publication of this book as painless as possible. Rafael Chimicatti did a wonderful job of design.

I hope that readers will find some enjoyment in my stories and what they reveal about a woman coming of age as traditions were questioned but not broken initially and, more recently, as they were challenged and rejected. To be caring and compassionate persons is a life-long occupation testing all of us, and we continue to evolve and change until we reach that final frontier.

ABOUT THE AUTHOR

ADRIANA A. DAVIES, Order of Canada and Cavaliere d'Italia recipient, was born in Italy, grew up in Canada and has BA and MA degrees from the University of Alberta, and a doctorate from the University of London, England. She has worked as an editor, museum curator and in the heritage field as an executive director. Publications include *The Dictionary of British Portraiture* (two volumes); *The Canadian Encyclopedia* (Science and Technology Editor); *From Realism to Abstraction: The Art of J. B. Taylor*; *The Rise and Fall of Emilio Picariello*; *The Frontier of Patriotism: Alberta and the First World War* (co-editor and contributor); *From Sojourners to Citizens: Alberta's Italian History*; poetry anthology *Changing My Skin: Dark Elegies and Other Poems*; and memoir *My Theatre of Memory: A Life in Words*.

Printed in December 2022
by Gauvin Press,
Gatineau, Québec